Expressing Oneself/
Expressing One's Self

Expressing Oneself/ Expressing One's Self

Communication, Cognition, Language, and Identity

Edited by

Ezequiel Morsella

Psychology Press
Taylor & Francis Group

New York   London

Psychology Press
Taylor & Francis Group
270 Madison Avenue
New York, NY 10016

Psychology Press
Taylor & Francis Group
27 Church Road
Hove, East Sussex BN3 2FA

International Standard Book Number: 978-1-84872-886-8 (Hardback)

**Visit the Taylor & Francis Web site at
http://www.taylorandfrancis.com**

**and the Psychology Press Web site at
http://www.psypress.com**

Contents

SECTION I   The Production of Gestures, Speech, and Action

SECTION II   Human Communication

SECTION III   The Perception of Speech and Identity

Contributors

John A. Bargh
Department of Psychology
Yale University

Laura L. Carstensen
New School for Social Research

Lei Chen
Speech & Language Processing Lab
School of Electrical & Computer
    Engineering
Purdue University

Shirley Y. Y. Cheng
Department of Psychology
University of Illinois at Urbana
    Champaign

Chi-yue Chiu
Department of Psychology
University of Illinois at Urbana
    Champaign

Susan Duncan
Department of Psychology
University of Chicago

Amy Franklin
Department of Linguistics
Rice University
Houston, TX

Susan R. Fussell
Department of Communication
Cornell University

Sam Glucksberg
Department of Psychology
Princeton University

James Goss
Department of Comparative
    Human Development
University of Chicago

Uri Hadar
Department of Psychology
Tel Aviv University

Mary Harper
Institute for Advanced
    Computer Studies
University of Maryland

Julian Hochberg
Department of Psychology
Columbia University

Sara Kiesler
School of Computer Science
Carnegie Mellon University

Irene Kimbara
Kushiro Public University
Kushiro, Japan

Satoro Kita
Department of Psychology
University of Birmingham

Lindsay R. L. Larson
Department of Psychology
Castleton College

David McNeill
Department of Psychology
University of Chicago

Ezequiel Morsella
Department of Psychology
San Francisco State University
Department of Neurology
UC San Francisco

Dafni Palti
Brain and Cognitive Sciences
Massachusetts Institute of
    Technology

Jennifer S. Pardo
Department of Psychology
Barnard College

Fey Parrill
Department of Cognitive Science
Case Western University

Francis Quek
Center for Human-Computer
    Interaction
Virginia Tech

Robert E. Remez
Department of Psychology
Barnard College

Miranda Rose
Department of Psychology
La Trobe University

Travis Rose
National Institute of Standards and
    Technology

Michael F. Schober
New School for Social Research

Cristen Torrey
Carnegie Mellon University

Ronald Tuttle
Air Force Institute of Technology

Haleema Welji
Department of Psychology
University of Chicago

Prologue: A Festschrift in Honor of Robert M. Krauss

Ezequiel Morsella

My first interaction with Professor Krauss was by telephone, when he called the drugstore I was working at to tell me that I had been admitted to the Psychology doctoral program at Columbia University, one of my dream schools. Both the content of what Krauss said that day and the manner in which he expressed it—with the thoughtfulness and cadence that only he carries—made that one of the most memorable days of my life. I now appreciate that it may have also been the most consequential day in my life, both professionally and personally. The young pharmacy technician at Robert's Drug Store could not have foreseen all that was to come from knowing Krauss's—that, for example, one day he would have the honor of organizing a conference in homage to his mentor and would also write the prologue to the Festschrift. Unlike any book before it, *Expressing Oneself/Expressing One's Self* embodies the state of the art regarding the experimental study of human communication, by bringing together cutting edge findings from psycholinguistics, communication, cognition, neuroscience, language, and identity in a manner reminiscent of the way that Krauss's own research has integrated knowledge from diverse disciplines in order to illuminate a phenomenon.

In the late 1990s, Krauss's Human Communication Laboratory at Columbia demonstrated that one could be brutally reductionistic about complex processes that, at first glance, appear incompatible with traditional experimental methods. Krauss broke down processes such as interpersonal communication into their component mechanisms—speech production, working memory, speech perception, semantic processing, and perspective taking. The culture of the laboratory was based on the idea that, to appreciate the great feat of linguistic communication, one must possess a solid understanding of all else that is achieved by the brain—perception, action production, and everything in between. Krauss would often seek reductionistic answers to questions such as, "What does it mean to know something?", or "What does it mean to communicate successfully?" Because of his influence, I find great comfort in reducing things to more manageable, sometimes primitive, components. From this standpoint, for example, brains are dauntingly sophisticated and versatile, yet, at the same time, neurons are unthreateningly "dumb" and higher-level modularized systems may function in reflexive, inflexible ways. In that environment, one immediately appreciated that, through their interactions (or communications), constituent subsystems—neurons, modules, representations, or even members of a social group—could render the higher-level system of which they are a part (e.g., an organism or group of people), a form of complexity that looks magical.

Like the sociolinguist William Labov, whom he greatly admires, Krauss displays a knack for taking a hard-nosed approach to subjects that are traditionally regarded as "soft." His nuts-and-bolts approach to how movements can indirectly influence the contents of working memory, how speech can convey identity, or how interpersonal communication can be greater than the sum of its parts reflects his fascination with the ways that simple things—levers, cogs, and cranks—can give rise to complicated functions, even if in roundabout and inefficient ways. I recall him explaining how automotive automatic transmissions work with an eagerness that few would express toward the topic. The enthusiasm reflected his joy at simplifying the complex. Speaking of reductionism, he once stated, "I can't imagine another way of understanding things."

With video cameras, editing consoles, polygraphs, oscilloscopes, and an assortment of high tech gadgets, his lab exemplified more of an engineering than a humanistic approach to human communication. Krauss was unsatisfied with dead-end generalizations (e.g., that language makes humans "special"), which do not explain our place in the larger biological and physical universe of which we are a part. Like the ethologist Tinbergen, Krauss was less concerned about the origin of a mechanism (whether it be from phylogeny, ontogeny, or from a "special module") than he was with how the mechanism works. Facetiously, he would often remark that, just as humans are special because of their unique linguistic ability, opossums are special because of their unique ability to sleep while hanging from their tails. Saying that opossums are special because of this does not at all explain how they achieve this feat. He was also skeptical of indiscriminate Whorfian views of the role of language in intrapersonal cognitive processing. Although the lungs are used when performing an aria, their primary function is breathing. Similarly, linguistic representations can be used to do various things (e.g., rehearse a telephone number in working memory), but their primary function is interpersonal communication, and things such as colors, beliefs, and stomachaches would certainly exist without them. Specifically, the primary function of language is to convert "non-serial" mental representations (e.g., the perceptual representation of a flower) into a serial propositional code that could be transmitted through one of the body's effector systems. One can convey the idea of a red flower piecemeal, through the vocal apparatus for speech or the hands and arms for sign language, consistent with Wundt's assertion that the sentence (a sequential structure) reflects an instantaneous mental event (a nonsequential structure).

When we first met in person in the spring of 1997, we spoke about Lashley, Tolman, the problem of serial order, and the nature of mental representation (e.g., propositional vs. modal accounts). He gave me a reprint of "Nonverbal Behavior and Nonverbal Communication: What Do Conversational Hand Gestures Tell Us?" (Krauss, Chen, & Chawla, 1996), which features a box-and-arrows process model illustrating how arm movements (a motor process) could influence semantic processing (a mental process), which could in turn influence speech production (related to another motor process; see Chapter 5). I still ponder about the implications of this loop-like process model for understanding top-down control in general (see Chapter 12). Looking back, I can conclude with great certainty that

Krauss's thinking was ahead of its time. Many of the ideas he proposed then were seen as controversial or misguided (e.g., that semantic representations of concrete words are "embodied" in sensorimotor-like states). Sometimes, it was difficult for general editors to find suitable reviewers for our research reports. Today, the ideas then espoused by Krauss form part of dominant lore (e.g., Kosslyn, Thompson, & Ganis, 2006; Pulvermuller, 2005).

As an advisor, Krauss had the reputation of being impatient, demanding, and holding students to high standards. He often used biting humor to convey his assessments. After reading one of my poorly crafted drafts of a manuscript, he commented, "Tomorrow I'll use your paper to soak up the extra bacon fat in my frying pan," a style of humor that I happen to relish. His no-frills, forward-looking impatience was tempered with wisdom: He never pushed students to abandon research paths that might not be fruitful in the long run. He demonstrated profound patience when it mattered and reminded students to not "outsophisticate" themselves and to simply let the data speak to them. He used to say, "The data will always tell you something important. It's our job to figure out what that is." As an investigator, Krauss enjoys what he calls "deep thinking," a form of thinking that through him has yielded great and durable fruits. Cynicism, and the ability to cleverly shoot down ideas, was not valued. One also had to build. In his lab, students were free to pursue the directions their curiosity and findings led them. One consequence of this was to break down the boundaries between social, cognitive, and psychophysiological psychology, which Krauss saw as faddish divisions that existed in the academic, but not in the natural, world. He constantly reminded students to "enjoy the process." "We're not paid enough to do something that we don't love to do," he would say. For example, Krauss encouraged me to keep trying to answer the question that perturbed me most, "What is consciousness for?" even though addressing this question interfered to some extent with the goals of his own research program. This led to my single-authored theoretical article on the topic (Morsella, 2005). Few laboratory directors would permit such "distractions." One could not ask for a better doctoral advisor, nor for a more excellent friend. As those who know him can attest, of the many things that Krauss is not, he is certainly not a fair-weather friend.

To understand why Krauss is the way he is, it is time now to use his own reductionistic approach to complex problems and "deconstruct" him into the historical factors that have helped shape him.

THE LIFE OF ROBERT M. KRAUSS

Robert M. (for Meyer—named after a deceased maternal uncle) Krauss was born on August 19, 1931, to Milton Krauss and May Temkin Krauss in Newark, New Jersey. His parents were working-class first-generation Americans, whose main concerns were paying bills and being able to put food on the table. Neither had finished high school. Milton worked for most of his life as a haberdashery sales clerk; May was a full-time homemaker. During the Great Depression, which followed shortly after Krauss's birth, the family shared an apartment with May's two brothers, sister, and father, who was between marriages. They lived in the Weequahic section of Newark, a predominantly Jewish neighborhood that is the setting for many of Phillip Roth's early stories. Over a five-year period, one by one May's relatives (her father included) married and moved out and in 1936, the Krauss family, which a year earlier had been augmented by the birth of a sister, Rhoda Jane, moved to Irvington, a nearby industrial suburb. A third child, Kenneth, was born in 1947. Krauss attended local schools and graduated in 1949 from Irvington High School, where he was an indifferent student.

In September 1949, he enrolled at New York University's (NYU) Washington Square College, planning to major in English, with the vague intention of becoming a novelist. However, he found living in New York and writing for the school newspaper more stimulating than his classes, and by the end of the year he was on academic probation and warned that if his performance did not improve he would have to withdraw from school. As he put it, "I was on the Dean's list, but not the one that people wanted to be on."

The following summer Krauss was hospitalized with what was initially believed to be a mild case of poliomyelitis, but quickly developed into total paralysis. Unable to breathe on his own, he spent the next five weeks in an "iron lung." After a year of hospitalization and another year of outpatient rehabilitation, he was able to walk with the aid of crutches, which he continued to use into his sixties. He returned to NYU in the fall of 1952 and, whether due to the sobering effect of his new physical state or simply the maturing effects of the passage of time, his academic performance improved markedly. During his rehabilitation, he had spent much of his free time browsing the local public library, and among the books he read was an urban sociology textbook, Svend Riemer's *The Modern City*. He found its objective and quantitative analysis of social life appealing, and on his return to school he registered for a course in urban sociology. He enjoyed it, and it was followed by several more undergraduate and graduate sociology courses, where he encountered sociological classics such as Weber, Durkheim, Mead, and Simmel, and modernists like Merton, Lazarsfeld, Parsons, Bales, Goffman, and Sherif. He also began taking psychology courses.

In the summer of 1954, Krauss worked as a research assistant at the Sociology Department of Rutgers University in New Brunswick, New Jersey, for Matilda White Riley, a research scientist at Rutgers who taught a graduate research methods course at New York Uuniversity that he had taken. Riley and her husband John W. Riley, Jr., chair of the Rutgers Sociology Department, had strong ties to the Sociology Department at Harvard and encouraged Krauss to pursue graduate work there, offering to arrange a research assistantship with Talcott Parsons, the eminent social theorist. However, after trying unsuccessfully to read Parsons's epic *The Social System* (Parsons, 1951), Krauss decided his future lay elsewhere, and focused his attention on psychology with a special emphasis on social psychology.

In the fall of 1955, he entered the PhD program in psychology at NYU. The graduate program was relatively large and most of the faculty did not teach undergraduates (none of the faculty with whom Krauss had studied as an undergraduate taught graduate courses). At the time, the social program had four members:

Stuart W. Cook, a soft-spoken and distinguished-looking Southern gentleman who was a staunch civil rights advocate; Marie Jahoda, co-author with Paul Lazarsfeld and Hans Zeisel of *Die Arbeitslosen von Marienthal,* an epic study of unemployment in an Austrian town (Jahoda, Lazarsfeld, & Zeisel, 1933); M. Brewster Smith, then editor of *Journal of Personality and Social Psychology* and co-author with Jerome Bruner and others of the influential *Opinions and Personality*; Isidor Chein; and Irwin Katz. Morton Deutsch and Richard Christie, former members of the department, had recently left the program—Deutsch for Bell Labs and Christie for Columbia.

Despite the large and distinguished contingent of social psychologists, not a lot of the research going on in the program was of great interest to Krauss, who had become fascinated with the study of social interaction. According to Krauss, neither Cook, who was department chair and had heavy administrative responsibilities, nor Brewster Smith, who was preoccupied with the editing of *JPSP*, had active research programs. Jahoda headed a group studying the social psychology of mental health. Chein directed a large team of researchers studying heroin addiction (Chein, Gerard, Lee, & Rosenfeld, 1964). Katz had not yet begun his program of research on interracial interaction.

In 1956, experimental social psychologist Murray Horwitz left the University of Illinois to join the NYU social program. Horwitz's MIT dissertation, done under the supervision of Kurt Lewin, had shown that the Zeigarnik effect could be moderated by the actions of another group member—that is, the effect of task interruption on recall was diminished when another member of one's group completed the task. The finding, interesting in its own right, was interpreted by Horwitz in the abstruse terms of Lewin's topological and vector theory, which he (unlike most of Lewin's former students) continued to espouse literally. Horwitz thought that electromyography could be used to measure Lewinian tension systems directly and had mounted a research program to pursue this idea. Krauss was assigned as Horwitz's research assistant, and Horwitz set him to work on the project.

Although electromyography is now a standard part of the psychophysiologist's armamentarium, in the 1950s it was more often used for medical diagnosis than for psychological research. Its output was difficult to quantify, the equipment Horwitz's team used to input and record the muscle action potential (essentially a modified vacuum tube electroencephalograph) was cantankerous and unstable, and the surface electrodes used as pick-ups made the apparatus susceptible to a variety of artifacts. Krauss, who had had no training in psychophysiology and relatively little technical knowledge, set about learning how to do electromyographic (EMG) recording (some of the kinesiology he had picked up in rehabilitation was helpful) and how to quantify the EMG output. The year was spent planning an experiment with Horwitz, purchasing and modifying an EEG machine, and building an apparatus.

For a variety of reasons, by the beginning of the 1957 spring semester the experiment had not yet been run. Krauss became discouraged and seriously contemplated dropping out of graduate school. To complicate matters, his wife (he had married

Iseli Koenig, a fellow graduate student in the fall of 1957) became pregnant; a single research assistant stipend would be insufficient to support the family.

Fortunately, Morton Deutsch was seeking a full-time research assistant at Bell Labs. While visiting Horwitz, Deutsch had seen a demonstration of the equipment Krauss had built for the aborted EMG experiment and was impressed by it. Not only did the assistantship carry with it a salary sufficient to support the small family (in October of 1958, Krauss's wife gave birth to a daughter, Pam; a second daughter, Erika, was born four years later), but the Labs would underwrite his tuition for graduate courses. Deutsch offered him the job with the stipulation that he continue to work toward his doctorate, and Krauss gratefully accepted.

The Bell Labs psychology research group had been organized by Yale's Carl Hovland. At one time or another, it included such luminaries-to-be as Deutsch, Roger Shepard, Bela Julesz, George Sperling, Herbert Jenkins, Saul Sternberg, Thomas Landauer, Seymour Rosenberg, J. Douglas Carroll, Ernst Z. Rothkopf, and John Krauskopf. In those days the Labs was a researcher's paradise. Investigators were given adequate funding and the freedom to pursue their projects, without the teaching and administrative responsibilities that complicate academic life. There was little concern for disciplinary lines (Max Mathews, who headed the group, was an engineer; Julesz's PhD was in applied mathematics). Distinguished outside speakers from a variety of fields visited the Labs frequently to lecture on their research. In addition to the small cadre of psychologists, the Labs had a distinguished group of statisticians led by John Tukey, such eminent speech scientists as James Flanagan, Bishnu Atal, Peter Denes, and Elliot Pinson, and what was arguably the world's preeminent cohort of computer scientists. The atmosphere was informal, congenial, and intellectually stimulating; cross-disciplinary collaboration and unconventional thinking was encouraged. Much of this spirit was later imbued into Krauss's own Human Communication Laboratory.

In his doctoral dissertation (done under the supervision of Kurt Lewin), Deutsch had studied the effect of cooperative and competitive situations on group performance and attitudes. Subsequently, influenced by the writings of the economist Thomas Schelling, he studied performance in "mixed motive" games that contained both cooperative and competitive elements. Deutsch and Krauss devised a "bargaining game" (often called the Acme-Bolt Trucking Game), and Krauss designed and built the apparatus, using counters manufactured for pinball machines, telephone switchboard keys, and pushbuttons salvaged from telephones. It proved a fertile set-up for studying interaction in mixed motive settings. The research found (among other things) that having a means of threatening their partners adversely affected bargainers' ability to coordinate mutually advantageous agreements––a finding that had special resonance during the tense years of the Cold War (Deutsch & Krauss, 1960; Deutsch, Krauss, & Rosenau, 1962; Krauss, 1966; Krauss & Deutsch, 1966). In 1962, Deutsch and Krauss received the AAAS Socio-Psychological Essay Prize for this research. They also began collaborating on a book, *Theories in Social Psychology,* for a series that E. G. Boring was editing for Basic Books. Published in 1965, *Theories* was well received and was later translated into four languages.

By 1964, Deutsch, a confirmed New Yorker, had grown tired of the daily com-
mute to rural New Jersey and accepted a professorship at Columbia University's
Teachers College. He recommended Krauss as his replacement, and the Bell Labs
management accepted his recommendation. Krauss, who had recently completed
his PhD at NYU, was promoted and encouraged to develop a research program
that was not simply a continuation of Deutsch's work on bargaining.

In their studies, Deutsch and Krauss had found that allowing bargainers to
communicate over a voice channel often complicated the process of reaching an
accommodation (Deutsch, Krauss, & Rosenau, 1962; Krauss & Deutsch, 1966).
The participants' exchanges were recorded and transcribed, and Krauss, who
studied them intensively, began to find the subjects' ineffectual attempts to reach
an accommodation by communicating more interesting than their bargaining
behavior. His interest in language and communication was further stimulated by
Roger Brown's research and the two chapters on language that appeared in the
first edition of Brown's *Social Psychology* (Brown, 1965). What Krauss found
frustrating about analyzing the bargainers' interactions, and indeed about most
studies of "communication," was the lack of a clear idea of what communication consisted of and how it was accomplished. Although the information theorist Claude Shannon, a Bell Labs icon, had defined communication in terms of
uncertainty reduction (Shannon & Weaver, 1975), that approach did not work
for what had come to be called interpersonal communication. Roger Brown's
seminal essay "How Shall a Thing Be Called?" (Brown, 1958) got Krauss thinking about the basic language function of *reference*—using language to designate
objects, events, relationships, etc. As Brown argued, even for objects that have
well-established names, the relationship of the referring expression to its referent
is far from simple; the same object can felicitously be referred to as *coin, dime,
money,* etc., depending on circumstances. As regards communication, deciding what a thing should be called depended both on to whom the message was
addressed and the context in which the communication was set.

For his research, Krauss devised a simple referential communication task utilizing specially designed "nonsense figures" that did not have conventional names.
In the task, a sender had to refer to the figures in communicating with a receiver,
who had to make a selection based on the message the sender had conveyed. This
provided an objective way of assessing the effectiveness of communication and
an opportunity to observe the way dyads converged on a referring expression over
the course of successive references. The task proved to be a convenient method
for studying a variety of communicative phenomena, among them effects of feedback, audience design, and perspective taking.

In collaboration with Sam Glucksberg of Princeton University (see Chapter 1),
a friend from graduate school, Krauss also began a program of research on the
development of communication. The research had its inception at a get-together
of the two families when Glucksberg tried to run their children on Krauss's referential communication task. Although the children had no difficulty understanding the task, to the surprise of both fathers they seemed incapable of formulating
referring expressions that would allow their partner to choose the desired stimulus.

Using a modified version of the task in which the children tried to build identical stacks of blocks marked with the novel forms of communicating, Glucksberg and Krauss ran students in the Princeton public school system and a local nursery school. The studies confirmed what they had found with their own children. Although the performance of children eight years and older on the task was virtually errorless from the outset, younger children performed poorly because the idiosyncratic expressions they used to refer to the novel forms seemed not to take their partners' perspective into account (Glucksberg & Krauss, 1967; Glucksberg, Krauss, & Weisberg, 1966; Krauss & Glucksberg, 1969, 1970, 1977).

Despite the productive and supportive atmosphere of Bell Labs, Krauss had always imagined himself returning to academia. In 1965, he accepted an assistant professorship at Princeton, and in the fall of 1966 moved there with his family. The rather traditional and formal Princeton department contrasted sharply with the freewheeling workplace he had just left at the Labs, and Krauss had difficulty adjusting to it. To complicate matters, soon after they arrived in Princeton, he and his wife separated. Krauss found himself living alone in reduced circumstances and wondering whether his decision to leave the Labs had been wise.

At just about the time his spirits were at their lowest ebb, he was invited by Roger Brown to spend the next year at Harvard as visiting lecturer in the Department of Social Relations. The opportunity seemed heaven sent. Although psychology at Harvard was fractionated and some of its most eminent figures had either retired or moved on, it still retained much of its former luster. Krauss would co-teach a graduate seminar on language with Brown and small undergraduate courses on social psychological theory and interpersonal conflict. He would have plenty of opportunity to interact with Brown and his graduate students, with members of the Center for Cognitive Studies and its director, Jerome Bruner, and with other members of the Harvard faculty, principally Robert Rosenthal and Roger Shepard, an old friend who had moved there from Bell Labs. The year was a good one for Krauss, despite the fact that he did not accomplish much of a concrete nature. Brown was a gracious and intellectually generous host, and Krauss had useful interactions with many of the senior and junior faculty. The Cambridge academic community was itself lively and intellectually stimulating—a welcome change from what Krauss considered a staid environment at Princeton.

Around the middle of the academic year, Krauss was introduced to Ernest Lynton, a charismatic Rutgers physicist and dean, who was organizing a new undergraduate division of the university scheduled to open in the fall of 1969, to be called Livingston College. Although Rutgers was the state university of New Jersey, it was then a relatively small, rather traditional school able to accommodate only a small fraction of the state's college-bound population. Because of its size, it admitted relatively few minority students. Lynton's charge was to make Livingston an "urban" undergraduate school.

While Krauss was at Harvard, the Princeton Psychology Department was undergoing a series of changes. As part of the process, Glucksberg was made acting chairperson, and a search outside the department for a chairperson resulted in Leo Kamin, former chair of the department at McMaster University, taking the helm with a mandate to modernize and rebuild the department. Krauss was invited by Lynton to organize and chair the nascent Livingston College department and, after a brief conversation with Kamin about the future of social psychology at Princeton, he decided to accept the Rutgers offer.

The Livingston College campus was to be located on the former site of Camp Kilmer, a decommissioned army base across the river from the main Rutgers campus. Dean Lynton had recruited a surprisingly strong core faculty, largely by involving them in his vision of a modern undergraduate school that was open to nontraditional students and not bound by traditional academic conventions. Perhaps most important was that the college was to have a large minority representation both in the faculty and the student body. The core faculty Lynton had recruited were mostly young and quite liberal politically, excited by this opportunity to put their values into practice. They included notables such as Roy D'Andrade, Robin Fox, and Lionel Tiger in anthropology; Irving Louis Horowitz in sociology; and George Levine, the novelist Tony Cade Bambara, and poet Niki Giovanni in English literature. In psychology, in addition to Krauss's, Lynton had recruited Seymour Rosenberg (a former Bell Labs colleague of Krauss's), who transferred from Rutgers College, and Sylvan Tomkins, a distinguished personality theorist, whom Krauss knew from his brief stint at Princeton. In addition, the department would be allowed to hire three assistant professors. The challenge of participating in the development of a new college appealed to Krauss, as did the prospect of living near his daughters, who had remained with their mother in Princeton.

The 1968-1969 academic year was spent recruiting faculty and developing a set of operating principles and procedures for the new college. Ultimately, Krauss hired three newly minted PhDs—Richard Ashmore (from UCLA), Russell Jones (from the University of North Carolina), and Melvin Gary (from Ohio State). In the fall of 1968, he was invited by Academic Press to take over the editorship of *Journal of Experimental Social Psychology* from John Thibaut, who had been its founding editor. Krauss agreed and served as editor of *JESP* from 1969 to 1974.

Early in 1969 Krauss was offered a professorship in the Psychology Department at Columbia University. A once distinguished department that, according to Krauss, had fallen on hard times, the Columbia department was undergoing a restructuring not unlike that at Princeton. The department was narrowly focused on two areas: operant conditioning and visual perception. Cognition, personality, and development were largely absent. Social psychology was located in a separate department, which included notable figures such as Stanley Schachter, Richard Christie, Bibb Latané, and (earlier) William McGuire. Columbia had selected Robert Bush, an eminent mathematical psychologist who had rebuilt the department at the University of Pennsylvania, as department head to expand and modernize the department and broaden its focus. An experienced administrator, Bush had negotiated a package with the Columbia administration that included additional faculty lines and renovated laboratory and office space. As part of the agreement, Stanley Schachter and Richard Christie, the remaining members of the autonomous social psychology program, would join the Psychology Department and three additional people in the social-personality area would be recruited. In addition to Krauss, the department hired Jonathan Freedman of Stanford and Phillip Shaver, who had just received his doctorate at the University of Michigan. Among the department's other hires were the psycholinguist Thomas Bever and developmental psychologist Deanna Kuhn. Krauss found the Columbia offer attractive both because of Bush's plans for rebuilding the department and the opportunity to have Schachter, Freedman, and Bever as colleagues. He also found life in New Brunswick, a small, gritty industrial city, unrewarding and the prospect of living in New York City was attractive. Krauss decided to accept the Columbia offer, after acceding to Lynton's request that he stay at Rutgers an additional year to see the department through the school's opening. He moved to Columbia in June 1970.

As it turned out, Columbia was unable to fulfill many of the commitments it had made to Bush and to the psychology faculty. The student disorders of 1968 had rocked the university and precipitated a change of administration. Alumni, alienated by the actions of both students and administration, withheld their support, and the university found itself unable to keep many of the promises it had made. Psychology was hit particularly hard because the departmental retrenchment was aborted midway through the process. As a result, hiring plans were curtailed and commitments for space and construction were cut back.

Despite these distractions, Krauss found Columbia much to his liking. The students, both graduate and undergraduate, were superb and his colleagues in the social area were congenial and supportive. Although the university was not able to provide much in the way of support for his research, his continued collaboration with former Bell Labs colleagues proved valuable. Krauss had become interested in nonverbal communication, and the Labs provided him with professional quality videotape recorders and a computer-based editing system that he needed to study it. They also sent a technician to install the equipment in the small lab space he had been allotted. Part of the set-up included video cameras that could be remotely controlled from a small control room. While the set-up would not seem impressive today, at the time it was state of the art.

THE HUMAN COMMUNICATION LAB AT COLUMBIA

In much of the research on nonverbal communication in the 1970s, nonverbal behavior was conceived of as a separate or independent communication system, distinct from language—"... an elaborate and secret code that is written nowhere, known to none, and understood by all" is the way the linguist Edward Sapir (1949, p. 556) put it. Krauss was more interested in the way talkers combined nonverbal behavior with speech to communicate and the way nonverbal components of speech could convey information that was independent of the speech's verbal content. In his earliest work at Columbia, he collaborated with Bell Labs colleague Lynn Streeter to study vocal changes during dissimulation (Streeter, Krauss, Geller, Olson, & Apple, 1977) and emotional stress (Streeter, Macdonald, Apple, Krauss, & Galotti, 1983). He also studied how acoustic properties of speech affected listeners' attributions about the talkers (Apple, Streeter, & Krauss, 1979), using advanced speech synthesis technology developed at the Labs. With former Bell Labs colleague Peter Bricker, he studied how communicators used nonverbal signals as back channels in a referential communication task (Krauss, Bricker, McMahon, & Garlock, 1977).

Krauss's interest in nonverbal behavior led directly to the study of emotional expressiveness. The earliest studies examined the relative contributions of visible nonverbal behavior and the verbal and paralinguistic contents of speech to the perception of emotion (Krauss, Apple, Morency, Wenzel, & Winton, 1981). In 1974, Lois E. Putnam, a developmental psychophysiologist who had just received her degree at the University of Wisconsin, joined the department. She and Krauss became friends, and in a short time the friendship developed into a close personal relationship. It also led to productive research collaboration. In a series of studies they examined the relationship between nonverbal expressiveness and autonomic (heart rate and skin conductance response [SCR]) responding (Winton, Putnam, & Krauss, 1984). They also examined the effects of dissimulation on vocal and autonomic responding (Putnam, Winton, & Krauss, 1982). Putnam and Krauss were married in January 1981. The following October a son, Max, was born.

During this period, Krauss also began a series of studies on the role of perspective taking in communication with graduate student Susan Fussell. Using a variant of the referential communication paradigm, they were able to demonstrate that communicators varied their messages to accord with the perspectives of their intended audiences, and that these variations affected the communicative effectiveness of their messages (Fussell & Krauss, 1989a, 1989b, 1992; Krauss & Fussell, 1991). They also investigated the perspective-taking process itself, finding both accuracy and systematic bias in people's ability to estimate the way knowledge was distributed in a population (Fussell & Krauss, 1991).

Krauss spent the 1983-1984 year in Palo Alto, California as a fellow at the Center for Advanced Study in the Behavioral Sciences. His original plan was to write a book on the relationship of speech and nonverbal behavior, but as the year passed he found himself increasingly intrigued by recent research and theory about speech-accompanying gestures. The prevailing wisdom was that these gestures functioned communicatively and served as an independent channel of communication. However, Krauss found the empirical evidence for this claim unconvincing, and mused about other functions these gestures might serve. The following year back at Columbia, he launched a series of studies that had two goals: to assess quantitatively the amount and significance of the information actually conveyed by gesture and to understand the role gesturing played in speech production. In a series of studies, Krauss and his students demonstrated that gesturally conveyed information tended to be redundant with speech and played a relatively insignificant role in communication (Krauss, Morrel-Samuels, & Colasante, 1991; Krauss, Dushay, Chen, & Rauscher, 1995). They also found that gesturing seemed to facilitate speech production by aiding in the retrieval of word forms from lexical memory (Morrel-Samuels & Krauss, 1992; Chawla & Krauss, 1994; Rauscher, Krauss, & Chen, 1996). Krauss was conducting this research when I arrived at Columbia.

From this line of research evolved the gestural feedback model (GFM; Morsella & Krauss, 2004), in which some of the gestures that accompany speech, a species of movement known as lexical gestures, can facilitate lexical retrieval by sustaining the activation of a target word's semantic features long enough in working memory for the process of word production to take place. The GFM proposes that, during lexical search, gestures continually reactivate semantics through feedback from effectors or motor commands, in much the same way that vocal (or subvocal) rehearsal keeps echoic representations active in the phonological loop (Baddeley, 1986; Burgess & Hitch, 1999). (See supporting evidence for the GFM in Chapter 5.) From this standpoint, lexical gestures activate the semantics of words that are "grounded" (Harnad, 1990) in sensorimotor states (see Barsalou, 2008). This line of research helped bring back into discussion non-traditional approaches in which the nature of mental representation is based in part on motor processing, as in "peripheralist," "motor," "efferent," and "reafferent" theories of thought (e.g., Festinger, Ono, Burnham, & Bamber, 1967; Hebb, 1968; Held & Rekosh, 1963; McGuigan, 1966; Münsterberg, 1891; Sperry, 1952; Washburn, 1928; Watson, 1924). For contemporary treatments regarding how action influences the nature of conscious percepts, see Gray (1995), Hochberg (1998), and O'Regan and Noë (2001); see Sheerer (1984) and Mahon and Caramazza (2008) for reviews of the shortcomings of these approaches.

As he approached his sixties, it became obvious that Krauss was becoming progressively more infirm. Walking with crutches was increasingly effortful, forcing him to drastically restrict his activities. By the mid-1990s, he was diagnosed as having post-polio syndrome, a condition that affects polio survivors years after recovery from an initial acute attack of the poliomyelitis virus. Although its cause is not well understood, post-polio syndrome is believed to result from the degeneration of individual nerve terminals in the motor units that remain after the initial illness. In the year 2000, Krauss gave up crutch walking for a motorized wheelchair. Although the wheelchair restricted him to accessible venues (travel became especially problematic), the increased mobility it afforded allowed him to pursue a number of activities he had been forced to give up.

A long-standing interest for Krauss had been how people used nonverbal behaviors to convey information about themselves. Rereading Erving Goffman's classic study *The Presentation of Self in Everyday Life* (Goffman, 1959) led Krauss to speculate about the information that a speaker's voice conveyed (quite apart from the semantic content of the utterance) and how that was related to the speaker's identity. Although traditional psycholinguistic models of speech perception viewed the variability that characterizes speech production as a kind of noise that listeners got rid of by "normalization" (see Chapter 10 and Chapter 11), there was increasing evidence that such "indexical information" was both retained and utilized.

The first study examined the extent to which voices conveyed information about the speaker's physical characteristics (Krauss, Freyberg, & Morsella, 2002). Using voice samples collected from Sunday strollers in New York's Central Park, the investigators found that naïve listeners could estimate speakers' age and height from their voices nearly as well as they could from their pictures. Further studies, some under way and others completed, have examined acoustic, articulatory, and lexical differences in males' and females' speech, how such differences affect listeners' evaluations of the speaker, and how voice fundamental frequency differentially affects the evaluations of male and female speakers.

Just as I could not foresee what was to come following that fateful telephone call when Professor Krauss invited me to be a graduate student at Columbia, I strongly believe that not even Krauss himself could foresee the various ways in which his efforts will continue to benefit the various fields of cognitive science. For example, Krauss's contributions to understanding the nature of communication and social interaction have led to hypotheses that have strong implications, not just for interpersonal processes, but also for *intracranial* (for lack of a better word) communication. The principles of interpersonal communication espoused by Krauss (e.g., Krauss & Fussell, 1996; see Chapter 6) will be instrumental in unraveling the ways in which different systems of the brain, having distinct operating principles and phylogenetic origins, are capable of cross-talking and yielding integrated behavior (cf., Morsella, Krieger, & Bargh, 2009). In this vein, research today has begun to identify, not only the networks of neuroanatomical regions that constitute the mechanisms underlying cognitive functions (e.g., visual working memory), but the ways in which these regions must interact in order to instantiate these functions. For a given mental process, it seems that the mode of interaction (or communication) among brain regions is as important as the nature and loci of the regions (Buzsáki, 2006). For instance, the presence or lack of interregional synchrony leads to different cognitive and behavioral outcomes (Hummel & Gerloff, 2005; see review of neuronal communication through "coherence" in Fries, 2005). The brain is all about communication. In this way, Krauss's findings and his rigorous and reductionistic approach to traditionally experimentally intractable puzzles such as social interaction and communication (whether it be *inter-* or *intracranial*) will continue to benefit the quest to understand the mind from a scientific standpoint.

In 2001, Krauss was elected a fellow of the American Academy of Arts and Sciences. In 2003, he was elected to membership in the Society of Experimental Psychologists. In July 2008, Krauss retired after 38 years of service at Columbia, taking the title of Professor Emeritus. His Human Communication Lab continues to operate, and he teaches a graduate seminar, Contemporary Topics in Language and Communication each year.

ACKNOWLEDGMENTS

This Festschrift was a wonderful group effort of which I have been very proud to be a part. On June 10, 2006, researchers from around the globe gathered at Columbia University to celebrate the science and person of Robert Krauss. For their contributions to both this wonderful event and the present book, I would like to acknowledge and thank (in alphabetical order) John Bargh, Niall Bolger, Purnima Chawla, Yihsiu Chen, Shirley Y. Y. Cheng, Chi-yue Chiu, Kay Deaux, Geraldine

Downey, Paul Dukes (Taylor & Francis Press), Phoebe Ellsworth, Lawrence Erlbaum Associates (LEA), Susan Fussell, Sam Glucksberg, Anthony Greenwald, Uri Hadar, Tory Higgins, Julian Hochberg, Shane Jones, Sotaro Kita, Max Krauss, Stephen Krieger, David McNeill, Walter Mischel, Jennifer Pardo, Lois Putnam, Robert Remez, Miranda Rose, Michael Schober, Gün R. Semin, and Lisa Son, as well as Taylor & Francis Group, LEA, and the Department of Psychology and the office staff at the Department of Psychology at Columbia University.

REFERENCES

Apple, W., Streeter, L. A., & Krauss, R. M. (1979). Effects of pitch and speech rate on personal attributions. *Journal of Personality and Social Psychology, 37,* 715–727.

Baddeley, A. D. (1986). *Working memory.* Oxford, UK: Oxford University Press.

Barsalou, L.W. (2008). Grounded cognition. *Annual Review of Psychology, 59,* 617–645.

Brown, R. (1958). How shall a thing be called? *Psychological Review, 65,* 14–21.

Brown, R. (1965). *Social psychology.* New York: Free Press.

Burgess, N., & Hitch, G. J. (1999). Memory for serial order: A network model of the phonological loop and its timing. *Psychological Review, 106,* 551–581.

Buzsáki, G. (2006). *Rhythms of the brain.* New York: Oxford University Press.

Chawla, P., & Krauss, R. M. (1994). Gesture and speech in spontaneous and rehearsed narratives. *Journal of Experimental Social Psychology, 30,* 580–601.

Chein, I., Gerard, D. L., Lee, R. S., & Rosenfeld, E. (1964). *The road to H.* New York: Basic Books.

Deutsch, M., & Krauss, R. M. (1960). The effect of threat upon interpersonal bargaining. *Journal of Abnormal and Social Psychology, 61,*181–189.

Deutsch, M., Krauss, R. M., & Rosenau, N. (1962). Dissonance or defensiveness? *Journal of Personality, 30,* 16–28.

Deutsch, M., & Krauss, R. M. (1965). *Theories in social psychology.* New York: Basic Books.

Festinger, L., Ono, H., Burnham, C. A., & Bamber, D. (1967). Efference and the conscious experience of perception. *Journal of Experimental Psychology Monograph, 74,* 1–36.

Fries, P. (2005). A mechanism for cognitive dynamics: Neuronal communication through neuronal coherence. *Trends in Cognitive Sciences,* 9, 474–480.

Fussell, S. R., & Krauss, R. M. (1989a). The effects of intended audience on message production and comprehension: Reference in a common ground framework. *Journal of Experimental Social Psychology, 25,* 203–219.

Fussell, S. R., & Krauss, R. M. (1989b). Understanding friends and strangers: The effects of audience design on message comprehension. *European Journal of Social Psychology, 19,* 509–526.

Fussell, S. R., & Krauss, R. M. (1991). Sensitivity and bias in estimates of others' knowledge. *European Journal of Social Psychology, 21,* 445–454.

Fussell, S. R., & Krauss, R. M. (1992). Coordination of knowledge in communication: Effects of speakers' assumptions about others' knowledge. *Journal of Personality and Social Psychology, 62,* 378–391.

Glucksberg, S., & Krauss, R. M. (1967). What do people say after they have learned how to talk? Studies of the development of referential communication. *Merrill-Palmer Quarterly, 13,* 309–316.

Glucksberg, S., Krauss, R. M., & Weisberg, R. (1966). Referential communication in nursery school children: Method and some preliminary findings. *Journal of Experimental Child Psychology, 3,* 333–342.

Goffman, E. (1959). *The presentation of self in everyday life.* Garden City, NY: Doubleday.

Gray, J. A. (1995). The contents of consciousness: A neuropsychological conjecture. *Behavioral and Brain Sciences 18,* 659–676.

Harnad, S. (1990). The symbol grounding problem. *Physica D, 42,* 335–346.

Hebb, D. O. (1968). Concerning imagery. *Psychological Review, 75,* 466–477.

Held, R., & Rekosh, J. (1963). Motor-sensory feedback and the geometry of visual space. *Science, 141,* 722–723.

Hochberg, J. (1998). Gestalt theory and its legacy: Organization in eye and brain, in attention and mental representation. In J. Hochberg (Ed.), *Perception and cognition at century's end. Handbook of perception and cognition* (2nd ed., pp. 253–306). San Diego, CA: Academic Press.

Hummel, F., & Gerloff, C. (2005). Larger interregional synchrony is associated with greater behavioral success in a complex sensory integration task in humans. *Cerebral Cortex, 15,* 670–678.

Jahoda, M., Lazarsfeld, P. F., & Zeisel, H. (1933). *Die arbeitslosen vom marienthal. ein soziographischer versuch über die wirkungen von langandauernder arbeitslosigkeit.* Leipzig: Hirzel.

Kosslyn, S. M., Thomspon, W. L., & Ganis, G. (2006). *The case for mental imagery.* New York: Oxford University Press.

Krauss, R. M. (1966). Structural and attitudinal factors in interpersonal bargaining. *Journal of Experimental Social Psychology, 2,* 42–55.

Krauss, R. M., Apple, W., Morency, N., Wenzel, C., & Winton, W. (1981). Verbal, vocal and visible factors in judgments of another's affect. *Journal of Personality and Social Psychology, 40,* 312–320.

Krauss, R. M., Bricker, P. D., McMahon, L. E., & Garlock, C. M. (1977). The role of audible and visible back channel responses in interpersonal communication. *Journal of Personality and Social Psychology, 35,* 523–529.

Krauss, R. M., Chen, Y., & Chawla, P. (1996). Nonverbal behavior and nonverbal communication: What do conversational hand gestures tell us? *Advances in Experimental Social Psychology, 28,* 389–450.

Krauss, R. M., & Deutsch, M. (1966). Communication in interpersonal bargaining. *Journal of Personality and Social Psychology, 4,* 572–577.

Krauss, R. M., Dushay, R. A., Chen, Y., & Rauscher, F. (1995). The communicative value of conversational hand gestures. *Journal of Experimental Social Psychology, 31,* 533–552.

Krauss, R. M., Freyberg, R., & Morsella, E. (2002). Inferring speaker's physical attributes from their voices. *Journal of Experimental Social Psychology, 38,* 618–625.

Krauss, R. M., & Fussell, S. R. (1991). Perspective-taking in communication: Representations of others' knowledge in reference. *Social Cognition, 9,* 2–24.

Krauss, R. M., & Fussell, S. R. (1996). Social psychological models of interpersonal communication. In E. T. Higgins & A. Kruglanski (Eds.), *Social psychology: A handbook of basic principles* (pp. 655–701). New York: Guilford.

Krauss, R. M., & Glucksberg, S. (1969). The development of communication: Competence as a function of age. *Child Development, 40,* 256–266.

Krauss, R. M., & Glucksberg, S. (1970). Socialization of communication skill. In R. A. Hoppe, G. A. Milton, & E. C. Simmel (Eds.), *Early experience and the processes of socialization.* New York: Academic Press.

Krauss, R. M., & Glucksberg, S. (1977). Social and nonsocial speech. *Scientific American, 236,* 100–105.

Krauss, R. M., Morrel-Samuels, P., & Colasante, C. (1991). Do conversational hand gestures communicate? *Journal of Personality and Social Psychology, 61,* 743–754.

Mahon, B. Z., & Caramazza, A. (2008). A critical look at the embodied cognition hypothesis and a new proposal for grounding conceptual content. *Journal of Physiology–Paris, 102,* 59–70.

McGuigan, F. J. (1966). *Thinking: Studies of covert language processes.* New York: Appleton-Century-Crofts.

Morrel-Samuels, P., & Krauss, R. M. (1992). Word familiarity predicts the temporal asynchrony of hand gestures and speech. *Journal of Experimental Psychology: Learning, Memory and Cognition, 18,* 615–623.

Morsella, E. (2005). The function of phenomenal states: Supramodular interaction theory. *Psychological Review, 112,* 1000–1021.

Morsella, E., & Krauss, R. M. (2004). The role of gestures in spatial working memory and speech. *American Journal of Psychology, 117,* 411–424.

Morsella, E., Krieger, S. C., & Bargh, J. A. (2009). The function of consciousness: Why skeletal muscles are "voluntary" muscles. In E. Morsella, J. A. Bargh, & P. M. Gollwitzer (Eds.), *Oxford handbook of human action* (pp. 625–634). New York: Oxford University Press.

Münsterberg, H. (1891). Über aufgaben und methoden der psychologie. *Schriften der Gesellschaft für psychologische Forsschung, 1,* 93–272.

O'Regan, J. K., & Noë, A. (2001). A sensorimotor account of vision and visual consciousness. *Behavioral and Brain Sciences, 24,* 939–973.

Parsons, T. (1951). *The social system.* New York: Free Press.

Pulvermuller, F. (2005). Brain mechanisms linking language and action. *Nature Reviews Neuroscience, 6,* 576–582.

Putnam, L. E., Winton, W., & Krauss, R. M. (1982). Effects of nonverbal affective dissimulation on phasic autonomic and facial responses. *Psychophysiology, 19,* 580–581.

Rauscher, F. B., Krauss, R. M., & Chen, Y. (1996). Gesture, speech and lexical access: The role of lexical movements in speech production. *Psychological Science, 7,* 226–231.

Riemer, S. (1952). *The Modern City: An Introduction to Urban Sociology.* New York: Prentice-Hall, Inc.

Sapir, E. (1949). The unconscious patterning of behavior in society. In D. Mandelbaum (Ed.), *Selected writings of Edward Sapir in language, culture and personality* (pp. 544–559). Berkeley: University of California Press.

Shannon, C. E., & Weaver, W. (1975). *The mathematical theory of communication* (6th ed.). Urbana: University of Illinois Press.

Sheerer, E. (1984). Motor theories of cognitive structure: A historical review. In W. Prinz & A. F. Sanders (Eds.), *Cognition and motor processes.* Berlin: Springer-Verlag.

Smith, M. B., Bruner, J. S., & White, R. W. (1956). *Opinions and Personality.* New York: Wiley.

Sperry, R. W. (1952). Neurology and the mind-brain problem. *American Scientist, 40,* 291–312.

Streeter, L. A., Krauss, R. M., Geller, V., Olson, C. T., & Apple, W. (1977). Pitch changes during attempted deception. *Journal of Personality and Social Psychology, 35,* 345–350.

Streeter, L. A., Macdonald, N. H., Apple, W., Krauss, R. M., & Galotti, K. M. (1983). Acoustic and perceptual indicators of emotional stress. *Journal of the Acoustical Society of America, 73,* 1354–1360.

Washburn, M. F. (1928). Emotion and thought: A motor theory of their relation. In C. Murchison (Ed.), *Feelings and emotions: The Wittenberg Symposium* (pp. 99–145). Worcester, MA: Clark University Press.

Watson, J. B. (1924). *Behaviorism.* New York: W. W. Norton.

Winton, W. M., Putnam, L. E., & Krauss, R. M. (1984). Phasic autonomic correlates of facial and self-reported affective responses. *Journal of Experimental Social Psychology, 27,* 195–216.

Section I

The Production of Gestures, Speech, and Action

1 On the Occasion of the Festschrift in Honor of Robert M. Krauss

The Science of Communication, Cognition, Language, and Identity

Sam Glucksberg

Bob and I met in graduate school at New York University in 1956. The cognitive revolution was on the near horizon, but at that time, in that department, it had not yet made any impression, let alone impact. Bob was in the social psychology program; I was in the experimental one. Despite our being in separate programs, we shared many first- and second-year courses that were common across the department, such as the beginning statistics and history of psychology courses. My very first publication arose from a summer research assistantship that Bob and I held with Irwin Katz, during which we found that wives of graduate students were more satisfied with their lives if they scored highly on a measure of nurturance (Katz, Glucksberg, & Krauss, 1960). That the entire sample of subjects consisted of male graduate students and their wives did not dampen our (that is, Bob's and my) enthusiasm for our very first publication! We have learned a lot since then.

Behaviorism was the dominant ideology in the experimental program. With the exception of social learning theory, social psychology found little of relevance in what was then known as experimental psychology. Indeed, experimental psychology was not just a method of doing psychology. It also explicitly laid out the appropriate topics for study within experimental psychology.* I chose problem solving as my dissertation topic, which led one of our more behaviorally oriented clinical psychologist faculty to observe, in a somewhat accusatory tone, that I was really a social psychologist in disguise. This attitude persisted until at least the late 1980s, when the National Institute of Mental Health review committee for "Cognition" was titled the "Review Committee for Cognition, Emotion and

---

* The canon concerning the content of experimental psychology was Woodworth and Schlossberg's text, *Experimental Psychology* (1954).

Personality." Even the subject of language was suspect, as reflected in the rather awkward name for a new journal within experimental psychology, *Journal of Verbal Learning and Verbal Behavior*—now more appropriately titled *Journal of Memory and Language*.

While Experimental Psychology (caps intended) excluded such an eminently human accomplishment as language, what was social psychology's position on language and human communication? For reasons too complex to consider here, social psychology was (and still largely is) unconcerned with language and language use, with the notable exception of the long-standing and intense interest in persuasion, propaganda, and attitude change. Social psychologists in Europe were not quite as disinterested in language as their counterparts in the United States and Canada but, still, work on language was surprisingly sparse. In a volume that came out in 1982, *Advances in the Social Psychology of Language* (Fraser & Sherer, 1982), the editors noted, with a hint of perplexity, that social psychologists had largely ignored language as an object of study. As I suggested in my review of that volume (Glucksberg, 1984), there was good reason for social psychology to ignore language. From the beginnings of the Chomskian and cognitive revolutions (Danks & Glucksberg, 1980), language had not been viewed as either social or interactive. Instead, language was seen as an encapsulated system, isolated not only from interpersonal and social contexts but also from *intrapersonal* contexts—the linguistic faculty was considered to be distinct and independent of other cognitive systems, including world knowledge (cf., Fodor, 1983). Given this zeitgeist, when Roger Brown turned his social-psychological lens onto language, that lens was highly focused on language as a thing unto itself, and not as a component or product of social interaction (cf., Brown, 1958). In Brown's groundbreaking study of language acquisition (Brown, 1973), the primary unit of analysis was the MLU—the mean length of a child's utterance as the child's linguistic processor progressed toward the linguistic gold standard, the sentence. The proverbial Martian, upon observing the linguistic and psycholinguistic literature of the time, could have easily inferred that people spoke primarily to utter grammatical utterances and to avoid uttering ungrammatical ones.

Within this context, Bob Krauss forged his own independent path for an explicitly social-psychological study of language and communication. From the beginning of his research career, Bob always held the interaction among people in clear focus. His first major research accomplishment concerned communication between people in the context of interpersonal bargaining (Deutsch & Krauss, 1960, 1962). Next, he turned to interpersonal communication, partly out of interest in the problem area per se, and partly to develop a measure of interpersonal communication efficiency under degraded circumstances. At the time, he was working at Bell Laboratories, where communication via satellite was being developed. Satellite voice communication—from earth to the orbiting station and back—entailed a noticeable time delay because of the distances involved. Would this delay impair communication? Bob developed a referential communication task to provide a measure of communication efficiency (Krauss & Bricker, 1966) and made a significant discovery. People were extraordinarily adept at communicating with one another if they could interact freely. However, when communication was one-sided, efficiency deteriorated (Krauss & Weinheimer, 1964, 1966). In his typical fashion, Bob took an applied human engineering problem and in solving that problem advanced our social-psychological understanding of interpersonal communication processes. His experimental paradigm was then extended to study the development of referential communication skills in children (Glucksberg, Krauss, & Weisberg, 1966; Krauss & Glucksberg, 1969), and this line of work has recently become a major topic in social-cognitive psychology. Bob's original paradigm has been extended and refined to enable the development of sophisticated models of perspective and role taking in referential communication (Clark & Brennan, 1991; Keysar, 2007)

In the course of his work on interpersonal communication, Bob became interested in nonverbal aspects of communication, such as the role of gestures. Here again, Bob made a significant discovery. While gestures may contribute to a speaker's messages (Krauss, Dushay, Chen, & Rauscher, 1995), gestures also serve an important *intrapersonal* function. In a series of ingenious studies, Bob and his colleagues demonstrated how gestures can serve as an aid to word retrieval (see review in Krauss, 1998; Krauss, Chen, & Gottesman, 2000). Finally, in addition to interesting forays into various aspects of communication and social interactive processes, Bob considered yet another integral aspect of interpersonal communication, what people infer about a speaker based on the speaker's speech and voice. Amazingly, listeners do quite well inferring a number of physical characteristics, including a speaker's height and weight (Krauss, Freyberg, & Morsella, 2002; Krauss & Pardo, 2005).

The contributions in this book represent Bob's considerable influence on students and colleagues alike as they extend, and in some cases respond to, his body of work. The contributions are organized into three sections, each reflecting a different aspect of Bob's varied interests and contributions over the years. Section I, The Production of Gestures, Speech, and Action, consists of chapters on the production of gestures, speech, and action, beginning with Sotaro Kita's presentation of a model of speech–gesture production (Levelt, 1989). The literature on speech production is sizable, much of it inspired by Levelt's speech production model. Kita adopts Levelt's general scheme, applying it not just to speech, but also to the integrated production of speech and accompanying gestures. Miranda Rose takes up Krauss's hypothesis that gestures facilitate lexical/word retrieval to ask whether gestures can be used in the treatment of aphasia. This is a promising line of both theoretical and clinical research. Further investigation of the integration of gesture and speech is described in Palti and Hadar's report on functional imaging of the hand motor cortex during linguistic tasks, providing further evidence on the close interaction of speech and gesture. The final chapter in this section, by Morsella, Larson, and Bargh, analyzes the determinants and purposes of spontaneous movements during working memory tasks, using the framework of Morsella and Krauss's (2004) gestural feedback model. Their claim is that all movements have meaning in the sense that they are relevant to the ongoing cognitive activity at the time—sometimes facilitating, sometimes interfering with task performance. Identifying the relations between movements of various kinds and cognitive task performances should be most useful in helping us to understand both action and cognitive processes, and the studies reported here are significant contributions to this goal.

Returning to Bob's initial set of interests, Section II, Human Communication, is devoted to work on human communication, beginning with a paradoxical chapter by Torrey, Fussel, and Kiesler on what robots, rather than humans, could teach us about perspective taking. Torrey and her colleagues argue cogently that if we could program robots to engage in perspective taking, we would further our understanding of how people do it. This is the classic argument on the utility of simulation models and artificial intelligence. These analytic modeling methods force us to be explicit about the processes of interest, and so this line of work should advance our understanding of human perspective taking. Turning to humans, Michael Schober asks whether people who have known one another for years (e.g., older married couples) communicate with one another more efficiently than people who are not familiar with one another. His surprising answer is "not necessarily," and he presents some elegant experiments to support this conclusion.

What do Apple users have in common with members of a minority religious sect? This bold question is addressed by Cheng and Chiu, who argue that brand cultures—groups of people who are loyal to a minority brand, such as Apple computers in a world populated by PC owners—are analogous to world cultures such as religions. Drawing on optimal distinctiveness theory (Brewer, 1991), Cheng and Chiu make a convincing case that the two kinds of cultures employ the same processes and strategies to create and maintain themselves. These include an articulated minority ideology, with founders who have incredibly strong beliefs. The members of the cultures are marginalized and hence proselytize, and they develop narratives in support of their ideology. As a PC user who is constantly beset by friends and colleagues eager to convert me to Apple products, Cheng and Chiu's arguments strike a chord, as they quote Bob Krauss, "Think…Think different."

The last chapter in this section, by David McNeill and his colleagues, presents a most ambitious research program, one that attempts to describe and assess group communication and decision processes among people during U.S. Air Force gaming sessions. McNeill et al. point out that any attempts to account for alignment of speakers in such complex situations in terms of mechanistic priming (as argued by Pickering & Garrod, 2004) ignores the reflective and dynamic interactions in dialogue, echoing the critique put forward by Krauss and Pardo (2004). Overall, the contributions of this chapter are in the tradition of Bob's research and thought: Complex phenomena processes cannot be captured fruitfully in simplistic, mechanistic terms.

The contributions in Section III, The Perception of Speech and Identity, deal with three aspects of speech perception in different contexts. Robert Remez shows how people express their personal identity in their speech, conditioned by their anatomy and physiology. One result is that listeners may mistakenly ascribe personal speech characteristics to qualitative, often negative, attributes of a speaker. Consistent with the notion of optimal distinctiveness mentioned earlier, Remez observes that speakers must use phonetic perception to regulate their own articulation so that their speech is within the range of their speech community, yet personally identifiable as an individual. This sort of adaptive self-regulation requires, of course, perceptual sensitivity, and this in turn enables people to calibrate the speech of others by their phonetic characteristics. How this is accomplished remains to be understood. Jennifer Pardo addresses a variant of Remez's work—how people's phonetic productions converge among partners in conversational interactions. While maintaining personal identity, the acoustic-phonetic repertoires of conversational partners gradually become more similar to one another, and this similarity persists as the conversational tasks and settings differ. Again, optimal distinctiveness seems to be an important factor, as conversational partners adapt to one another and still maintain personal identity markers. In both Remez's and Pardo's contributions, the hallmark of Bob Krauss's scientific approach is evident: the concern with and focus on social interaction.

As counterpoint to these two contributions, Julian Hochberg extends the concept of gestural interaction to visual perception during interpersonal interaction, beginning with infant–caretaker interactions. In such interactions, glances of both pre-verbal infants and their caretakers serve the same purposes as do gestures during conversational interactions: "to direct attention at …[the]…pre-speech period during which so many of our gesture-supported behaviors and our visuo-motor planning must originate" (this volume, p. 200). Hochberg's essay, concluding this volume, extends the applicability and relevance of the Krauss–Morsella gestural feedback model from the linguistic to the visual mode, providing a rich source of hypotheses for further experimentation and theoretical development. This final chapter is thus not a mere wrap-up, but a set of signposts for further work on human interaction.

REFERENCES

Brewer, M. B. (1991). The social self: On being the same and different at the same time. *Personality and Social Psychology Bulletin, 17*, 475–482.

Brown, R. (1958). *Words and things*. Glencoe, IL: The Free Press.

Brown, R. (1973). *A first language: The early stages*. Cambridge, MA: Harvard University Press.

Clark, H. H., & Brennan, S. A. (1991). Grounding in communication. In L. B. Resnick, J. M. Levine, & S. D. Teasley (Eds.), *Perspectives on socially shared cognition* (pp. 27–149). Washington, DC: APA Books.

Danks, J. H., & Glucksberg, S. (1980). Experimental psycholinguistics. In M. R. Rosenzweig & L. W. Porter (Eds.), *Annual review of psychology* (pp. 391–417). Palo Alto, CA: Annual Reviews, Inc.

Deutsch, M., & Krauss, R. M. (1960). The effect of threat upon interpersonal bargaining. *Journal of Abnormal and Social Psychology, 61*,181–189.

Deutsch, M., & Krauss, R. M. (1962). Studies of interpersonal bargaining. *Journal of Conflict Resolution, 6*, 52–76.

Fodor, J. (1983). *The modularity of mind*. Cambridge, MA: The MIT Press.

Fraser, C., & Sherer, K. R. (Eds.). (1982). *Advances in the social psychology of language*. Cambridge: Cambridge University Press.

Glucksberg, S. (1984). Social psychology discovers a social phenomenon: Language. Review of *Advances in the Social Psychology of Language,* C. Fraser and K. R. Scherer (Eds.), *Contemporary Psychology, 29,* 798–799.

Glucksberg, S., Krauss, R. M., & Weisberg, R. (1966). Referential communication in nursery school children: Method and some preliminary findings. *Journal of Experimental Child Psychology, 3,* 333–342.

Katz, I., Glucksberg, S., & Krauss, R. M. (1960). Need satisfaction and Edwards PPS scores in married couples. *Journal of Consulting Psychology, 24,* 205–208.

Keysar, B. (2007). Communication and miscommunication: The role of egocentric processes. *Intercultural Pragmatics, 4,* 71–84.

Krauss, R. M. (1998). Why do we gesture when we speak? *Current Directions in Psychological Science, 7,* 54–59.

Krauss, R. M., & Bricker, P.D. (1966). Effects of transmission delay and access delay on the efficiency of verbal communication. *Journal of the Acoustical Society, 4,* 286–292.

Krauss, R. M., Chen, Y., & Gottesman, R. F. (2000). Lexical gestures and lexical access: A process model. In D. McNeill (Ed.), *Language and gesture* (pp. 261–283). New York: Cambridge University Press.

Krauss, R. M., Dushay, R. A., Chen, Y., & Rauscher, F. (1995). The communicative value of conversational hand gestures. *Journal of Experimental Social Psychology, 31,* 533–552.

Krauss, R. M., Freyberg, R., & Morsella, E. (2002). Inferring speakers' physical attributes from their voices. *Journal of Experimental Social Psychology, 38,* 618–625.

Krauss, R. M., & Glucksberg, S. (1969). The development of communication: Competence as a function of age. *Child Development, 40,* 256–266.

Krauss, R. M., & Pardo, J. S. (2004). Is alignment always the result of automatic priming? *Behavior and Brain Sciences, 27,* 203–204.

Krauss, R. M., & Pardo, J. S. (2005). Speaker perception and social behavior: Bridging social psychology and speech science. In P. A. M. van Lange (Ed.), *Bridging social psychology and speech science: Benefits of transdisciplinary approaches* (pp. 273–278). Mahwah, NJ: Lawrence Erlbaum Associates.

Krauss, R. M., & Weinheimer, S. (1964). Changes in reference phrases as a function of frequency of usage in social interaction: A preliminary study. *Psychonomic Science, 1,* 113–114.

Krauss, R. M., & Weinheimer, S. (1966). Concurrent feedback, confirmation and the encoding of referents in verbal communication. *Journal of Personality and Social Psychology, 4,* 343–346.

Levelt, W. J. M. (1989). *Speaking: From intention to articulation.* Cambridge, MA: The MIT Press.

Morsella, E., & Krauss, R. M. (2004). The role of gestures in spatial working memory and speech. *American Journal of Psychology, 117,* 411–424.

Pickering, M., & Garrod, S. (2004). Toward a mechanistic psychology of dialogue. *Behavioral and Brain Sciences, 27,* 169–190.

Woodworth, R. S., & Schlossberg, H. (1954). *Experimental psychology* (rev. ed.) New York: Henry Holt.

2 A Model of Speech– Gesture Production

Sotaro Kita

INTRODUCTION

Speaking and gesturing are tightly coupled systems. For example, infants at the one-word stage of language development already produce speech and gesture in a coordinated way (Capirci, Iverson, Pizzuto, & Volterra, 1996; Goldin-Meadow & Butcher, 2003), and co-speech gestures are produced even when the listener cannot see the speaker's gestures (e.g., Alibali, Heath, & Myers, 2001; Cohen, 1977; Krauss, Dushay, Chen, & Rauscher, 1995). In addition, people with left hemisphere dominance for language processing have a stronger right-hand preference for gesturing than do those with weaker left hemisphere dominance (Kimura, 1973a, 1973b), and prohibiting gestures makes the speech less fluent (Rauscher, Krauss, & Chen, 1996). These indications of strong ties between speaking and gesturing demand explanation.

One of Bob Krauss's important contributions to the study of gesture is to provide detailed information-processing models to account for the relationship between speech production and gesture production (Krauss, Chen, & Chawla, 1996; Krauss, Chen, & Gottesman, 2000; Krauss & Hadar, 1999). Information-processing models require clear, specific, and detailed theoretical claims and assumptions that allow one to draw new predictions that can be tested in subsequent studies. The models of Krauss and his colleagues have indeed inspired subsequent studies and generated many constructive discussions in the literature (e.g., Beatie & Shovelton, 2006; de Ruiter, 2000, 2006; Frick-Horbury & Guttentag, 1998; Hadar & Butterworth, 1997; Hostetter & Alibali, in press; Kita & Özyürek, 2003; Melinger & Levelt, 2004; Rose, Douglas, & Matyas, 2002; Seyfeddinipur, 2006). The models of Krauss and his colleagues have been an important catalyst for the advancement of our knowledge about the relationship between gesture and speech.

Inspired by these developments, my collaborator and I developed our own model of speech–gesture production (Kita & Özyürek, 2003) to account for the results that did not fit existing models. As illustrated by the work of Krauss and colleagues, a model is most useful when it is specific. Thus, in this chapter, I aim to further specify and develop the Kita–Özyürek (2003) model. More specifically, the goal of this chapter is threefold. First, I will describe the Kita–Özyürek (2003) model. Second, I will present additional evidence supporting different aspects of the model. Third, I will discuss the addition of new features in the model, features based on recent findings about gesture production.

THE KITA–ÖZYÜREK (2003) MODEL

This section describes the empirical results that motivated the Kita–Özyürek (2003) model and then describes the model. We investigated how language influences gesture production. More specifically, we compared gestural depictions of motion events (e.g., events in animated cartoons) in three languages that, linguistically, "package" the events differently. We did this in order to see how the syntax and lexicon of a particular language influences how gesture packages information.

EMPIRICAL FINDINGS GIVING RISE TO THE MODEL

In this study, speakers of Japanese, Turkish, and English viewed an animated cartoon (Warner Brothers' *Sylvester and Tweety*) and retold the story to a listener. Two motion events in the cartoon were chosen for analysis because they elicited different linguistic descriptions in English, on one hand, and Japanese and Turkish, on the other hand. In the first motion event, Sylvester (the cat) swung across a street on a rope like Tarzan to get to Tweety's (the bird's) room. In English, the verb, *to swing,* can exactly depict the cat's change of location with an arc trajectory, and all English speakers used this verb. However, in Japanese and Turkish, it is difficult to describe the change of location with an arc trajectory because there is no agentive intransitive verb to describe the arch-shaped movement. Consequently, none of the Japanese and Turkish speakers linguistically encoded the arc trajectory. Instead, they used motion verbs without any trajectory shape specifications such as *to go* and *to jump/fly.*

Similar to the linguistic difference among the three languages, the gestures that depicted the swing event also differed cross-linguistically. The gestures were categorized into two types: arc gestures, which encoded the arc trajectory, and straight gestures, which encoded only change of location. It was found that Japanese and Turkish speakers were more likely to produce straight gestures than English speakers were. Virtually all English speakers exclusively produced arc gestures. This supports the idea that linguistic formulations can influence the contents of gestures.

We analyzed another event in which the three languages gave rise to different linguistic descriptions. This was a scene in which Sylvester, having swallowed a bowling ball, rolled down the street into a bowling alley. All three languages can describe the rolling-down event equally well; however, the languages differed as to the syntactic structures they used (Talmy, 1985). Japanese and Turkish speakers all used two separate verbs to encode the manner of motion (i.e., rolling) and the path (or trajectory) of motion (i.e., downward direction). Thus, they used a two-clause description (e.g., "*he descended as he rolled*") to describe the event. In contrast, English speakers all used a one-clause description (e.g., "*he rolled down*"). Since the clause is considered an important unit for the speech production process (Bock & Cutting, 1992; Garrett, 1982), Japanese and Turkish speakers presumably needed to distribute the information about manner and path over two processing units. Thus, it would have been necessary for Japanese and Turkish speakers to separate the representations of manner and path at the stage of conceptual planning. In line with this prediction, it was found that, when gesturally depicting the rolling-down event, Japanese and Turkish speakers were more likely than English speakers to produce manner gestures and path gestures, which represented manner and path separately (e.g., first a hand rotated in one location to represent rolling, and then the hand moved linearly to represent descending). English speakers mostly produced just manner-path conflated gestures, in which manner and path were expressed in a single gesture (e.g., a hand circled repeatedly as it moved across in front of the torso at the same time). This provides evidence for the claim that gestures reflect representations that are "pre-processed" into a form that is suitable for speech production in a specific language.

In addition to these linguistic effects on iconic gestures, we found that gestures systematically encoded spatial information that was never encoded in speech. Namely, the left-right direction of the movements in the stimuli was encoded in gesture very accurately. For example, when the stimulus event was to the left on the video monitor, the gesture describing the event tended to move to the speaker's left. This was the case for the speakers of all three languages. Thus, gestures were *simultaneously* influenced by spatial details that were never verbalized and by the linguistic formulations of ideas in a given language. This leads us to conclude that iconic gestures are generated from the "interface mechanism" between spatial cognition and speech production, in which imagistic information is packaged into chunks that are suitable for the processes of speech formulation.

Description of the Model

To account for these results, Kita and Özyürek (2003) proposed a model of how contents of speech and gesture are determined and coordinated with each other. (The synchronization of speech and gesture is outside the scope of the model.) Figure 2.1 is a graphic representation of the model. The rectangles are various computational processes, which receive an input and compute an output. The arrows between the rectangles represent the input-output relationships between the processes. The ovals represent databases, and the broken lines represent the access link to the databases.

Like other information processing models of speech–gesture production (de Ruiter, 2000, 2006; Hadar & Butterworth, 1997; Krauss et al., 1996; Krauss et al., 2000; Krauss & Hadar, 1999) is the model that is based on Levelt's (1989) speech production model, which distinguishes the conceptualization and formulation processes. The conceptualization process corresponds to the Communication Planner and the Message Generator in our model, and it determines what information needs to be encoded in the next utterance, and generates a propositional message representation. The Formulator transforms the message representation into a linguistic representation by specifying lexical items, syntactic structure, morpho-syntax, and phonology.

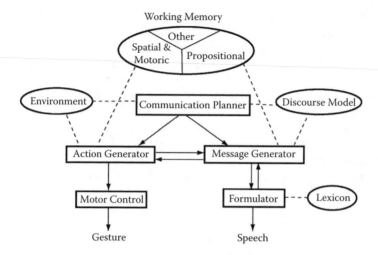

FIGURE 2.1 The model of speech–gesture production by Kita and Özyürek. (From Kita, S., & Özyürek, A. (2003). *Joural of Memory and Language*, 48, 16–32. With permission.)

The model has the following key characteristics (Kita & Özyürek, 2003, p. 28):

1. The Communication Planner decides what modalities of expression should be involved, although it does not necessarily determine exactly what information is to be expressed in each modality.
2. The content of a gesture is determined by
   a. "communicative intention," generated in the Communication Planner,
   b. action schemata selected on the basis of features of imagined or real space, and
   c. online feedback from the Formulator via the Message Generator. Together, these factors jointly determine gestural content, and none of the factors alone fully specifies gestural content. In other words, gestural content is not fully specified in mechanisms dedicated to communication, such as Levelt's Conceptualizer, but rather gestural content is specified in a more general mechanism that is responsible for generating actions (Action Generator).
3. There is online bidirectional information exchange between the Message Generator and the Action Generator, and between the Formulator and the Message Generator. This allows gestural content to be shaped online by linguistic formulation possibilities.

Characteristic 3 is the key feature that accounts for the linguistic effects on iconic gestures, as seen in the cross-linguistic comparison discussed previously. Characteristic 2b accounts for the fact that gestures can systematically encode spatial details, such as left-right directionality, that are never verbalized.

Based on what has been communicated about a given discourse, and on various demands in the environment in which the communication takes place, the Communication Planner generates communicative intention at what can be conceptualized as a gross level. For example, when describing the swing event, it might generate the intention, *I want to convey, using both speech and gesture, the event in which the cat tried to get to where the bird is in a particular way.* This rough intention will be developed into more detailed plans in the Message Generator and the Action Generator.

The Communication Planner only roughly specifies what needs to be conveyed. For example, when describing the swing event, the left-right directionality of the event may not be a part of the communicative intention. After all, none of the speakers mentioned the directionality in speech even though it was straightforward to do so in any of the three languages. The directionality might have come "for free" when the Action Generator accessed the spatio-motor representations in the working memory. This gross-level specification in communicative intention is in contrast with some of the existing models. For example, in de Ruiter's (2000) model, the content of gesture is fully specified by communicative intention generated in the Conceptualizer (*à la* Levelt, 1989). Krauss et al. (2000) proposed, on the contrary, that in most cases gestural contents are not determined by communicative intention.

Furthermore, the Communication Planner has access to the discourse model so that it can decide what information is important and needs to be conveyed at a given point in discourse. The Communication Planner also has access to the information in the environment so that it can determine the use of expression modalities. If, for example, the listener cannot see the gestures, the Communication Planner may be less likely to send the communicative intention to the Action Generator. In such situations, the speaker indeed produces fewer gestures (e.g., Cohen, 1977; Krauss et al., 1995), especially fewer iconic and deictic gestures (Alibali et al., 2001).

The Message Generator receives communicative intention from the Communication Planner and generates a representation of a message for an utterance that would achieve the communicative goal specified in the communicative intention. When describing a motion event, it consults the propositional representations about the event in working memory and the discourse model to determine the propositions to be verbalized that are true of the event and are appropriate for the particular discourse context (e.g., the choice of passive vs. active voice, use of pronouns, etc.).

The bidirectional feedback between the Message Generator and the Formulator is one of the key features for the explanation of the linguistic effect on gestural contents (Kita & Özyürek, 2003). This contrasts with Levelt's (1989) and de Ruiter's (2000) assumption that the Formulator is a "module" in Fodor's (1983) sense, and with the idea that there is no feedback from the Formulator back to the Message Generator.

The Action Generator accesses the spatio–motoric representations about the event in working memory. It also examines whether there are any features in the environment (e.g., physical obstacles, the location of the addressee) that must be taken into account for the unencumbered and successful execution of gestures (de Ruiter, 2000; Özyürek, 2002). The Action Generator and the Message Generator influence the representations of each other so that the contents of speech and gesture converge. This is the other key feature explaining the linguistic effect on gestural contents.

From this standpoint, the Action Generator is a general-purpose process for generating actions for both communicative and practical purposes. It is responsible for generating not only speech-accompanying gestures but also practical actions such as grasping objects. The confluence of communicative and practical action at the Action Generator is compatible with the idea that gestures have origins in practical actions (Streeck, 1996; Müller, 1998). However, it contrasts with theories that assume that gestures are generated from a mechanism dedicated solely to communication (de Ruiter, 2000; McNeill, 1992).

Thus, the Kita–Özyürek (2003) model consists of a set of theoretical claims that explain key findings from the cross-linguistic comparison of gestures. Some of these theoretical claims contradict those posited in other models and theories about the link between speech and gesture production. In the next section, I present further evidence that supports various features of the Kita–Özyürek (2003) model.

FURTHER EVIDENCE FOR FEATURES OF THE KITA–ÖZYÜREK (2003) MODEL

BIDIRECTIONAL LINKS AMONG THE ACTION GENERATOR, MESSAGE GENERATOR, AND FORMULATOR

The bidirectional links among the Action Generator, Message Generator, and Formulator were essential in explaining the cross-linguistic difference in gestural depiction of events. In recent years, more evidence has been found for this key feature of the model. (For a more detailed review of linguistic effects on iconic gestures, see Kita & Özyürek, 2007.)

In Özyürek, Kita, Allen, Furman, and Brown (2005), Turkish and English speakers described ten different motion events, all involving simultaneous manner and path, as in the rolling-down event in Kita and Özyurek (2003). The authors again found that Turkish speakers typically produced two-clause descriptions of the events, whereas English speakers typically produced one-clause descriptions of the events. They compared the gestural depiction of manner and path that accompanied these language-typical descriptions, and found that Turkish speakers were more likely to produce separate manner gestures and path gestures, whereas English speakers were more likely to produce manner-path conflated gestures. This replicated the finding from Kita and Özyürek (2003).

Furthermore, it was also found that the speakers of both languages sometimes produced a sentence that encoded only manner information (e.g., "he was rolling") or that encoded only path information (e.g., "he was going down"). The types of gestures (manner, path, or conflated) that co-occurred with manner only sentences and path only sentences were compared between the two languages.

It was found that manner gestures were most frequent in the context of manner only sentences, and path gestures were most frequent in the context of path only sentences. More crucially, the distribution of the three gesture types did not differ between the two languages in these sentential contexts. Thus, the cross-linguistic difference in gesture was found only when the co-occurring sentences had different syntactic structures. This means that the cross-linguistic differences in gestures found in this study and in Kita and Özyürek (2003) were not due to some general cultural variables that differed between Turkish speakers and American English speakers. Rather, the difference in gesture stemmed from the way in which information was syntactically packaged in the co-occurring utterance.

There is further evidence against the alternative hypothesis that such findings are based on general cultural variables. Kita et al. (2007) investigated gestural representations of manner and path in motion event among English speakers. They constructed stimulus animations that were designed to elicit both one-clause descriptions of manner and path (e.g., "*he rolled down*") and two-clause descriptions (e.g., "*he rolled as he went down*"). They examined the type of gestures that accompanied one-clause descriptions and two-clause descriptions, and found that the speakers were more likely to produce manner-path conflated gestures with one-clause descriptions, and were more likely to produce separate manner and path gestures with two-clause descriptions.

This finding is significant in that it replicates Kita and Özyürek (2003) and Özyürek et al. (2005) within a single language. Here, an explanation for the finding based on cultural variables is not viable. Rather, the results indicate that the speaker's online choice of the *syntactic packaging of information* influences the *gestural packaging of information*. These results provide a clear support for the online information flow from the Formulator to the Message Generator and to the Action Generator. The contents in speech and gesture probably converge, however, in repeated bidirectional exchanges between speech and gesture production processes (as opposed to there being only unidirectional information from speech production processes to gesture production processes).

There is also evidence for the claim that the Action Generator can influence the Message Generator. The support comes from studies demonstrating that the content of speech changes when the speaker is prohibited from gesturing. In Rimè, Shiaratura, Hupet, and Ghysselinckx (1984) it was found that when gestures were prohibited, speakers produced utterances with lower "imagery scores." In Hostetter, Alibali, and Kita's (2007) study, participants described how to change tires and how to wrap a present (the tasks used in Feyereisen & Havard, 1999). It was found that speakers used semantically generic words (such as "*to pull*," "*to put*") in the prohibited condition, and semantically more specific words (such as "*to slide*," "*to cross*") in the gesture allowed condition. Thus, gesturing caused speech to be more spatio-motorically rich. In Alibali and Kita (2007; see also Albali, Kita, Bigelow, Wolfman, & Klein, 2001), children performed Piagetian conservation tasks and explained their answers in the gesture prohibited or allowed condition. It was found that children's explanations referred to perceptually nonpresent information (e.g., the past state of the task objects or hypothetical operations on the task objects) in the gesture prohibited condition, and to perceptually present information (e.g., how task objects were at that time) in the gesture allowed condition. Thus, gesturing caused the explanations to be more closely bound to the present state of the environment. Taken together, there is evidence that the Action Generator influences the Message Generator.

ACTION GENERATOR WITH ACCESS TO THE ENVIRONMENT

The Action Generator has access to the environment (as suggested by de Ruiter, 2000) so that gesture production can be modulated according to the conditions in the current environment. For example, gestural hand movement may be needed to avoid obstacles in the environment (de Ruiter, 2000). In addition, the speaker changes the direction of gestures to depict motion events depending on how many listeners there are and where they are situated (Özyürek, 2002).

Recent studies have also shown that the information about the environment is important not only for how we execute gestures but also for how we construct gestural representations. Goodwin (2003) investigated gestures produced during an archaeological excavation. He showed that many of the gestural representations were inherently linked to the environment. Some gestures traced a feature on the ground. Other gestures even actually changed the environment as they "inscribed" a mark on the ground to highlight important areas for excavation. Haviland (2003) described a case in which objects in the environment were used as a "prop" in gestural representation. A Mayan farmer in Mexico described a sugar cane press, in which two logs are mounted on supporting posts. In his description, he used a real house post conveniently located near him as the representation of supporting posts, and he gestured in relation to the house post to depict how the contraption was constructed. Similarly, LeBaron and Streeck (2000) described gestures produced in an architecture class. The professor commented on a miniature model of a structure, designed by students. The professor produced gestures that highlighted some features of a model (e.g., tracing a curved shape), and such gestures later became more detached from the object and performed in midair to represent the same concept. Finally, Chu and Kita (2008) examined gestures that were produced during a mental rotation task. The participants were presented with two views of an object on a computer screen and were instructed to describe how the object from one view can be rotated into the object from the other view. In this task, the participants often gestured near the computer screen as if to grasp the object and turn it, especially at the initial trials of the experiment. These examples all show that the environment is a part of gestural representation, and thus the Action Generator needs access to the information about the environment.*

---

* In a trivial way, the information about the environment is also necessary when we point to an object. The examples discussed previously show that the need for an access to the environment goes beyond pointing gestures. Elaborate iconic representation by gestures may require the environment to be a crucial component.

COMMUNICATIVE INTENTION, DISCOURSE MODEL, AND THE COMMUNICATION PLANNER

The Communication Planner generates a communicative intention, which roughly specifies what information needs to be encoded in speech and gesture. It does this in consultation with the Discourse Model. A recent study by Melinger and Levelt (2004) supports this view. In their study, participants described a path through a network of colored dots to a listener. Some participants spontaneously gestured in this task, and others did not. It was found that participants who gestured were more likely to omit directional information in the path description in speech (e.g., "*it goes to an orange dot*" as opposed to "*it goes left to an orange dot*"). This indicates that the speaker intended the gesture to be a part of an overall communicative act and coordinated what contents should be expressed in the two modalities. Thus, when the directional information was encoded in gesture, it was omitted in the accompanying speech.

Another related finding from this study highlights the importance of the access to the Discourse Model. At the beginning of a description, the speaker sometimes provided an overview of the shape of the network. For example, the speaker might trace the overall shape that looks like an F with an utterance such as "*the figure looks like this.*" The overview could also be given in speech only with an utterance such as "*the figure looks like an F,*" or it could be given in both modalities at the same time. It was found that when a preview was given in any of the modalities, the speakers were more likely to omit directional information in the subsequent description of a path than when the speakers did not give any previews. This indicates that the speaker keeps track of the information expressed in speech and gesture in the Discourse Model, and this information influences the decision as to what information to encode in speech, namely, the content of communicative intention. This finding provides further evidence that gestures are intended to convey specific information to the addressee in the same way as speech and that the speaker registers both gesturally and linguistically encoded information in the Discourse Model.

FURTHER SPECIFICATION OF THE MODEL: THE EFFECT OF COMMUNICATIVE CONTEXTS

In this section, we discuss further specifications of the model, based on recent findings regarding how communicative contexts influence gesture production. It has been known for a long time that communicative contexts can influence gesture frequencies. People produce more gestures in a face-to-face condition than in a visual-blockage condition (Alibali et al., 2001; Cohen, 1977; Krauss et al., 1995). In the model, this was handled by the access link from the Communication Planner to the environment.

The gesture frequency is also influenced by how the speaker conceptualizes features of the communicative context (as opposed to the features of the physical context such as visibility). For example, people produce more gestures in a context with a visually blocked interlocutor (e.g., speaking on the intercom) than in a context without an interlocutor (e.g., speaking into a tape recorder; Bavelas, Gerwing, Sutton, & Prevost, 2008; Cohen, 1977). In addition, when people are told to describe something in such a way that others can decode the message based on either video or audio recording, they produce more gestures in the video recording condition than in the audio recording condition (Bavelas, Kenwood, Johnson, & Phillips, 2002; Fujii, 2000). The model can account for such findings if we extend the notion of the Discourse Model.

The Discourse Model has thus far been taken as a depository of information about what the speaker has said or gestured. However, this is not sufficient information to plan communicative moves, and thus it is natural to posit that the Discourse Model also holds information about various properties of the addressee. The recent literature uncovered at least three different types of addressee properties that affect gesture production.

The first type is the communicative potential of the addressee. Is the addressee interactable online, as in the case of face-to-face or telephone conversation? Alternatively, is the addressee merely imagined or just a future possibility, as in the case of talking into audio or video recorders? Another related property of the addressee depends on which modalities the addressee has access to (e.g., just audio or both audio-visual).

The second type is the "knowledge state" of the addressee. What does the addressee know about what I am about to say or gesture? This information should also be represented in the Discourse Model. In the recent literature, it has been reported that the knowledge state of the addressee influences gesture frequency and physical form of gestures. The speaker produces more gestures when the speaker and the listener share "common ground" (Clark, 1992) about the topic than when they do not (Holler & Stevens, 2007; Jacobs & Garnham, 2007). The speaker produces more complex and precise gestures when the speaker and the listener share common ground than when they do not (Enfield, Kita, & de Ruiter, 2007; Gerwing & Bavelas, 2004; Holler & Stevens, 2007).*

The third type is the communicative motivation or engagement of the addressee. The speaker produces more gestures when the listener is attentive than when the listener is not (Jacobs & Garnham, 2007). One way to interpret this result is that when the listener is perceived to have high motivation to obtain information from the speaker or to be engaged in the communication in general, the speaker increases the gesture frequency.

If the Discourse Model is enriched with addressee properties, the Communication Planner can modulate the probability of using the gesture modality, based on those properties. This would lead to the systematic variation of gesture frequency. The change in physical properties of the gestures, however, requires further extension of the model. Note that the Communication Planner in the Kita–Özyürek (2003) model

---

* In case of Enfield et al. (2007), the speaker assumes (rather than knows) that the speaker and the listener share common ground.

can generate information about what needs to be conveyed and which modalities to be used, but not about how to produce a gesture (e.g., the physical shape, size, and detail of a gesture). Thus, the new specification we need for the model is to posit that the Communication Planner can send out information about the desired level of explicitness or elaboration or precision of expressions. The addition of this feature is also justified from the viewpoint of speech production because the knowledge status of the addressee can modulate the degree of explicitness or elaboration or precision in verbal referring expressions (Clark, 1992).

This addition would also allow the model to account for the recent finding of the effect of visibility between the speaker and the listener on the precision in gestural representation. Gullberg (2006) analyzed the consistency in the use of gesture space when a referent in discourse is repeatedly mentioned. It was found that gestures more consistently placed a particular referent in the same location in gesture space when the speaker and the listener can see each other, than when they cannot. This phenomenon can be accounted for if the Communication Planner accesses the environment to assess potential visual blockage, and specifies the desired degree of precision in gestural expressions, which are to be generated in the Action Generator.

CONCLUSIONS

The goal of this chapter was to further develop a model of speech and gesture production by Kita and Özyürek (2003). New pieces of evidence were provided that corroborate existing features of the model. Two new features were also added to the model based on recent evidence regarding how communicative contexts influence gesture production. First, the Discourse Model stores not only the information about preceding discourse but also properties of the addressee such as communicative potentials, the knowledge state, and communicative motivation or engagement. Second, the Communication Planner can send an additional type of information to the Action Generator and the Message Generator. Kita and Özyürek (2003) posited that the Communication Planner could send a rough specification of what needs to be conveyed to the listener and what modality (gesture or speech) needs to be used. In addition to these pieces of information, the Communication Planner can specify the desired level of explicitness or elaboration or precision of expressions (in both speech and gesture). This accounts for the recent findings that communicative contexts influence not only the gesture frequency but also the physical shape and size of gestures with different degrees of explicitness, elaboration, and precision.

It is important for researchers in the study of gesture to develop information-processing models of speech–gesture production that are as specific as possible. The more specific the model is, the more it will further our understanding of the relationship between speech and gesture. It is hoped that my humble attempt in this chapter will also have a positive effect on the development of gesture study, just as the models of Krauss and colleagues have been having.

ACKNOWLEDGMENT

I would like to thank Mingyuan Chu and Ezequiel Morsella for their valuable comments on an earlier version of this chapter.

REFERENCES

Alibali, M. W., Heath, D. C., & Myers, H. J. (2001). Effects of visibility between speaker and listener on gesture production: Some gestures are meant to be seen. *Journal of Memory and Language, 44*, 169–188.

Alibali, M. W., Kita, S., Bigelow, L. J., Wolfman, C. M., & Klein, S. M. (2001). Gesture plays a role in thinking for speaking. In C. Cavé, I. Guaïtella, & S. Santi (Eds.), *Oralité et gesturalité: Interactions et comportements multimodaux dans la communication* (pp. 407–410). Paris: L'Harmattan.

Bavelas, J., Kenwood, C., Johnson, T., & Phillips, B. (2002). An experimental study of when and how speakers use gestures to communicate. *Gesture, 2*(1), 1–17.

Bavelas, J. B., Gerwing, J., Sutton, C., & Prevost, D. (2008). Gesturing on the telephone: Independent effects of dialogue and visibility. *Journal of Memory and Language, 58*, 495–520.

Bock, K., & Cutting, J. C. (1992). Regulating mental energy: Performance units in language production. *Journal of Memory and Language, 31*, 99–127.

Beattie, G., & Shovelton, H. (2006). A critical appraisal of the relationship between speech and gesture and its implications for the treatment of aphasia. *Advances in Speech-Language Pathology, 8*(2), 134.

Capirci, O., Iverson, J. M., Pizzuto, E., & Volterra, V. (1996). Gestures and words during the transition to two-word speech. *Journal of Child Language, 23*(3), 645–673.

Chu, M., & Kita, S. (2008). Spontaneous gestures during mental rotation tasks: Insights into the microdevelopment of the motor strategy. *Journal of Experimental Psychology: General, 137*, 706–723.

Clark, H. H. (1992). *Arenas of language use*. Chicago: University of Chicago Press & Center for the Study of Language and Information.

Cohen, A. A. (1977). The communicative functions of hand illustrators. *Journal of Communication, 27*(4), 54–63.

de Ruiter, J. P. (2000). The production of gesture and speech. In D. McNeill (Ed.), *Language and gesture* (pp. 284–311). Chicago: University of Chicago Press.

de Ruiter, J. (2006). Can gesticulation help aphasic people speak, or rather, communicate? *Advances in Speech-Language Pathology, 8*(2), 124.

Enfield, N. J., Kita, S., & de Ruiter, J. P. (2007). Primary and secondary pragmatic functions of pointing gestures. *Journal of Pragmatics 39*(10), 1722–1741.

Feyereisen, P., & Havard, I. (1999). Mental imagery and production of hand gestures while speaking in younger and older adults. *Journal of Nonverbal Behavior, 23*, 153–171.

Fodor, J. A. (1983). *Modularity of mind*. Cambridge, MA: The MIT Press.

Frick-Horbury, D., & Guttentag, R. (1998). The effects of restricting hand gesture production on lexical retrieval and free recall. *American Journal of Psychology, 111*(1), 43–62.

Fujii, M. (2000). Jesucha no sanshutu ni kakawaru shakaiteki yoin: Washa no jesucha seikiryo to shiten no ichi ni eikyo o oyobosu kikite no sonzai [Communicative factors on the production of gesture: The effect of listener's presence on the frequency and the viewpoint of gesture]. *Ninchikagaku [Cognitive Studies], 7*(1), 65–70.

Garrett, M. F. (1982). Production of speech: Observations from normal and pathological language use. In A. W. Ellis (Ed.), *Normality and pathology in cognitive functions* (pp. 19–76). London: Academic Press.

Gerwing, J., & Bavelas, J. (2004). Linguistic influences on gesture's form. *Gesture, 4*(2), 157–195.

Goldin-Meadow, S., & Butcher, C. (2003). Pointing toward two-word speech in young children. In S. Kita (Ed.), *Pointing: Where language, culture, and cognition meet* (pp. 85–107). Mahwah, NJ: Lawrence Erlbaum Associates.

Goodwin, C. (2003). Pointing as situated practice. In S. Kita (Ed.), *Pointing: Where language, cognition, and culture meet* (pp. 217–241). Mahwah, NJ: Lawrence Erlbaum Associates.

Gullberg, M. (2006). Handling discourse: Gestures, reference tracking, and communication strategies in early L2. *Language Learning, 56*(1), 155–196.

Hadar, U., & Butterworth, B. (1997). Iconic gestures, imagery, and word retrieval in speech. *Semiotica, 115*, 147–172.

Haviland, J. B. (2003). How to point in Zinacantán. In S. Kita (Ed.), *Pointing: Where language, cognition, and culture meet* (pp. 139–169). Mahwah, NJ: Lawrence Erlbaum Associates.

Holler, J., & Stevens, R. (2007). The effect of common ground on how speakers use gesture and speech to represent size information. *Journal of Language and Social Psychology, 26*(1), 4–27.

Hostetter, A. B., & Alibali, M. W. (2008). Visible embodiment: Gesture as simulated action. reflect embodied thinking. *Psychonomic Bulletin and Review, 15*(3), 495–514.

Hostetter, A. B., Alibali, M. W., & Kita, S. (2007). Does sitting on your hands make you bite your tongue? The effects of gesture inhibition on speech during motor descriptions. In D. S. McNamara & J. G. Trafton (Eds.), *Proceedings of the 29th annual meeting of the Cognitive Science Society* (pp. 1097–1102). Mawhah, NJ: Lawrence Erlbaum Associates.

Jacobs, N., & Garnham, A. (2007). The role of conversational hand gestures in a narrative task. *Journal of Memory and Language, 56*(2), 291–303.

Kimura, D. (1973a). Manual activity during speaking—II. Left-handers. *Neuropsychologia, 11*, 51–55.

Kimura, D. (1973b). Manual activity during speaking—I. Right-handers. *Neuropsychologia, 11*, 45–50.

Kita, S., & Alibali, M. W. (2007). Role of gusture in thinking and speaking: Insights from Piagetion conservation tasks. In T. Sakamoto (Ed.), *Intentions of communication* (pp. 121–129). Tokyo: Hitsuji Shobo.

Kita, S., & Özyürek, A. (2003). What does cross-linguistic variation in semantic coordination of speech and gesture reveal? Evidence for an interface representation of spatial thinking and speaking. *Journal of Memory and Language, 48*, 16–32.

Kita, S., & Özyürek, A. (2007). How does spoken language shape iconic gestures? In S. Duncan, J. Cassell, & E. T. Levy (Eds.), *Gesture and the dynamic dimension of language: Essays in honor of David McNeill* (pp. 67–74). Amsterdam: John Benjamins.

Kita, S., Özyürek, A., Allen, S., Brown, A., Furman, R., & Ishizuka, T. (2007). Relations between syntactic encoding and co-speech gestures: Implications for a model of speech and gesture production. *Language and Cognitive Processes, 22*(8), 1212–1236.

Krauss, R. M., Chen, Y., & Chawla, P. (1996). Nonverbal behavior and nonverbal communication: What do conversational hand gestures tell us? In M. Zanna (Ed.), *Advances in experimental social psychology, Vol. 28* (pp. 389–450). Tampa, FL: Academic Press.

Krauss, R. M., Chen, Y., & Gottesman, R. F. (2000). Lexical gestures and lexical access: A process model. In D. McNeill (Ed.), *Language and gesture* (pp. 261–283). Cambridge, UK: Cambridge University Press.

Krauss, R. M., Dushay, R. A., Chen, Y., & Rauscher, F. (1995). The communicative value of conversational hand gestures. *Journal of Experimental Social Psychology, 31*, 533–522.

Krauss, R. M., & Hadar, U. (1999). The role of speech-related arm/hand gestures in word retrieval. In L. Messing & R. Campbell (Eds.), *Gesture, speech, and sign* (pp. 93–116). Oxford, UK: Oxford University Press.

LeBaron, C. D., & Streeck, J. (2000). Gesture, knowledge, and the world. In D. McNeill (Ed.), *Gestures and language* (pp. 118–138). Chicago: University of Chicago Press.

Levelt, W. J. M. (1989). *Speaking*. Cambridge, MA: The MIT Press.

McNeill, D. (1992). *Hand and mind*. Chicago: University of Chicago Press.

Melinger, A., & Levelt, W. J. M. (2004). Gesture and the communicative intention of the speaker. *Gesture, 4*(2), 119–141.

Müller, C. (1998). *Redebegleitende gesten: Kutturgeschichte-theorie-sprachvergleich.* Berlin: Berlin Verlag.

Özyürek, A. (2002). Do speakers design their cospeech gestures for their addressees? The effects of addressee location on representational gestures. *Journal of Memory and Language, 46*(4), 688–704.

Özyürek, A., Kita, S., Allen, S., Furman, R., & Brown, A. (2005). How does linguistic framing of events influence co-speech gestures? Insights from crosslinguistic variations and similarities. *Gesture, 5*, 219–240.

Rauscher, F. H., Krauss, R. M., & Chen, Y. (1996). Gesture, speech, and lexical access: The role of lexical movements in speech production. *Psychological Science, 7*, 226–230.

Rimè, B., Shiaratura, L., Hupet, M., & Ghysselinckx, A. (1984). Effects of relative immobilization on the speaker's nonverbal behavior and on the dialogue imagery level. *Motivation and Emotion, 8*, 311–325.

Rose, M., Douglas, J., & Matyas, T. (2002). The comparative effectiveness of gesture and verbal treatments for a specific phonologic naming impairment. *Aphasiology, 16*(10/11), 1001–1030.

Seyfeddinipur, M. (2006). *Disfluency: Interrupting speech and gesture*. Unpublished Doctoral dissertation, Radboud University, Nijmegen, The Netherlands.

Streeck, J. (1996). How to do things with things: Objects trouvés and symbolization. *Human Studies, 19*, 365–384.

Talmy, L. (1985). Lexicalization patterns: Semantic structure in lexical forms. In T. Shopen (Ed.), *Grammatical categories and the lexicon, Vol. III* (pp. 57–149). Cambridge, UK: Cambridge University Press.

3 Expressing One's Self in the Context of Aphasia

The Utility of Arm and Hand Gestures in Aphasia Treatments

Miranda Rose

Humans rely heavily on language skills for communication. The sudden and dramatic reduction in language skills caused by brain damage resulting from stroke has significant and far-reaching consequences for the individual, their family, and their community. It is estimated that over one million people in the United States have significant aphasia, an acquired language impairment, following stroke (Chapey, 2008). The aphasic impairments can manifest in some or all four language domains: speaking, comprehending speech, reading, and writing. The impairments interfere with the exchange of thoughts and feelings in both transactional and interactional genres. The aphasic language impairment radically affects communication skills and can mask the aphasic individual's intellectual and social competence (Kagan, 1995). Such radical change to communication skills has been shown to negatively affect social relationships (Pound, 2004) and seriously threaten self-identity (Shadden, 2005). People with aphasia report dramatic changes to their friendship groups and high rates of depression and social isolation (Byng & Duchan, 2005). Therefore, finding treatments aimed at reducing the aphasic language impairment and the resulting communication disability is important and has been a major focus of the field of speech–language pathology for the past 50 years.

There has been much work investigating the effects of spoken and written word treatments for aphasic deficits (for a recent review see Murray & Clarke, 2006). However, investigations of competencies and treatment modalities beyond the linguistic system (e.g., drawing, arm and hand gesture, music) have been relatively limited in the aphasia literature. This is surprising given the definition of aphasia as being primarily a linguistic deficit and by definition the likelihood that nonlinguistic skills such as imagistic, sensory, and kinetic processing are relatively maintained. Such strengths in nonlinguistic skills could be harnessed in therapy. One potentially potent nonlinguistic treatment for aphasia is the use of arm and hand gestures (Rose, 2006).

This chapter briefly discusses the rationale for exploring gesture-based treatments in aphasia before describing gesture-speech interaction models as a theoretical framework to guide the development of gesture-based aphasia treatment studies. Our research on the impact of limb apraxia on gesture use by aphasic speakers is discussed before we review findings from our and others' research into the effectiveness of gesture treatments for aphasic noun and verb retrieval deficits. Finally, I recommend greater interdisciplinary research into the utility of gesture in the treatment of aphasia.

A RATIONALE FOR CONSIDERING GESTURE PRODUCTION AS A TREATMENT FOR APHASIA

The idea that nonlinguistic modalities such as gesture could be useful in aphasia therapy is not new. Luria (1973) discussed the notion of intersystemic reorganization of function, whereby intact modalities could be exploited to work toward restoration of impaired functions. Similarly, Weigl (1968) discussed "deblocking" as a therapy technique where the use of one or more intact functions could directly facilitate the use of the impaired function. For example, target words are named more accurately after reading them aloud. However, it was not until the 1970s that Skelly (1979) presented a systematic approach for utilizing gesture in aphasia treatments in the speech–language pathology literature.

Skelly's 1979 text outlined the Amer-Ind hand signals that previously were used by North American indigenous communities to communicate with each other in the absence of a shared oral language. In their seminal article, Skelly, Schinsky, Smith, and Fust (1974) presented the results of therapy using the highly transparent Amer-Ind hand signals with six individuals with severe aphasia and apraxia of speech. Fifty signals were paired with target words and practiced in question and answer drills, structured conversations, and elicited in spontaneous conversation. The authors argued that the use of the Amer-Ind signals directly facilitated recovery of oral language for all six participants, with one participant acquiring 10 words, another 50, two other participants using 200 words, and two others using three-word phrases following the therapy. However, it is difficult to interpret the gains made by the participants as being a direct result of the Amer-Ind component on the therapy, as the signals were always paired with the verbal model of the target oral word. Further, in this simple A-B intervention study, multiple baselines were not taken during the six-month course of twice-weekly group therapy and no tests of statistical significance were applied to the changed test scores.

In my own early clinical practice in the 1980s, I observed that gesture seemed a potent treatment modality for some clients with aphasia but not for others. I also noted that there were some people with aphasia whose word retrieval abilities appeared to be directly facilitated by the production of arm and hand gesture, while for other people with aphasia, the production of the gesture had no apparent effect on their word retrieval and production. In turning to the speech-language pathology literature, I found little research that could explain this apparent selective phenomenon, nor directly guide clinical reasoning about when and with whom to use gesture in therapy. On the one hand, there appeared to be inflated claims of the word retrieval facilitation effects of gesture production, and on the other hand, there were overly negative views with respect to the gesture abilities of people with aphasia when a co-occurring limb apraxia was present. Further, there was little in terms of models to explain the behavioral interactions or to underpin the generation of research hypotheses.

MODELS OF SPEECH AND LANGUAGE INTERACTION

The dominant model of gesture in the speech–language pathology literature has been based on notions of limb praxis and limb apraxia. Figure 3.1 presents a cognitive neuropsychological model of limb praxis as proposed by Rothi and Heilman (1997) based on an information-processing model initially described by Patterson and Shewell (1987). The model has been utilized to understand the various impairments that underpin the three major types of limb apraxia (ideomotor, ideational, and conceptual). A dominant axiom in speech-language pathology literature has been that clients with limb apraxia would necessarily have impaired naturalistic gesture use and would therefore be poor candidates for gesture-based treatments (Duffy, Watt, & Duffy, 1994; Goodglass & Kaplan, 1963; Wang & Goodglass, 1992). This axiom probably developed from a limited understanding of the spectrum of arm and hand gestures as described by McNeill (2005) from gesticulation (beats, iconics, pointing/deictics, metaphorics), to pantomimes, emblems, and sign languages, and from an overemphasis on investigating frankly

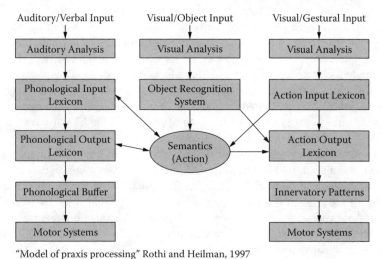

"Model of praxis processing" Rothi and Heilman, 1997

FIGURE 3.1 A cognitive neuropsychological model of limb praxis as proposed by Rothi and Heilman (1997).

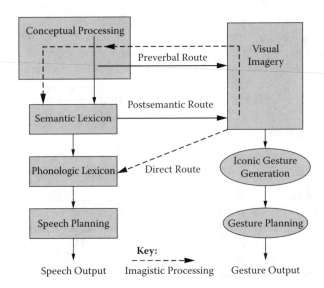

FIGURE 3.2   Hadar and Butterworth's model of the relationship between iconic gesture and speech production.

communicative gestures, such as pantomime and emblems. Before we began to publish our results, very few researchers in speech–language pathology utilized the more specific lexical gesture/gesticulation models to guide the development of research hypotheses about gesture use in aphasia.

In turning to the psycholinguistic and cognitive neuropsychology literature, I found greater insights into the issue of how gesture production might affect language and speech production, the work of Robert Krauss whom we honor in this publication being a significant source. Several models of normal speech and gesture interaction have been posed that suggest how the production of a gesture might facilitate word retrieval and production in aphasia. The models reflect the differences in theories about the origins and functions of gesture. Hadar and Butterworth (1997) presented a model of speech and gesture interaction that suggests three sources of imagistic/gestural assistance for lexical retrieval (see Figure 3.2). The model assumes that conceptual processing automatically activates visual imagery to the extent that the concepts in mind are imageable. A second assumption is that visual images mediate between conceptual processing and the generation of iconic gesture. The visual image is then able to facilitate word retrieval in three different ways: via a preverbal route by refocusing conceptual processing, via a postsemantic route by holding core features during semantic reselection, and via a direct route by directly activating word forms in the phonological lexicon. Thus, word retrieval difficulties will elicit imagery and its associated gesture.

A second model as shown in Figure 3.3 was proposed by Krauss, Chen, and Gottesman (2000). Following Levelt's (1989) successive stages of

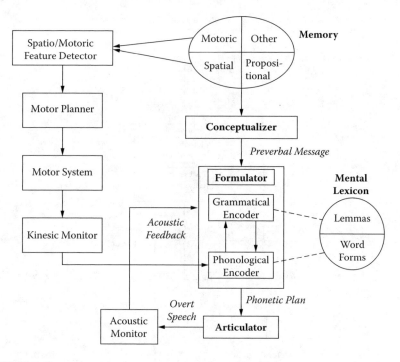

FIGURE 3.3 A processing model of gesture and speech production (Krauss, Chen, & Gottesman, 2000).

conceptualizing, formulating, and articulating, the model posits a gesture production system that articulates directly with the formulator. Memory employs a number of different formats and the content of memory is encoded in more than one representational format. Activation of a concept in one representational format will tend to activate related concepts in other formats. These different representations are activated during the precommunication phase. The conceptualizing phase draws on these knowledge stores in order to construct a communicative intention. Gesture production facilitates word retrieval by cross-modal priming via a direct route from the kinesics monitor, which monitors the gesture output, to the formulator of the speech production process. Morsella and Krauss (2004) proposed an updated version of the model, the gestural feedback model, which emphasizes the role gesture plays in activating and sustaining semantic representations of words, particularly those that involve the body and space.

A third model, which also builds on Levelt's speech production model, has been suggested by de Ruiter (1998) (see Figure 3.4). In the sketch model, gestures originate from the conceptualizer as a gesture sketch is generated. The information to either be conveyed in the verbal or gesture modalities is decided upon, and a sketch is produced in relation to the spatial-temporal/imagistic properties of the concepts to be conveyed. Different processes and knowledge stores are

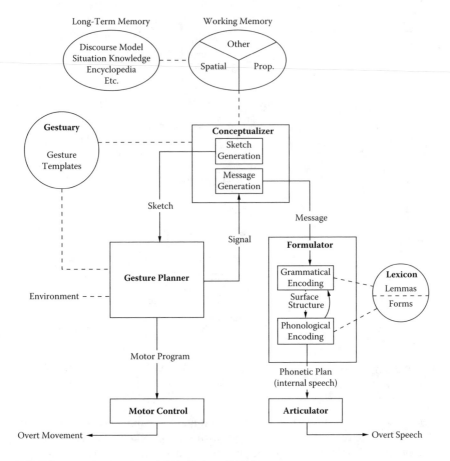

FIGURE 3.4   The sketch model (de Ruiter, 1998).

drawn upon depending on the specific type of gesture that is to be produced. De
Ruiter's sketch model is based on research data from healthy speakers. However,
in separating the processes underlying production of gesticulation, emblems, pantomimes, and pointing gestures we can begin to understand how an individual
with brain damage might show varying impairments and competencies in these
gesture elements and how the usual tight "coupling" of gesture and speech production processes may be "decoupled" in aphasia. For example, to produce iconic
gestures it is necessary to extract information from imagery processes in a novel
way and online each time. This compares to producing an emblem whereby a store
of conventionalized hand shapes, a "gesture syllabary," is accessed. Although the
sketch model was based on notions that the reasons for gesture production are
largely communicative, the model does not preclude the possibility of facilitation
effects (de Ruiter, 2006). The mechanism underlying possible gesture facilitation
of word retrieval in the sketch model is through reactivating visual representations in short-term memory, which then assists lexical access. All three models

suggest that the production of a gesture may facilitate lexical retrieval in normal speakers. However, what do we know about the gesture abilities and possible gesture facilitation effects in people with aphasia?

THE GESTURE ABILITIES OF PEOPLE WITH APHASIA AND THE THORNY ISSUE OF LIMB APRAXIA

The early work investigating the gesture abilities of people with aphasia and the utility of gesture in aphasia treatments was framed following detailed and careful observation rather than with the benefit of the more elaborated models of cognition, language, and praxis that we have today. Thus, without such models, the interpretation of results was often made whereby constructs that we now know to be reasonably discrete functional units capable of double dissociation were erroneously integrated. One example of this faulty reasoning concerned the suggestion that people with aphasia and concomitant limb apraxia (defined by Rothi & Heilman, 1997 as a neurological disorder of learned purposive limb movement that is not explained by deficits of elemental motor or sensory systems) would have poor conversational gesture skills and would therefore be poor candidates for gesture-based therapies. This argument arose from several group studies that employed correlational designs to examine the relationships between linguistic, cognitive, and praxic skills (Duffy, Duffy, & Pearson, 1975; Duffy & Duffy, 1981; Pickett, 1974). However, the bivariate correlational analyses failed to control for the considerable covariance that exists among the variables studied (Duffy et al., 1994). Further, these early researchers approached the notion of gesture from a limited framework that emphasized the more transparent and communicative pantomime and emblem-type gestures over the more frequently occurring gesticulations or iconic gestures that accompany spontaneous verbal output (see McNeill, 2005 for a detailed description of gesture taxonomies). Thus, the researchers examined the gesture skills of aphasic speakers only in terms of their performance on formal tests of limb praxis rather than in more spontaneous and less consciously driven tasks. Limb apraxia tests require a person with aphasia to represent an object or activity with a pantomime or emblem-type gesture following the examiner's command or to imitation. The tests do not take into account gesticulations that are tightly temporally coupled with natural speaking (McNeill, 2005).

We have argued that people with mild and moderate degrees of limb apraxia still have gestural competence and ability. In a study of seven people with moderate to severe nonfluent aphasia, ideomotor apraxia, and pantomime deficits on formal tests of pantomime, we found that all participants produced large amounts of meaning-laden gesture (iconics, pantomime, emblems) in natural conversational (Rose & Douglas, 2003) (see Table 3.1 and Table 3.2). It has been suggested that tests of limb apraxia require the person with aphasia to adopt an abstract attitude and to use meta-linguistic skills (Borod, Fitzpatrick, Helm-Estabrooks, & Goodglass, 1989; Rose, 2006). Thus, poor performance on limb apraxia tests may reflect these later skills rather than have any direct bearing on how well

TABLE 3.1
Participant Demographic and Linguistic Data

	SA	BO	KC	WS	CC	RG	JS
Age	80	68	38	63	42	61	72
Gender	Female	Male	Female	Female	Female	Male	Male
Months post-onset	18	60	31	192	13	216	15
Hemiplegia	Absent	Present	Present	Present	Present	Present	Present
Aphasia type	Broca's	Broca's	Broca's	Broca's	Global	Global	Broca's
WAB AQ	40.6	59.7	63	NA	NA	NA	NA
BDAE severity rating	NA	NA	NA	2	1	1	2

Note: WAB AQ—Western Aphasia Battery Aphasia Quotient (Kertesz, 1982); BDAE severity
rating—Boston Diagnostic Aphasia Examination ranging from 0 = no usable speech to
5 = minimal discernible handicap.

a person uses co-verbal gesture and gesticulation in a natural setting. Recently, Matsumoto, Suzuki, and Tanaka (2003) made suggestions concerning the possible neural architecture that could support dissociations between limb praxis and gesticulation skills. They argued that the ventral premotor area of the left hemisphere supports extrinsically motivated action such as imitation and performing movements to command (as required in tests of limb apraxia), while the medial premotor area supports intrinsically motivated action (such as that seen

TABLE 3.2
Percentage of Gestures Produced During a 6-Minute Conversation Sample for Each Participant

Participant	Speech-Focused Movements	Descriptive Gesture	Codified Gesture	Pantomime
SA	27.3 (9)	30.3 (10)	30.3 (10)	12.1 (4)
BO	46.4 (13)	25 (7)	18 (5)	10.6 (3)
KC	54 (19)	23 (8)	9 (3)	14 (5)
WS	32.5 (13)	35 (14)	15 (6)	17.5 (7)
GC	3 (1)	15 (5)	12 (4)	70 (24)
RG	34 (12)	37 (13)	26 (9)	3 (31)
JS	14 (5)	25 (9)	19 (7)	42 (15)

Note: Figures in parentheses refer to actual number of gestures produced in the sample.

in spontaneous gesture production). Therefore, selective lesions could potentially underlie a limb apraxia/gesticulation skill dissociation.

Small group studies using cognitive neuropsychological approaches and samples of conversational gesture and speech have found that people with aphasia use more gestures per spoken word than do normal speakers (Behrmann & Penn, 1984) and that the type of aphasia is strongly related to the type and amount of co-verbal gesture used (Hadar, Wenkert-Olenik, Krauss, & Soroker, 1998; LeMay, David, & Thomas, 1988). For example, Carlomango, Pandolfi, Martini, Di Iasi, and Cristilli (2005) found people with anomic aphasia produced four times more iconic gestures per spoken word than did normal control speakers. Similarly, in a recent study of eighteen people with nonfluent aphasia, we found that speakers used significantly more meaning-laden gestures (iconic, pantomimes, emblems) than beat gestures, and significantly more meaning-laden gestures during instances of word retrieval difficulty than during fluent clauses, in 20-minute samples of natural conversation (Lanyon & Rose, 2009).

GESTURE FACILITATION OF WORD RETRIEVAL

Motivated by the fact that people with aphasia do use large amounts of gesture, and by the speech/gesture interaction models reviewed earlier in this chapter that suggest possible mechanisms for gesture facilitation effects, we examined the facilitation effects of gesture production on word retrieval in six individuals with aphasia in a pilot study (Rose & Douglas, 2001). Four females and two males with aphasia who had sustained a single left-hemisphere stroke at least six months prior to the study participated. They were right-handed premorbidly, monolingual English speakers, had no history of drug or alcohol abuse, and had not had gesture targeted in previous speech pathology interventions. Following three baseline picture naming trials, 100 object pictures were divided into five groups balanced for all relevant psycholinguistic variables and individual baseline error rates. In the experimental phase, participants were asked to name the same pictures over five trials following instructions to either point at the picture, close their eyes and imagine the object, close their eyes and imagine using the object, make an iconic gesture representing the object, or produce a cued articulation gesture representing the first phoneme of the target object name. Significant facilitation effects were demonstrated after making an iconic gesture but only for three participants whose word retrieval difficulties were underpinned by a phonological access/ encoding impairment (see Figure 3.5). The facilitation effects were not demonstrated for participants with a primary semantic or phonetic encoding impairment or for the two visualizing or other general motor movement conditions (pointing, cued articulations).

The fact that the facilitation effects were not present until the gesture was actually physically produced (as compared to during earlier stages of processing such as imagining) argues for interactions between later stages of gesture

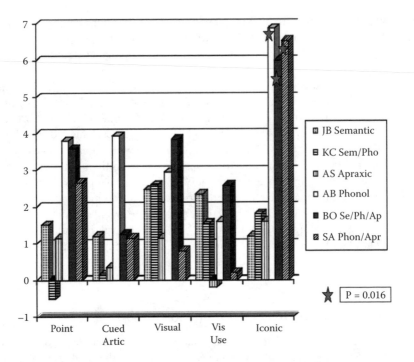

FIGURE 3.5 Facilitation trial results for the pointing, cued articulation, visualizing object, visualizing object use, and iconic gesture conditions, expressed as the difference between the mean facilitation trial scores and the mean baseline phase scores.

production and language production, perhaps as late as phonological access/encoding. Such late stage processing is consistent with the model of Krauss et al. (2000). Similarly, in our recent work investigating the possible facilitation effects of gesture production on word retrieval in conversational settings, a particular impairment pattern was consistent with the facilitation effects observed. Five of the eighteen participants who demonstrated the most significant amounts of iconic gesture production during instances of resolved word retrieval difficulties also demonstrated word retrieval error patterns consistent with phonological level impairments (Lanyon & Rose, 2009).

Together, the results from these two studies suggest that gesture facilitation of word retrieval may well be possible for some individuals with aphasia, and in particular, those who have predominantly phonological level impairments underlying their word retrieval difficulties. These data require replication across a larger number of participants but we feel motivated to search further for this "needle in the haystack." We are grateful for the work of Krauss and colleagues whose models have underpinned this exploration. The short-term facilitation effects captured in the studies discussed previously do not necessarily equate to the longer term and more conscious use effects of gesture in aphasia treatments. The following section reviews the effects of gesture use in aphasia treatments.

GESTURE PRODUCTION AS A TREATMENT FOR APHASIA

During the 1980s a raft of studies were published in the speech-language pathology literature concerning the possibility of utilizing gesture in treatments for aphasia. The majority of these studies focused on the compensatory use of gesture where verbal communication could not be restored. The studies were mostly case study designs concerning individuals with moderate to severe nonfluent or global aphasia. They demonstrate that people with moderate to severe aphasia are capable of acquiring a repertoire of arm and hand gestures in a therapeutic setting but the evidence for generalization of these gestures to use in everyday conversation is less compelling (see Rose, 2006 for an overview of this literature and Table 3.3 for a summary).

Gesture has also been employed with the aim to restore the impaired linguistic systems, with Skelly et al.'s (1974) research being the seminal study in the area. A summary of these studies is provided in Table 3.4. We have undertaken a series of studies examining the efficacy of verbal alone, gesture alone, and combined verbal + gesture treatments for aphasic noun and verb retrieval deficits (Rose & Douglas, 2002, 2006, 2008; Rose, Douglas, & Matyas, 2002; Rose & Sussmilch, 2008). Ten carefully controlled multiple-baseline single subject research designs have been utilized: seven investigating noun retrieval and three investigating verb retrieval.

All 10 participants sustained left-sided strokes at least 12 months prior to the therapy studies. They had English as their first and only language, were right-handed pre-morbidly (Bryden, 1982 Simplified Hand Preference score = +1.0), had no history of drug or alcohol abuse, and gesture had not been targeted in any previous speech pathology interventions. Aphasia syndrome assignment and severity was based on the language profiles obtained from performance on the Western Aphasia Battery (Kertesz, 1982), the Test for Oral and Limb Apraxia (Helm-Estabrooks, 1992), the Apraxia Battery for Adults (Dabul, 1979), the Psycholinguistic Assessment of Language Processing in Adults (Kay, Lesser, & Coltheart, 1992), and the Pyramid and Palm Trees Test (Howard & Patterson, 1992).

Baseline naming rates were obtained by having participants name 80 or 100 object or action pictures on 10 separate occasions over a period of three weeks. Following the baseline naming phase, the 80 or 100 items were divided into four or five groups (groups A to D/E) of 20 items each, and were balanced for word frequency, imageability, number of syllables, number of phonemes, phonetic complexity, and individual error rates obtained during the baseline phase. For the three verb studies, the verb targets were also balanced for argument structure and age of acquisition. Group B was assigned to the verbal treatment condition, group C to the gesture treatment condition, and group D to the combined verbal and gesture treatment condition. In two studies, group E was assigned to a repetition only treatment (simply repeating the target word after the therapist-spoken model). Initially, group A was assigned to the control condition. Three 45-minute treatment sessions were held per week. Every session commenced with naming items from group A. Items from groups B to D/E were then trained in three/four different conditions.

TABLE 3.3
Summary of Case Reports Using Gesture as a Compensatory Communicative Method

Author	Year	Participants	Type of Aphasia	Severity of Aphasia	Gesture Used in Therapy	Amount of Treatment	Treatment Outcome
Skelly et al.	1974	6	Oral verbal apraxia	Moderate to severe	70–100 Amer-Ind	Not stated	Sign and improved speech
Bonvillian & Freidman	1978	1	T.B.I.*	Severe	117 signs	Not stated	Spontaneous use of 67%, unintelligible vocalization attempts
Simmons & Zorthian	1979	1	Jargon	Severe	24 Amer-Ind	7 months	Spontaneous use at home
Schlanger & Freimann	1979	4	Not stated	Severe	14 pantomimes	8 hours	14 used + generalized to 5 nontrained
Heilman et al.	1979	1	Global	Not stated	100 signals	Not stated	Used 100 and sequenced 3
Rao & Horner	1978	4	Expressive	Severe	Amer-Ind	Not stated	Spouse reports progress
Kirshner & Webb	1981	1	Global	Severe	127 Amer-Ind plus ASL signs	7 months	Phrase level spontaneous gesture
Guilford & Schuerle	1982	8	Not stated	Not stated	20 ASL 20 Amer-Ind	8 hours	Acquired 60% on testing
Kearns et al.	1982	2	Global	Moderate to severe	6 Amer-Ind	5 sessions	Spontaneous signing, some verbal skills
Helm-Estabrooks et al.	1982	8	Global	Severe	Visual action therapy (VAT)	1/2 hour per day for 4–14 weeks	Increased pantomime ability

Author	Year	N	Aphasia type	Severity	Treatment	Duration	Outcome
Moody	1982	1	Global	Severe	200 signs	Not stated	Sign learned
Tonkovich & Loverso	1982	4	Broca's	Not stated	Amer-Ind ASL 4 verbs 4 nouns	12 training sessions	Learned signs generalized to 25 other combinations
Baratz	1985	1	Global	Severe	VAT plus ASL signs	20 months of 4 hours per week	25 ASL signs, combinations of Amer-Ind, 20% effective
Code & Gaunt	1986	1	Broca's	Severe	20 Makaton signs	45 min per week for 24 weeks	Learned signs, increased verbal output
Coelho	1987	1	T.B.I. oral verbal apraxia	Severe	47 signs	13 months	47 signs no generalization
Coelho & Duffy	1990	2	Nonfluent	Moderate to severe	14 signs	180 min for 6 weeks	Learned all 14 signs
Cubelli et al.	1991	1	Global	Severe	23 gestures	180 min per week for 8 weeks	All gestures learned
Rao	1995	1	Jargon	Severe	50 Amer-Ind signs	Daily for 6 weeks	30 signs, reduced jargon

*T.B.I.—Traumatic brain injury.

TABLE 3.4
Summary of Treatments Using Gesture as a Restorative Method

Authors	Year	Participants	Aphasia Type and Severity	Apraxia of Speech (AOS) and Limb Apraxia	Study Design	Treatment Targets	Treatment Method	Outcomes	Experimental Control Demonstrated
Skelly et al.	1974	6	Moderate to severe aphasia	Severe AOS; No data on limb praxis	Small group	Amer-Ind gestures	Combined verbal plus gesture	Mixed results; 10–200 words; Some phrases	No control probes during treatment
Kearns et al.	1982	2	Moderate to severe anomia	No AOS; No limb apraxia	Multiple-baseline	6 Amer-Ind gestures and 6 verbs	A. Gesture only	Learned signs; No verbs	Yes
							B. Combined verbal plus gesture	Learned 6 verbs	Yes
Ramsberger & Helm-Estabrooks	1982	6	Severe aphasia	Bucco-facial apraxia; No data on limb praxis	Small group	Objects, object and action pictures	Bucco-facial Visual action therapy	Gesture increased; Word repetition skills increased	Participants 2–5 months post-onset, no controls for spontaneous recovery

Study	Year	N	Diagnosis	Praxis/AOS	Design	Stimuli	Conditions	Results	Stimuli variables
Hoodin & Thompson	1983	2	Moderate-severe nonfluent aphasia	No data provided	Alternating treatments	Amer-Ind gestures and nouns	Verbal alone Gesture alone Verbal plus gesture	Spoken noun acquisition Gestures acquired, no words Nouns and gestures acquired	No data provided on stimuli variables
Code & Gaunt	1986	1	Severe Broca's aphasia	Severe AOS Ideomotor and ideational apraxia	ABABA	10 iconic Makaton signs	Combined verbal plus gesture	40% improved cued noun production	Yes
Raymer & Thompson	1991	1	Severe Broca's aphasia	Severe AOS Reasonably intact limb praxis	Multiple-baseline	Amer-Ind gestures Pictured nouns	Combined verbal plus gesture	Improved noun repetition	Yes
Schneider et al.	1996	1	Primary progressive aphasia: nonfluent	No data on AOS Normal limb praxis	Multiple-baseline and matrix	108 NP + V + NP Sentences Amer-Ind gestures	Verbal alone, combined verbal plus gesture	Improved trained sentences Combined treatment superior	Yes

(continued)

TABLE 3.4 (CONTINUED)
Summary of Treatments Using Gesture as a Restorative Method

Authors	Year	Participants	Aphasia Type and Severity	Apraxia of Speech (AOS) and Limb Apraxia	Study Design	Treatment Targets	Treatment Method	Outcomes	Experimental Control Demonstrated
Pashek	1997	1	Severe Broca's aphasia	Severe AOS Mild ideomotor apraxia	Alternating treatments	60 nouns and verbs Amer-Ind gestures	Verbal only, left gesture, right gesture	Improved picture naming No generalization	Verbs not matched for argument structure; no statistical analysis of treatment differences across conditions
Pashek	1998	1	Not stated	Severe AOS No limb apraxia	Alternating treatments	28 nouns 28 verbs	Verbal alone, combined verbal plus gesture	Small improvement in nouns, generalized to conversation More improvement in verbs, no generalization to conversation Verb + gesture superior	Verbs not matched for argument structure; no statistical analysis of treatment differences across conditions

Study	Year	N	Aphasia type	AOS/apraxia	Design	Stimuli	Treatment	Outcome	Generalization	Notes
Marshall	1999	1	Severe Broca's aphasia	No data provided	Single case study	10 general verbs	Combined semantic, gesture, imagery, and narrative training	Significant increase in trained verbs, increase in verb arguments and communicative effectiveness in story re-tell	Yes	
Rose et al.	2002	1	Mild conduction aphasia	No AOS No limb apraxia	Multiple-baseline	80 nouns Iconic and cued articulation gestures	Verbal only Gesture only Combined verbal plus gesture	Significant increase in picture naming Generalized to conversation	Yes	
Rose & Douglas	2002	2	Moderate-severe Broca's	Severe AOS Moderate limb apraxia	Multiple-baseline	80 nouns Iconic and cued articulation gestures	Verbal only Gesture only Combined verbal plus gesture	Significant increase in picture naming Generalized to conversation	Yes	
Rodriguez, Raymer, & Rothi	2006	4	2 conduction 1 Wernicke's 1 Broca's	Moderate AOS		60 verbs	Combined verbal and gesture Semantic-phonologic	Only one conduction participant showed significant increase in picture naming		Partial stimuli groups not balanced for argument structure, homophonous nouns

(continued)

TABLE 3.4 (CONTINUED)
Summary of Treatments Using Gesture as a Restorative Method

Authors	Year	Participants	Aphasia Type and Severity	Apraxia of Speech (AOS) and Limb Apraxia	Study Design	Treatment Targets	Treatment Method	Outcomes	Experimental Control Demonstrated
Rose & Douglas	2006	1	Moderate Broca's aphasia	Severe AOS No limb apraxia	Multiple-baseline	80 nouns and cued articulation gestures	Verbal only Gesture only Combined verbal plus gesture	Significant increase in picture naming Generalized to conversation	Yes
Rose & Douglas	2008	1	Mild anomic aphasia	No AOS No limb apraxia	Multiple-baseline	80 nouns and iconic gestures	Verbal only Gesture only Combined verbal plus gesture	Significant increase in picture naming Generalized to conversation	Yes

| Rose & Sussmilch | 2008 | 3 | Moderate Broca's aphasia: Participant KC + MW word form verb impairment Participant MT semantic verb impairment | Moderate AOS Moderate limb apraxia | Multiple-baseline | 100 verbs and iconic gestures | Verbal only Gesture only Repetition only Combined verbal plus gesture | Significant increase in verb naming Verb + ing generalized to conversation for KC and MW Little improvement for MT | Yes |
| Rose et al. | In preparation | 2 | 1. Severe Broca's 2. Moderate Broca's | Moderate AOS Moderate limb apraxia | Multiple-baseline | 100 nouns and iconic gestures | Verbal only Gesture only Combined verbal plus gesture | Significant increase in picture naming Generalization to conversation naming | Yes |

The order of conditions was rotated every session, with a repeated cycle every three sessions. Training was applied to any items in sets B to D/E that were not spontaneously named within 20 seconds of presentation. Training continued in this way until one set reached 90% correct on three out of four consecutive sessions, at which time the condition applied to that successful set was then applied to the control set A. The remaining two/three sets continued to receive their respective treatments and all training continued until one set reached 100% correct on three consecutive occasions or twenty sessions were completed, whichever came first. All baseline and treatment sessions were videotaped with participant permission for later transcription and analyses. Follow-up naming trials were completed at one and three months after the final treatment session.

An example of the standard case charts displaying the naming results in baseline and intervention phases for the participants is presented in Figure 3.6 (see Rose et al., 2002; Rose & Douglas, 2006, 2008; Rose & Sussmilch, 2008 for further examples). In this series of studies, 9 of the 10 participants demonstrated significantly enhanced object or action naming following treatment as compared to the levels obtained during the baseline phase, with large effect sizes demonstrated. These improvements can be attributed to the interventions rather than spontaneous recovery or general therapeutic stimulation, as there was stability in naming scores in the control conditions until treatment was applied to those items. For 7 participants, all three treatment conditions produced significant improvements in naming with no condition being significantly better than another, that is gesture only, verbal only, and combined verbal plus gesture treatment were equally efficacious. In comparison, the gesture only treatment produced greater levels of naming accuracy for 1 participant (BO) as compared to the verbal only or the combined verbal plus gesture treatment conditions. BO evidenced a severe nonfluent aphasia with significant auditory and reading comprehension impairments such that the linguistic modality offered little assistance in communication. Therefore, it was not surprising to see that the gesture only condition produced significantly better results than the verbal conditions.

For 2 participants, EW and MW, the combined verbal and gesture treatments were more potent than the verbal alone or gesture alone treatments. These two participants demonstrated phonological level impairments underpinning their noun (EW) or verb (MW) retrieval difficulties. So again, the importance of the underlying linguistic impairment appears to be significant in terms of the response to combined verbal and gesture treatment, a finding in keeping with recent work by Rodriguez, Raymer, and Rothi (2006).

The majority of our data did not support the long held axiom in speech-language pathology that multimodality interventions are superior to single-modality interventions. Rather, the results highlight the need for clinicians to consider the underlying knowledge and processes generated by particular intervention tasks, rather than simply the modality in which the treatment is transmitted. Similarly, clinicians need to carefully consider each patient's strengths and weaknesses with respect to particular interventions and recognize that multimodality treatments may prove more difficult for some patients than single modality options. The

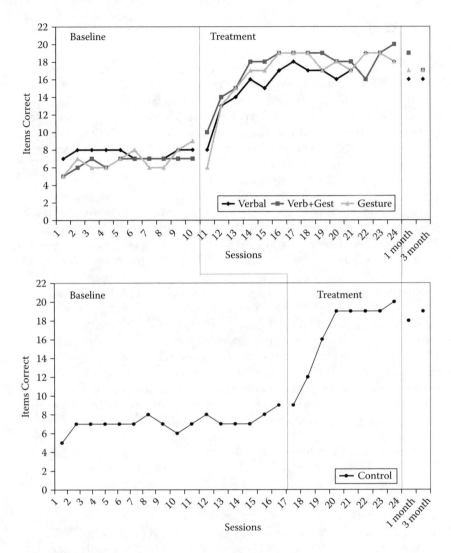

FIGURE 3.6 Comparative noun treatments results for JB, semantic level impairment.

superior results for the combined gesture and verbal treatment demonstrated for EW and MW are noteworthy given their underlying phonological level impairments. Again, the importance of phonological level impairment is highlighted in terms of achieving any significant boost from gesture treatments. We have only studied three participants in action naming studies to date and are encouraged by the large effect sizes demonstrated in two participants. It is possible that gesture treatments may well be more potent for verbs than nouns, and we believe this idea is worthy of further investigation.

FUTURE RESEARCH

To date, the majority of studies examining the effects of gesture treatments for aphasic language impairments have been focused on word retrieval. One study by Schneider, Thompson, and Luring (1996) examined the effects of gesture treatments on subject-verb-object sentence constructions in an individual with primary progressive aphasia. The combined verbal plus gesture treatment lead to higher levels of correct oral sentence production than verbal training alone. Future research should examine the effects of combined gesture and verbal treatments on tense morphology and sentence construction skills.

People with aphasia who, by definition, have poor linguistic processing skills may need to rely more heavily on spatial working memory and spatial motoric modes of thinking during conceptualization as compared to unimpaired speakers. That is, the "thinking for speaking" that we carry out silently is probably more difficult without ready access to language. When the spoken modality is compromised in normal speakers, for example during talking in noisy environments, speakers frequently resort to the increased use of pantomime and emblem codes for communication (McNeill, 2005). We and others (Behrmann & Penn, 1984; Duffy, Duffy, & Mercaitis, 1984) have observed that some people with aphasia, particularly fluent aphasia, have difficulty utilizing pantomime. When using pantomime for communication, there is a greater demand placed on visuo–motoric working memory and the need to synthesize perceptual inputs, knowledge of objects, action semantics, and action programs to produce the pantomime. It is possible that some people with aphasia are poor at utilizing pantomime because they have concurrent reduction in working memory. We recommend that future studies investigating gesture use in aphasia should report on working memory in their participants.

The exploration of gesture use, facilitation, and treatment methods in aphasia is a natural focus for interdisciplinary research. Future studies would be enhanced with the collaborative efforts of psycholinguistics, neuropsychology, neurology, and speech-language pathology. Such interdisciplinary research would help to further specify current models of speech/gesture interaction and integrate findings from neuro-imaging studies highlighting distributed functional interactive neurological systems and the mirror neuron systems (e.g., Pulvermuller, 2005; Rizzolatti, Sinigaglia, & Anderson, 2008). Ultimately, we believe the goal of finding effective treatments for aphasic language impairments will be met more rapidly through focused collaborative and interdisciplinary research. Robert Krauss's work had an impact on many disciplines. The challenge of working together is ready for the taking.

REFERENCES

Baratz, R. (1985). Manual communication training for a global aphasic patient. *Aphasia-Apraxia-Agnosia, 3*(4), 19–44.

Behrmann, M., & Penn, C. (1984). Non-verbal communication of aphasic patients. *British Journal of Disorders of Communication, 19*, 155–168.

Bonvillian, J. & Friedman, R. (1978). Language development in another mode: The acquisition of signs by a brain-damaged adult. *Sign Language Studies, 19*, 111–120.

Borod, J., Fitzpatrick, P., Helm-Estabrooks, N., & Goodglass, H. (1989). The relationship between limb apraxia and spontaneous use of communicative gesture in aphasia. *Brain and Cognition, 10,* 121–131.

Bryden, M. (1982). Handedness and its relations to cerebral function. In M. Bryden (Ed.), Laterality: Functional asymmetry in the intact brain (pp. 157–179). New York: Academic Press.

Byng, S., & Duchan, J. (2005). *Challenging aphasia therapies.* New York: Oxford University Press.

Carlomagno, S., Pandolfi, M., Martini, A., Di Iasi, G., & Cristilli, C. (2005). Coverbal gestures in Alzheimer's type dementia. *Cortex, 41,* 535–546.

Chapey, R. (2008). *Language intervention strategies in aphasia and related neurogenic communication disorders* (5th ed.). Philadelphia: Lippincott Williams & Wilkins.

Code, C. & Gaunt, C. (1986). Treating severe speech and limb apraxia in a case of aphasia. *British Journal of Disorders of Communication, 21,* 11–20.

Coelho, C. & Duffy, R. (1987). The relationship of the acquisition of manual signs to severity of aphasia: A training study. *Brain and Language, 31,* 328–345.

Coelho, C. & Duffy, R. (1990). Sign acquisition in two aphasic subjects with limb apraxia. *Aphasiology, 4,* 1–8.

Cubelli, R., Trentini, P. & Montagna, C. (1991). Re-education of gestural communication in a case of chronic global aphasia and limb apraxia. *Cognitive Neuropsychology, 8,* 369–380.

Dabul, B. (1979). *Apraxia battery for adults.* Tigard, OR: CC Publications.

de Ruiter, J. (1998). *Gesture and speech production.* Wageningen: Max Plank Institute.

de Ruiter, J. (2006). Can gesticulation help aphasic people speak, or rather, communicate? *Advances in Speech-Language Pathology, 8*(2), 124–127.

Duchan, J. & Byng, S. (2004). Challenging aphasia therapies: Broadening the discourse and extending the boundaries. New York: Psychology Press.

Duffy, J., Duffy, R., & Pearson, K. (1975). Pantomime recognition in aphasics. *Journal of Speech and Hearing Research, 18,* 115–132.

Duffy, R., & Duffy, J. (1981). Three studies of deficits in pantomime expression and pantomimic recognition in aphasia. *Journal of Speech and Hearing Research, 46,* 70–84.

Duffy, R., Duffy, J., & Mercaitis, A. (1984). Comparison of performance of a fluent and a non-fluent aphasic on a pantomimic referential task. *Brain and Language, 21,* 260–273.

Duffy, R., Watt, J., & Duffy, J. (1994). Testing causal theories of pantomime deficits in aphasia using path analysis. *Aphasiology, 8,* 361–379.

Goodglass, H., & Kaplan, E. (1963). Disturbance in gesture and pantomime in aphasia. *Brain, 86,*703–720.

Guilford, A. & Scheuerle, J. (1982). Manual communication skills in aphasia. *Archives of Physical Medicine and Rehabilitation, 63,* 601–604.

Hadar, U. & Butterworth, B. (1997). Iconic gestures, imagery, and word retrieval in speech. Semiotica, 115, 147–172.

Hadar, U., Wenkert-Olenik, D., Krauss, R., & Soroker, N. (1998). Gesture and the processing of speech: Neuropsychological evidence. Brain and Language, 62, 107–126.

Heilman, K., Rothi, L., Campanella, D. & Wolfson, S. (1979). Wernicke's and global aphasia without alexia. *Archives of Physical Medicine and Rehabilitation, 36,* 129–133.

Helm-Estabrooks, N., Fitzpatrick, P. & Barresi, B. (1982). Visual action therapy for global aphasia. *Journal of Speech and Hearing Disorders, 47,* 385–389.

Helm-Estabrooks, N. (1992). *Test of oral and limb apraxia.* Chicago: The Riverside Publishing Group.

Hoodin, R. & Thompson, C. (1983). Facilitation of verbal labeling in adult aphasia by gestural, verbal or verbal plus gestural training. In R. H. Brookshire (Ed). *Clinical aphasiology* (pp. 62–64). Minneapolis: BRK.

Howard, D., & Patterson, K. (1992). *The pyramid and palm trees test.* Suffolk, UK: Thames Valley Test Company.

Kagan, A. (1995). Revealing the competence of aphasic adults through conversation: A challenge to health professionals. *Topics in Stroke Rehabilitation, 2,* 15–28.

Kay, J., Lesser, R., & Coltheart, M. (1992). *Psycholinguistic assessments of language processing in aphasia.* Hove, UK: Lawrence Erlbaum Associates.

Kearns, K., Simmons, N. & Sisterhen, C. (1982). Gestural sign (Amer-Ind) as a facilitator of verbalisation in patients with aphasia. In R. Brookshire (Ed.) *Clinical aphasiology*, (pp.183–191). Minneapolis, MN: BRK Publishers.

Kertesz, A. (1982). *The western aphasia battery.* New York: Grune and Stratton.

Kirshner, H. & Webb, W. (1981). Selective involvement of the auditory-verbal modality in an acquired communication disorder: Benefit from sign language therapy. *Brain and Language, 13,* 161–170.

Krauss, R., Chen, Y., & Gottesman, R. (2000). Lexical gestures and lexical access: A process model. In D. McNeill (Ed.). *Language and gesture* (pp. 261–283). Cambridge, UK: Cambridge University Press.

Lanyon, L., & Rose, M. (2009). Do the hands have it? The facilitation effects of arm and hand gesture on word retrieval in non-fluent aphasia. *Aphasiology, 23*(7/8), 809–822.

LeMay, A., David, R., & Thomas, A. (1988). The use of spontaneous gesture by aphasic patients. *Aphasiology, 2,* 137–145.

Levelt, W. (1989). Speaking: From intention to articulation. Cambridge, MA: MIT Press.

Luria, A. (1973). *The working brain.* Harmondsworth, Middlesex: Penguin.

Marshall, J. (1999). Doing something about a verb impairment: Two therapy approaches. In S. Byng, Swinburn & C. Pound (Ed). *The Aphasia Therapy File* (pp.111–130). London: Psychology Press.

Matsumoto, K., Suzuki, W., & Tanaka, K. (2003). Neural correlates of goal-based motor selection in pre-motor cortex. *Science, 301,* 229–301.

McNeill, D. (2005). *Gesture and thought.* Chicago: University of Chicago Press.

Moody, E. (1982). Sign language acquisition by a global aphasia. *The Journal of Nervous and Mental Disease, 170*(2), 113–116.

Morsella, E., & Krauss, R. (2004). The role of gestures in spatial working memory and speech. *American Journal of Psychology, 117*(3), 411–424.

Murray, L., & Clarke, H. (2006). *Neurogenic disorders of language: Theory driven clinical practice.* Clifton Park, NY: Thomas Delmar Learning.

Pashek, G. (1997). A case study of gesturally cued naming in aphasia: Dominant versus nondominant hand training. *Journal of Communication Disorders, 30,* 349–366.

Pashek, G. (1998). Gestural facilitation of noun and verb retrieval in aphasia: A case study. *Brain and Language, 65*(1), 177–180.

Patterson, K., & Shewell, C. (1987). *The cognitive neuropsychology of language.* Hove, UK: Lawrence Erlbaum Associates.

Pickett, L. (1974). Assessment of gesture and pantomimic deficit in aphasic patients. *Acta Symbolica, 5,* 69–86.

Pound, C. (2004). Dare to be different: The person and the practice. In J. Duchan & S. Byng (Eds.), *Challenging aphasia therapies* (pp. 32–53). Hove, UK: Psychology Press.

Pulvermuller, F. (2005). Brain mechanisms linking language and action. *Nature Reviews Neuroscience, 6,* 576–582.

Ramsberger, G. & Helm-Estabrooks, N. (1989). Visual action therapy for bucco-facial apraxia. In T. Prescott (Ed). *Clinical aphasiology* (pp. 395–406). Massachusetts: College-Hill.

Rao, P. (1995). Drawing and gesture as communication options in a person with severe aphasia. *Topics in Stroke Rehabilitation, 2*(1), 49–56.

Rao, P. & Horner, J. (1978). Gesture as a deblocking modality in a severe aphasic patient. In R. Brookshire (Ed). *Clinical aphasiology conference proceedings*. Minneapolis, MN: BRK Publishers.

Raymer, A. & Thompson, C. (1991). Effects of verbal plus gestural treatment in a patient with aphasia and severe apraxia of speech. In T. Prescott (Ed). *Clinical aphasiology* (pp. 285–297). Austin, TX: Pro-Ed.

Rizzolatti, G., Sinigaglia, C., & Anderson, F. (2008). *Mirrors in the brain: How our minds share actions, emotions, and experience*. New York: Oxford University Press.

Rodriguez, A., Raymer, A., & Rothi, L. (2006). Effects of gesture and verbal and semantic-phonologic treatments for verb retrieval in aphasia. *Aphasiology, 20*(2–4), 286–297.

Rose, M. (2006). The utility of arm and hand gestures in the treatment of aphasia. *Advances in Speech-Language Pathology, 8*(2), 92–109.

Rose, M., & Douglas, J. (2001). The differential facilitation effects of gesture and visualisation processes on object naming in aphasia. *Aphasiology, 15* (10/11), 977–990.

Rose, M., & Douglas, J. (2002). Questioning an axiom of aphasia therapy: When multimodality treatment is not better. Paper presented at the International Aphasia Rehabilitation Conference, Brisbane, Australia.

Rose, M., & Douglas, J. (2003). Limb apraxia, pantomime, and lexical gesture in aphasic speakers: Preliminary findings. *Aphasiology, 17*(5), 453–464.

Rose, M., & Douglas, J. (2006). A comparison of verbal and gesture treatments for a word production deficit resulting from acquired apraxia of speech. *Aphasiology, 20*(12), 1186–1209.

Rose, M., & Douglas, J. (2008). Treating a semantic word retrieval problem with gesture and verbal methods. *Aphasiology, 22*(1), 20–41.

Rose, M., Douglas, J., & Matyas, T. (2002). The comparative effectiveness of gesture and verbal treatments for a specific phonologic naming impairment. *Aphasiology, 16*(10/11), 1001–1030.

Rose, M., & Sussmilch, G. (2008). The effects of semantic and gesture treatments on verb retrieval and verb use in aphasia. *Aphasiology, 22*(7&8), 691–706.

Rothi, L., & Heilman, K. (1997). *Apraxia. The neuropsychology of action*. Hove, UK: Psychology Press.

Schlanger, P. & Freimann, R. (1979). Pantomime therapy with aphasics. *Aphasia-Apraxia-Agnosia, 1*, 34–39.

Schneider, B., Thompson, C., & Luring, B. (1996). Effects of verbal plus gestural matrix training on sentence production in a patient with primary progressive aphasia. *Aphasiology, 10*(3), 297–317.

Shadden, B. (2005). Aphasia as identity theft. *Aphasiology, 19*, 11–29.

Simmons, N. & Zorthian, A. (1979). The use of symbolic gesture in a case of fluent aphasia. In R. Brookshire (Ed.). *Clinical aphasiology* (pp.278–284). Minneapolis, MN: BRK.

Skelly, M. (1979). *Amer-Ind gestural code based on universal American Indian hand talk*. New York: Elsevier.

Skelly, M., Schinsky, L., Smith, R., & Fust, R. (1974). American Indian sign (Amer-Ind) as a facilitator of verbalisation for the oral verbal apraxic. *Journal of Speech and Hearing Disorders, 34*, 445–455.

Tonkovich, J. & Loverso, F. (1982). A training matrix approach for gestural acquisition by the agrammatic patient. In R. Brookshire (Ed). *Clinical aphasiology: Conference proceedings* (pp.283–288). Minneapolis, MN: BRK.

Wang, L., & Goodglass, H. (1992). Pantomime, praxis, and aphasia. *Brain and Language, 42,* 402–418.

Weigl, E. (1968). On the problem of cortical syndromes: Experimental studies. In M. L. Simmel (Ed.), *The reach of the mind: Essays in memory of Kurt Goldstein.* New York: Springer.

4 Functional Imaging of the Hand Motor Cortex During the Performance of Linguistic Tasks

Dafna Palti and Uri Hadar

Over the last decade, functional brain imagining has been applied in a large number of studies in order to locate the neuronal substrates related to hand gestures. These studies investigated brain reactions during the viewing of hand gestures (e.g., Buccino et al., 2001; Decety et al., 1997; Fadiga, Fogassi, Pavesi, & Rizzolatti, 1995), during overt and covert production of gestures (e.g., Binkofski et al., 2000; Bonda, Petrides, Frey, & Evans, 1995; Parsons et al., 1995), or mental imagery of gestures and grasping movements (Grafton, Arbib, Fadiga, & Rizzolatti, 1996; Lotze et al., 1999). Most of the gestures that were used as stimuli in those experiments were instrumental in the sense that they referred to objects or tools (e.g., opening a bottle) or were functional in natural settings (e.g., drawing a line).

A different set of imaging studies tried to look for brain reaction during the observation of expressive gestures (also known as co-verbal or co-speech gestures) rather than instrumental gestures (Gallagher & Frith, 2004; Grosbras & Paus, 2006; Lotze et al., 2006). This research addressed more symbolic and nonfigurative roles of hand gesture during communication, such as threatening or waving. However, none of these studies actually involved any verbal stimuli. Those studies that tried to deal directly with the linguistic aspects of gesture concentrated mostly on sign languages (MacSweeney et al., 2006; MacSweeney et al., 2004; MacSweeney et al., 2002; Neville et al., 1998; Newman, Bavelier, Corina, Jezzard, & Neville, 2002). Yet, the signs in sign languages are lexicalized and are produced in hierarchic combinations, and therefore their neuronal correlates may not be comparable to those activated by co-verbal gestures, which, in normal speakers, are supplementary to the lexicalized units (Krauss & Hadar, 1999).

As far as we are aware, only one published study thus far has actually looked at the effect of speech–gesture interaction on brain reactions (Willems, Özyürek, & Hagoort, 2006). This study found that, in a sentential context, a local mismatch between a verb and the accompanying gesture, presented in an audio-visual setting, resulted in an effect both in Broca's area, considered to be mainly linguistic, and in the premotor cortex, which subserves more general motor processes.

The latter set of results may demonstrate the contribution of co-verbal hand gestures to the processing of a verbal message presented in face-to-face interaction. It is still unclear, however, to what extent the hand motor system in the brain is actually activated during the processing of linguistic inputs in other situations, for example, when the message is only auditory or during the production of speech.

In this chapter, we wish to present some indirect evidence of the link between language and hand gestures. This evidence was obtained from an imaging study that looked specifically at hand-related brain areas during listening to verbal linguistic inputs, as well as during the generation of single words. The problem of adducing direct evidence in these cases is that, during speech production, people tend to move their head (Hadar, Wenkert-Olenik, Krauss, & Soroker, 1998), implying severe distortion of the imaging data from the brain. Therefore, the subjects in our experiments did not actually gesture. The lack of supra-threshold brain activations in primary motor hand areas during many previous results of imaging studies that employed linguistic tasks (Figure 4.1) suggest that overt hand movements do not occur in correlation with linguistic processing. However, in

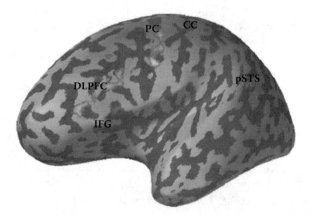

FIGURE 4.1 A statistical map on an inflated brain, representing activation of cortical regions during various comprehension tasks. The activations were obtained by contrasting periods of listening to real words with periods of listening to the same words played backward. The activated regions are part of a common network involved in language comprehension. IFG—inferior frontal gyrus, DLPF—dorsolateral prefrontal, PC—precentral sulcus (including the dorsal and ventral premotor), CC—central sulcus, pSTS—posterior superior temporal sulcus. Note the absence of activation in the primary motor area (around the central sulcus), including the areas corresponding to the hand.

the present chapter we report on the cortical motor regions whose activation correlates with activation in linguistic regions. This may indicate the existence of neuronal activation that reflects motor preparation or subliminal motor activity. Yet, our results still lack the evidence needed to show that the observed cortical activations in motor regions reflect gestural activity.

Any attempt to link the language and the motor neuronal systems must consider the theoretical framework associated with the so called "mirror neurons." These neurons were first discovered with electrophysiological recordings in monkeys that showed that neural activation during action *observation* is similar to the neuronal activation during action *execution* (Jeannerod, 2001; Nishitani, Schurmann, Amunts, & Hari, 2005; Rizzolatti et al., 1996; Rizzolatti, Fogassi, & Gallese, 2001). In humans, a large number of functional imaging studies have shown activation of premotor areas during action observation (Buccino et al., 2001; Costantini et al., 2005; Grezes, Armony, Rowe, & Passingham, 2003; Hari et al., 1998; Jeannerod, 2001; Nishitani & Hari, 2000; Rizzolatti & Luppino, 2001). This has been interpreted as evidence for the existence of a "mirror" or "action recognition" system in humans that is comparable to the one observed in monkeys.

The generalized notion of mirror activity, which has been revolutionary in the understanding of perceptual processes, may suggest that input information is fully appreciated by the cognitive system only after mapping it onto the corresponding output motor activity. Interestingly, the original site of mirror neurons in monkeys was F5. The human homologue to this region is Broca's area, which was conceived of, for many years, primarily as a language region. However, the findings of many recent imaging studies on humans (Heiser, Iacoboni, Maeda, Marcus, & Mazziotta, 2003; Nishitani & Hari, 2002) suggest that activity in Broca's area may possess mirror properties as well.

The involvement of a canonical language region in mirror activity in humans gave rise to the idea that mirror activity may play a crucial role not only in the visual perception of action but also in the understanding of speech (Arbib, 2006; Gallese & Lakoff, 2005), and that hand movements and the language system are in fact strongly linked. Following this line of thought, one can expect some kind of hand motor activity during speech comprehension because of the strong relationship between these two systems. This relationship may not necessarily be reflected in greater activity of hand-related areas during linguistic processing, but in the creation of resonances of activity among different regions instead. In this case, correlational patterns may be measured during continuous activity such as listening to a story. Those correlational patterns can be measured in the form of functional connectivity; that is, the amount of coupling between time courses of different brain regions (Ramnani, Behrens, Penny, & Matthews, 2004).

For our experiment, we used fMRI to examine the neural regions activated while subjects listened to continuous passages of speech that related a story. Specifically, we looked at the correlations between neural activity in Broca's area and the neural activity in various motor regions. Although the primary motor hand areas are not directly involved in brain activation related to language processing, we expected the dominant hand area to show a consistent coherence (correlation) with language-related activity more than the nondominant hand area. In other words, we expect "a lateralization of correlations." Let us label the correlation coefficient between Broca's area and the dominant hand area (left M1) as r_{left} and the correlation coefficient between Broca's area and the nondominant hand area (right M1) as r_{right}. A lateralization in correlations would thus be manifest as a significant difference between r_{left} and r_{right}. It is important to stress that we did not expect a lateralization of correlation in the primary motor areas of the feet as there is no reason to believe that feet movement play any role in language processing.

The relevant brain regions were identified in a separate scan ("a localizer") in which the subjects were asked to perform various motor and language tasks in a block design. Thus, to identify the right-hand area in the left motor cortex, subjects were asked to move only their right hand. This was repeated with the left hand, as well as with the right and left foot. In addition, in order to identify the brain areas related to language processing (i.e., Broca's and Wernicke's areas), the subjects were given an object name and were asked either to silently generate manual verbs related to the object ("Verb Generation," abbreviated here as VG) or to silently generate nouns related to the object in an associative manner ("Association Generation" abbreviated here as AG). Each of the above blocks lasted 9 seconds (repeated four times for each condition) and was separated by 6 to 9 seconds of rest. The design of the localizer as a whole is sketched in Figure 4.2.

The regions of interest (ROIs) on which we concentrated were Broca's area and the primary motor areas of the hands. We also identified those parts of the premotor areas involved in hand movement, the primary motor area of the foot, and Wernicke's area. Each of these regions was identified in both hemispheres (see Figure 4.3 for illustration of brain localizations).

In each subject, for each ROI, we computed the activation time course during listening to the story. These time courses reflected the continuous blood oxygenated level dependent (BOLD) activity while the subject was engaged in processing a natural and continuous linguistic stimulus. We then used the time course of Broca's area as a seed-signal, to which we correlated time courses of the other predefined brain regions. Within those predefined brain regions, we focused on

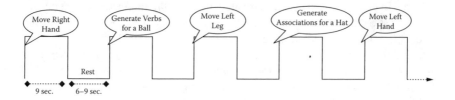

FIGURE 4.2 A sketch of the localizer scan used to identify language and motor areas in each subject. Callout drawings show the auditory instructions given before each block. The movement blocks were used to localize areas within the motor system. The word generation blocks were used to localize Broca's and Wernicke's areas.

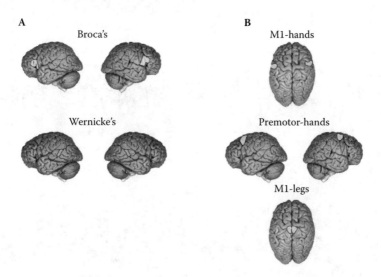

FIGURE 4.3 A general illustration of the brain loci within which we identified regions of interest in each subject individually. **A.** Areas related to language processing: Broca's area was restricted to the posterior part of the inferior frontal gyrus. Wernicke's area was identified in the posterior part of the superior temporal sulcus. **B.** Areas related to movement. The primary motor areas of both hands (M1-hands) were identified as the active areas around the central sulcus during hand movements. The premotor areas were identified as the active areas in the precentral gyrus during hand movements. The primary motor areas of both feet (M1-legs) were identified as the active areas in the medial part of the central sulcus during foot movement.

the primary motor hand areas (M1) on the left and right hemispheres. Figure 4.4 shows the superposition of the signal in Broca's area and M1 of the right and left hands throughout listening to the story.

We scanned 9 (4 women, 5 men) *right-handed* native speakers of Hebrew with a 1.5T scanner located at the Wohl Institute for Advanced Imaging at the Tel Aviv Sourasky Medical Center. The scanning parameters in the functional imaging were TR = 3000, TE = 55, FA = 90, with 27-29 axial slices, of 4-mm thickness and a gap of 0 mm. The parameters of the anatomical imaging were 3D SPGR (80 slices, thickness = 2 mm). In addition, MRI compatible headphones were used to deliver auditory stimuli, and BrainVoyager 4.9 and Matlab 6.5 were used for data analysis.

Figure 4.5 shows for each ROI the difference between the left and the right homologues in their correlation to Broca's area. As expected, Wernicke's area shows the highest correlations as well as the greatest left–right difference. Remarkably, M1 hand area also shows this significant "lateralization of correlation," whereas the lateralization of correlation in M1 foot area and the premotor area were not significant. In order to examine whether this finding was a mere result of synchronization within as opposed to across hemispheres, we performed the same analysis with respect to the right homologue of Broca's area. If inter-hemispheric

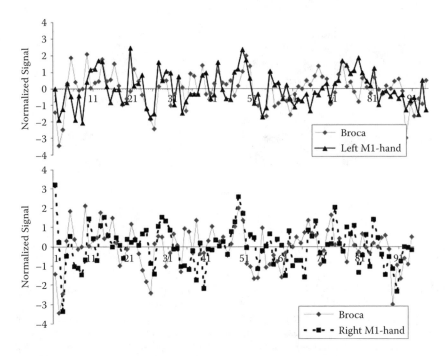

FIGURE 4.4   Superposition of signal time courses during listening to a story in one subject. The upper panel shows in grey and black lines the time course of Broca's area and M1 area of the right (on the left hemisphere), respectively. The lower panel shows in grey and dashed black lines the time course of Broca's area and M1 area of the left (on the right hemisphere), respectively. The x-axis represents time in scanning volumes (each scanning volume = 3 sec).

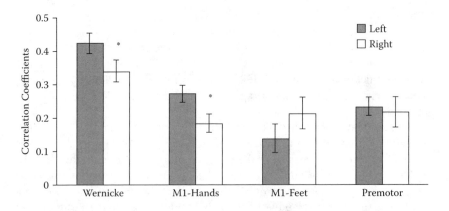

FIGURE 4.5   Correlation coefficients between Broca's area and the right and left homologues of the other ROIS. An asterisk marks a siginificant difference of $p < 0.05$.

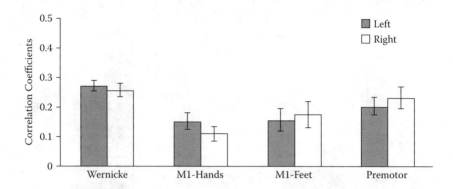

FIGURE 4.6 Correlation coefficients between the right homologue of Broca's area and the right and left homologues of the other ROIs.

synchronizations were indeed the origin of the lateralization of correlation on the left hemisphere, we should expect similar results also on the right hemisphere. That would not be the case when the lateralization of correlation is more specific to the left hemisphere and to the language system. As is shown in Figure 4.6, no areas revealed lateralization of correlation with respect to the right homologue of Broca's area. This control analysis suggests that our main finding is specific to activation in left Broca's area only. The fact that it was a comprehension task and that the subjects were actually not gesturing (gestures only occur during speech production; McNeill, 1992) suggests that our result may reflect some nonspecific, low-level coordination between language and gesture processing. This result is also in line with previous transcranial magnetic stimulation studies, in which motor event potentials measured from hand muscles were higher during tasks of linguistic processing compared to nonlinguistic tasks (Floel, Ellger, Breitenstein, & Knecht, 2003; Meister et al., 2003; Tokimura, Tokimura, Oliviero, Asakura, & Rothwell, 1996). Future research may determine whether the lateralization of correlation observed here is actually specific to language processing or is a more general property of the left hemisphere and whether it is dependent on the motor content of the linguistic stimuli.

The effect of motor contents on the activation of hand motor areas can be partially addressed here by using the data obtained from the localizer described previously (that was originally performed in order to identify several regions of interest). Specifically, we were able to contrast the generation of verbs (VG) with the generation of association (AG) in order to see whether activation in motor areas is sensitive to the content of the stimuli, but this time in production rather than in comprehension. The results of this contrast are presented in Figure 4.7.

As can be seen in Figure 4.7, only one of the three motor regions showed a significantly greater activation during VG than during AG, and this was the dorsal part of the left premotor area. Two things must be noted about this area. First, like Broca's area, this area is believed to have shown activity of mirror neurons during

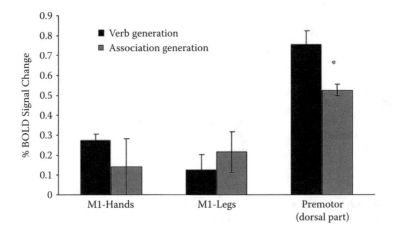

FIGURE 4.7 fMRI activation in motor areas on the left hemisphere during the two-word generation conditions of the localizer. The bars show percent signal changes relative to rest periods. M1-hands and M1-legs are the left primary motor area of the hand and leg, respectively. Premotor is the left dorsal precentral area activated during hand movement. * marks a significant difference of $p < 0.05$.

visual perception (Buccino et al., 2001; Jeannerod, 2001). Second, in this area we also see activation during language comprehension tasks (Palti et al., 2007). This suggests that premotor activation may be a crucial part of the system that connects motor with language processing. However, significant differences that are related to the content of speech are observed only in the premotor areas and not in M1. We therefore propose that this activation is not gestural in itself, but rather a *prerequisite* to gestural activation.

The two sets of results presented here reveal two orthogonal modes in which the hand motor system is participating in language processing networks. Thus, the primary and premotor areas, which act synergistically during hand movement, seem to show a dissociable pattern of activation in our linguistic tasks: Whereas the primary hand area shows lateralization of correlation during comprehension, the premotor area does not. Conversely, whereas the premotor area is sensitive to the motor contents of the stimuli during word generation, the primary motor hand area is not. This dissociation supports the claim that the premotor area takes an active part in semantic processing, as was suggested previously (e.g., Pulvermuller, Hauk, Nikulin, & Ilmoniemi, 2005). By contrast, during language processing, the primary motor area possibly maintains subliminal activational resonances with the language network, but at the same time, may be inhibited for larger, content-related activation. The manners in which these patterns of motor activation may contribute to our understanding of the cognitive conditions for gesture production remain underconstrained by the data and their explication must await further research.

REFERENCES

Arbib, M. A. (2006). A sentence is to speech as what is to action? *Cortex, 42*(4), 507–514.

Binkofski, F., Amunts, K., Stephan, K. M., Posse, S., Schormann, T., Freund, H. J., et al. (2000). Broca's region subserves imagery of motion: A combined cytoarchitectonic and fMRI study. *Human Brain Mapping, 11*(4), 273–285.

Bonda, E., Petrides, M., Frey, S., & Evans, A. (1995). Neural correlates of mental transformations of the body-in-space. *Proceedings of the National Academy of Sciences of the United States of America, 92*(24), 11180–11184.

Buccino, G., Binkofski, F., Fink, G. R., Fadiga, L., Fogassi, L., Gallese, V., et al. (2001). Action observation activates premotor and parietal areas in a somatotopic manner: An fMRI study. *European Journal of Neuroscience, 13*(2), 400–404.

Costantini, M., Galati, G., Ferretti, A., Caulo, M., Tartaro, A., Romani, G. L., et al. (2005). Neural systems underlying observation of humanly impossible movements: An fMRI study. *Cerebral Cortex, 15*(11), 1761–1767.

Decety, J., Grezes, J., Costes, N., Perani, D., Jeannerod, M., Procyk, E., et al. (1997). Brain activity during observation of actions. Influence of action content and subject's strategy. *Brain, 120* (Pt 10), 1763–1777.

Fadiga, L., Fogassi, L., Pavesi, G., & Rizzolatti, G. (1995). Motor facilitation during action observation: A magnetic stimulation study. *Journal of Neurophysiology, 73*(6), 2608–2611.

Floel, A., Ellger, T., Breitenstein, C., & Knecht, S. (2003). Language perception activates the hand motor cortex: Implications for motor theories of speech perception. *European Journal of Neuroscience, 18*(3), 704–708.

Gallagher, H. L., & Frith, C. D. (2004). Dissociable neural pathways for the perception and recognition of expressive and instrumental gestures. *Neuropsychologia, 42*(13), 1725–1736.

Gallese, V., & Lakoff, G. (2005). The brain's concepts: The role of the sensory-motor system in reason and language. *Cognitive Neuropsychology, 22*, 455–479.

Grafton, S. T., Arbib, M. A., Fadiga, L., & Rizzolatti, G. (1996). Localization of grasp representations in humans by positron emission tomography. 2. Observation compared with imagination. *Experimental Brain Research, 112*(1), 103–111.

Grezes, J., Armony, J. L., Rowe, J., & Passingham, R. E. (2003). Activations related to "mirror" and "canonical" neurons in the human brain: An fMRI study. *Neuroimage, 18*(4), 928–937.

Grosbras, M. H., & Paus, T. (2006). Brain networks involved in viewing angry hands or faces. *Cerebral Cortex, 16*(8), 1087–1096.

Hadar, U., Wenkert-Olenik, D., Krauss, R., & Soroker, N. (1998). Gesture and the processing of speech: Neuropsychological evidence. *Brain and Language, 62*(1), 107–126.

Hari, R., Forss, N., Avikainen, S., Kirveskari, E., Salenius, S., & Rizzolatti, G. (1998). Activation of human primary motor cortex during action observation: A neuromagnetic study. *Proceedings of the National Academy of Sciences of the United States of America, 95*(25), 15061–15065.

Heiser, M., Iacoboni, M., Maeda, F., Marcus, J., & Mazziotta, J. C. (2003). The essential role of Broca's area in imitation. *European Journal of Neuroscience, 17*(5), 1123–1128.

Jeannerod, M. (2001). Neural simulation of action: A unifying mechanism for motor cognition. *Neuroimage, 14*(1 Pt 2), S103–109.

Krauss, R. M., & Hadar, U. (1999). The role of speech-related arm/hand gestures in word retrieval. In L. Messing & R. Campbell (Eds.), *Gesture, speech, and sign* (pp. 93–116). Oxford: Oxford University Press.

Lotze, M., Heymans, U., Birbaumer, N., Veit, R., Erb, M., Flor, H., et al. (2006). Differential cerebral activation during observation of expressive gestures and motor acts. *Neuropsychologia, 44*(10), 1787–1795.

Lotze, M., Montoya, P., Erb, M., Hulsmann, E., Flor, H., Klose, U., et al. (1999). Activation of cortical and cerebellar motor areas during executed and imagined hand movements: An fMRI study. *Journal of Cognitive Neuroscience, 11*(5), 491–501.

MacSweeney, M., Campbell, R., Woll, B., Brammer, M. J., Giampietro, V., David, A. S., et al. (2006). Lexical and sentential processing in British Sign Language. *Human Brain Mapping, 27*(1), 63–76.

MacSweeney, M., Campbell, R., Woll, B., Giampietro, V., David, A. S., McGuire, P. K., et al. (2004). Dissociating linguistic and nonlinguistic gestural communication in the brain. *Neuroimage, 22*(4), 1605–1618.

MacSweeney, M., Woll, B., Campbell, R., McGuire, P. K., David, A. S., Williams, S. C., et al. (2002). Neural systems underlying British Sign Language and audio-visual English processing in native users. *Brain, 125*(Pt 7), 1583–1593.

McNeill, D. (1992). *Hand and mind: What gestures reveal about thought.* Chicago: University of Chicago Press.

Meister, I. G., Boroojerdi, B., Foltys, H., Sparing, R., Huber, W., & Topper, R. (2003). Motor cortex hand area and speech: Implications for the development of language. *Neuropsychologia, 41*(4), 401–406.

Neville, H. J., Bavelier, D., Corina, D., Rauschecker, J., Karni, A., Lalwani, A., et al. (1998). Cerebral organization for language in deaf and hearing subjects: Biological constraints and effects of experience. *Proceedings of the National Academy of Sciences of the United States of America, 95*(3), 922–929.

Newman, A. J., Bavelier, D., Corina, D., Jezzard, P., & Neville, H. J. (2002). A critical period for right hemisphere recruitment in American Sign Language processing. *Nature Neuroscience, 5*(1), 76–80.

Nishitani, N., & Hari, R. (2000). Temporal dynamics of cortical representation for action. *Proceedings of the National Academy of Sciences of the United States of America, 97*(2), 913–918.

Nishitani, N., & Hari, R. (2002). Viewing lip forms: Cortical dynamics. *Neuron, 36*(6), 1211–1220.

Nishitani, N., Schurmann, M., Amunts, K., & Hari, R. (2005). Broca's region: From action to language. *Physiology (Bethesda), 20*, 60–69.

Palti, D., Ben Shachar, M., Hendler, T., & Hadar, U. (2007). Neural correlates of sementic and morphological processing of Hebrew nouns and verbs. *Human Brain Mapping, 28*(4), 303–314.

Parsons, L. M., Fox, P. T., Downs, J. H., Glass, T., Hirsch, T. B., Martin, C. C., et al. (1995). Use of implicit motor imagery for visual shape discrimination as revealed by PET. *Nature, 375*(6526), 54–58.

Pulvermuller, F., Hauk, O., Nikulin, V. V., & Ilmoniemi, R. J. (2005). Functional links between motor and language systems. *European Journal of Neuroscience, 21*(3), 793–797.

Ramnani, N., Behrens, T. E., Penny, W., & Matthews, P. M. (2004). New approaches for exploring anatomical and functional connectivity in the human brain. *Biological Psychiatry, 56*(9), 613–619.

Rizzolatti, G., Fadiga, L., Matelli, M., Bettinardi, V., Paulesu, E., Perani, D., et al. (1996). Localization of grasp representations in humans by PET: 1. Observation versus execution. *Experimental Brain Research, 111*(2), 246–252.

Rizzolatti, G., Fogassi, L., & Gallese, V. (2001). Neurophysiological mechanisms underlying the understanding and imitation of action. *Nature Reviews Neuroscience, 2*(9), 661–670.

Rizzolatti, G., & Luppino, G. (2001). The cortical motor system. *Neuron, 31,* 889–901.

Tokimura, H., Tokimura, Y., Oliviero, A., Asakura, T., & Rothwell, J. C. (1996). Speech-induced changes in corticospinal excitability. *Annals of Neurology, 40,* 628–634.

Willems, R. M., Özyürek, A., & Hagoort, P. (2006). When language meets action: The neural integration of gesture and speech. *Cerebral Cortex, 17,* 2322–2333.

5 Indirect Cognitive Control, Working-Memory–Related Movements, and Sources of Automatisms

Ezequiel Morsella, Lindsay R. L. Larson,
and John A. Bargh

Why do people move their eyes, arms, and head as they try to keep information in working memory? Why do they twirl their hair and tap their feet while trying to sit still in a classroom or auditorium? Such actions can occur even when they interfere with the task at hand, consume energy, violate the *law of least work* (cf., Botvinick, 2007; Hull, 1943), or annoy others (Lorenz, 1963). In the controlled environment of a psychophysics experiment, for example, it is not uncommon for subjects to whimsically scratch their nose or, with one swift motion of the upper body, press their left cheek against their shoulder. Experimenters treat the effects of these "task-irrelevant" actions as "behavioral weeds" whose noise must be trimmed from the data set. But subjects are not to blame, for these actions arise, not from their conscious selves, but from some psychological ether. The onset and form of these actions—rubbing the nose versus twirling the hair—cannot be accounted for by observers or their authors (Carpenter, 1874). In everyday life, such out-of-the-blue actions seldom engender curiosity and are generally deemed useless and explained away (often by circular logic) as resulting from edginess, nervous energy, or from elusive entities such as a "jimmy leg." Scientifically, they have received little attention.

As a student of Robert Krauss, one of us (EM) quickly learned to pay attention to mental and behavioral phenomena that, at first glance, appear to serve no function. One can isolate the potential function of a phenomenon by examining why it occurs under some circumstances but not others. For example, why does conscious awareness accompany the organismic event of holding one's breath but not that of the pupillary reflex or peristalsis (cf., Morsella, 2005)? Why do people tend to gesture more when describing things from memory than when reporting about things that are visually present (cf., Morsella & Krauss, 2004)? In the spirit of the pioneering research by Robert Krauss on the counterintuitive *intra*personal functions of co-speech gestures, we regard *cognitive movements* (certain kinds of co-speech gestures and working-memory–related movements) and *automatisms** as motor processes that serve a functional role in the nervous system, a view that is in line with the proposals of the great theorists Margaret Floy Washburn, Hugo Münsterberg, and Donald Hebb.

In the following sections, we briefly review the growing literature about the various sources of spontaneous action and cognitive movements, the nature of indirect cognitive control, and examine in a series of experiments how the rate of occurrence of automatisms—the least understood class of spontaneous action—can be explained by psychological factors such as fatigue, low-arousal, cognitive load, and displacement activity. We view automatisms as forms of nonreflexive action production that are experimentally tractable and can inform theories about action production in general (cf., Morsella, Bargh, & Gollwitzer, 2009).

SOURCES OF SPONTANEOUS ACTION AND COGNITIVE MOVEMENTS

One class of spontaneous behavior stems from incidental, environmental stimuli, a dramatic case of "stimulus control" (Levine, Morsella, & Bargh, 2007; Wood, Quinn, & Kashy, 2002). Cognitive movements, another class of spontaneous behavior, stem from ongoing cognitive operations, usually involving speech production or working memory (for a more comprehensive review see Morsella & Krauss, 2004, 2005; Spivey, Richardson, & Dale, in press). The least understood class of spontaneous behavior falls under the rubric of automatism. Automatisms seem to reflect homeostatic cognitive mechanisms associated with maintaining optimal levels of arousal. They are examined in the section titled "Out of the Blue: Sources of Automatisms."

WORKING-MEMORY–RELATED MOVEMENTS

People often perform a variety of movements while engaged in working memory tasks. An attempt to imagine the shape of an inverted §, for example, may be accompanied by an averted gaze, a furrowed brow, and gesticulation. Similar sorts of movements accompany mental arithmetic (Graham, 1999), spatial reasoning, and musical imagery (Goldin-Meadow & Wagner, 2005; Laeng & Teodorescu, 2002; Lawrence, Myerson, Oonk, & Abrams, 2001). The view that these movements play a functional role in cognition has a long history in psychology. Nearly 85 years ago, Washburn (1928) contended "...the motor innervations underlying

---

* Classic, and more dramatic, forms of automatisms involve the movements associated with the Chevreul pendulum, dowsing, automatic writing, and Ouija boards (see review in Wegner, 2002, Chapter 4). In neurology, the term also refers to the unintended behaviors exhibited in psychomotor epilepsy.

the consciousness of effort are not mere accompaniments of directed thought, but an essential cause of directed thought" (p. 105). Forty years later, Hebb (1968) espoused a similar notion—that the movements coincidental with mental events are not adventitious, but necessary for the mental events to occur.

Although working-memory–related movements, or the processes involved in their planning and execution, may not be essential to mental functioning, there is considerable evidence that they can facilitate cognitive processing, as in *indirect cognitive control* (see section titled "Indirect Cognitive Control"). Some motor events reduce unwanted sensory inputs that may interfere with cognitive goals, and by so doing modulate the kinds of information that enter the perceptual system. Other movements increase desired sensory input. We will refer to movements that facilitate cognitive functioning by attenuating sensory inputs that would impede performance as *subtractive movements* and movements that facilitate functioning by selectively introducing, maintaining, or increasing the activation of information as *additive movements*.

Subtractive Movements

A familiar subtractive movement is the tendency to shift gaze from complex to less complex visual arrays while performing tasks involving language. Gaze aversion in this situation serves to reduce potential informational input that would compete for the cognitive resources required by the complex task of speech production (Beattie, 1980; Butterworth, 1978; Glenberg, Schroeder, & Robertson, 1998). In a set of experiments, Glenberg et al. (1998) found the tendency to avert gaze to be positively related to the difficulty of the cognitive task at hand, and that averting gaze improves performance in memory tasks. Chiu, Hong, and Krauss (unpublished) found that subjects required to visually fixate on their conversational partner's face while describing a route to a destination spoke less fluently than those required to fixate on an inanimate object or allowed to look where they chose. Whether a particular signal will impede cognitive processing depends on the task. In a classic series of experiments, Brooks (1968, 1970) demonstrated that "recall of verbal information is most readily disrupted by concurrent vocal activity; recall of spatial information is most readily disrupted by concurrent spatially monitored activity," [1968], p. 349) such as monitoring movements (see also Kim, Kim, & Chun, 2005).

Additive Movements

In contrast, additive movements facilitate cognition by introducing, or increasing the accessibility of, inputs that enhance a cognitive operation. An example is the (often subvocal) articulation involved in the phonological loop, whereby representations (e.g., of a telephone number) are kept in working memory through the active process of rehearsal. In the loop, proprioceptive (or re-afferent) inputs from vocalization or subvocalization are believed to reactivate quickly, decaying phonemic representations in a working-memory buffer (Baddeley, 1986; see also Burgess & Hitch, 1999). See Buchsbaum and D'Esposito (2008) for a recent treatment of the neural correlates of this process. Analogously, it is believed that, in visuo-spatial working memory, movements can reflect the workings of the "inner scribe" (Logie, 1995) that continually refreshes visuo-spatial representations.

CO-SPEECH GESTURES AND SPEECH PRODUCTION

In the complex cognitive task we call conversation, there are postural shifts, changes in gaze direction, sweeping movements of the arms, and an elaborate medley of hand and finger movements. The way conversational gestures are coordinated with speech has led researchers to speculate about the functions they serve. One hypothesis is that gestural movements facilitate the retrieval of words from the mental lexicon (Butterworth & Hadar, 1989; De Laguna, 1927; Dobrogaev, 1929; Krauss & Hadar, 1999; Mead, 1934; Rose & Douglas, 2001; Rose, Douglas, & Matyas, 2002; Werner & Kaplan, 1963), and there is some empirical support for this view (see review in Krauss, 1998). It has also been proposed that these gestures decrease cognitive load during language processing (Goldin-Meadow, Nusbaum, Kelly, & Wagner, 2001), and that they play a role in the conceptual processes that precede language production (Alibali, Kita, & Young, 2000; see Chapter 2). Alternatively, others have contended that *lexical gestures** are primarily communicative in nature and play little or no role in speech production (e.g., Beattie & Coughlan, 1999; Kendon, 1994).

In the gestural feedback model (GFM; see also Chapters 2 and 12) of Morsella and Krauss (2004), lexical gestures are additive movements that facilitate retrieval by sustaining the activation of a target word's semantic features long enough in working memory for the process of word production to take place. According to this model, such gestures continually reactivate semantics through feedback from effectors or motor commands, in much the same way that vocal (or subvocal) rehearsal keeps echoic representations active in the phonological loop (Baddeley, 1986; Burgess & Hitch, 1999; see also Figure 5.1). Thus, lexical gestures function as self-generated cues (Frick-Horbury & Guttentag, 1998). Consistent with this model, gesturing facilitates object naming in aphasics with phonological access, storage, or encoding difficulties (Rose & Douglas, 2001). Conversely, immobilizing subjects' hands increases the number of retrieval failures in a tip-of-the-tongue (TOT) experiment (Frick-Horbury & Guttentag, 1998) and leads to speech dysfluencies (Morsella & Krauss, 2004; Rauscher, Krauss, & Chen, 1996). Similar effects have been found with children (cf., Pine, Bird, & Kirk, 2007). In addition, Morsella and Krauss (2004) demonstrated that speakers gesture more when describing visual objects from memory than they do when the objects are visually accessible, and that speakers gesture more when describing objects that tax spatial working memory, such as drawings that are difficult to remember and encode verbally. It was concluded that movements are prevalent when spatial

---

* The hand-arm actions that often accompany everyday conversation, variously called "representational gestures" (McNeill, Cassell, & McCullough, 1994), "illustrators" (Ekman & Friesen, 1972), and "gesticulations" (Kendon, 1980, 1983), constitute another important class of additive movements. We refer to them as "lexical gestures" (Krauss, Chen, & Gottesman, 2000).

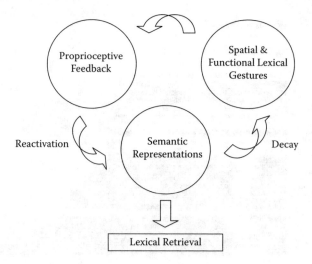

FIGURE 5.1   The gestural feedback model.

working memory is taxed, and it is reasonable to assume that these movements facilitate the recall of spatial information.

According to the GFM, gestures can only activate the semantics of words that are "grounded" (Harnad, 1990) in *sensorimotor* states (see Barsalou, 1999, 2003, 2008; Borghi, Glenberg, & Kaschak, 2004; Glenberg, 1997; Hostetter & Alibali, 2008; Kosslyn, Thompson, & Ganis, 2006). Accordingly, it has been well documented that speakers are more likely to gesture while articulating phrases with spatial, imageable, or concrete semantic content than during phrases with more abstract content (Beattie & Shovelton, 2002; Rauscher et al., 1996; Sousa-Poze, Rohrberg, & Mercure, 1979). Morsella and Krauss (2005) demonstrated in an electromyographic (EMG) study that, during lexical retrieval, muscular activation is positively correlated with words rated high on concreteness—the kinds of words that seem to be grounded in sensorimotor states. Use of the EMG as an index of muscle activation is superior to the observational methods used in previous studies of gesture because it is less subjective and permits quantification of activation that does not result in overt movement, which occurred quite often in the experiment by Morsella and Krauss (2005).

To gain some insight into the semantic properties of words whose retrieval is accompanied by muscular activity, Morsella and Krauss (2005) correlated EMG amplitude with several word-concept attributes. The four attributes most highly correlated ($rs > .30$, $ps < .05$) with EMG amplitude were *concrete*, *drawable*, *spatial*, and *manipulable*. In addition, Morsella and Krauss (1999) found similar psychophysiological results from the variable of *word concreteness* in a task in which subjects had to generate sentences with abstract or concrete words (Figure 5.2). For this task, the attributes that were highly correlated with EMG amplitude were *manipulable*, *concrete*, *spatial*, and *drawable*. This finding is particularly

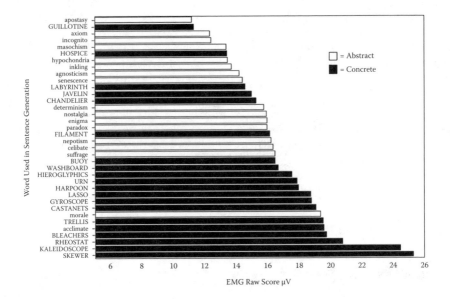

FIGURE 5.2 Mean raw EMG scores (peak amplitude in μV) for each sentence during a task in which subjects had to construct a sentence with concrete words (filled bars) and abstract words (unfilled bars).

interesting given that the experimenters could not control the words that subjects selected to construct a sentence incorporating the target word.

Together, these findings are consistent with the GFM (see also Krauss & Hadar, 1999; Morsella, 2002), in which lexical gestures facilitate word retrieval by sustaining the activation of semantic representations (e.g., of words that are grounded in sensorimotor states). It should be noted that this is not to argue that the sole function of co-speech gestures is to facilitate lexical retrieval. Like many behaviors, gestures can have more than one function, and we have no doubt that they do sometimes function communicatively.

INDIRECT COGNITIVE CONTROL

Purposefully activated mental representations tend to be transient and the process of activating them is effortful (Farah, 2000). As a result, it is difficult to hold them in mind for lengthy intervals, as can occur in mental rotation and lexical search (e.g., in a TOT state). When *phonological encoding* (i.e., the process that converts semantic information such as the concept CAT into the phonological representation such as /k/, /œ/, and /t/) cannot be controlled directly by top-down processing (assuming that it can ever be controlled directly), top-down processes can still influence phonological encoding, but indirectly. The GFM proposes that lexical gestures, as a compensatory mechanism, can serve as self-generated cues that help keep semantic representations activated long enough for lexical retrieval to occur, much like vocal (or subvocal) rehearsal keeps echoic representations activated long enough for one to be able to dial a telephone number moments after hearing it for the first time. Activating semantic representations is the key by which top-down processes can indirectly unlock the process of retrieval. This form of control is a roundabout way of influencing a cognitive process that, at the moment, cannot be modulated by *direct cognitive control.*

One's ability to immediately control thinking (or imagining) and movements of a finger, arm, or other skeletal muscle effector perhaps best exemplifies direct cognitive control. Interestingly, all these kinds of processes require the activation of perceptual-like representations, one for constituting mental imagery (Farah, 2000) and the other for the instantiating *ideomotor* mechanisms (Hommel, Müsseler, Aschersleben, & Prinz, 2001). When direct control cannot be implemented, indirect forms of control can be used. The architecture of the GFM yields insights into the ways by which indirect cognitive control may influence the cognitive apparatus.

For example, it is clear that one may not be able to directly influence one's affective state at will. One cannot make oneself frightened, happy, angry, sad, or excite a desired appetitive state (being hungry) if the adequate conditions are absent. It is for this reason that people seek and even pay for certain experiences (e.g., going to movies or comedy clubs) to put themselves in a desired state that cannot be instantiated by an act of will. Although direct control cannot activate incentive or affective states (Öhman & Mineka, 2001), it is possible to indirectly stimulate these states by activating the kinds of perceptuo-semantic representations that, as *releasers* (to use an ethological term), can trigger the networks responsible for these states. For instance, *method* actors spend a great deal of time and effort imagining certain events in order to put themselves into a certain state (e.g., to make themselves sad in order to portray a sad personage). This is done to render the acting performance more natural and convincing. To make oneself hungry, one can imagine a tasty dish; to make oneself angry, one can recall an event that was frustrating or unjust. Similarly, players preparing for a soccer match often rile themselves up to get into the aggressive mindset that may improve performance.

Indirect cognitive control illustrates how a system with limited cognitive control—one that can directly activate only, say, perceptual-like representations—can still influence the functioning of otherwise encapsulated processes. Understanding indirect cognitive control may also illuminate the way in which controlled processes can influence automatic processes (Lieberman, 2007; Strack & Deutsch, 2004) and how the conscious "perception pathway" can influence the unconscious "action pathway" (Goodale & Milner, 2004), a cross-talk mechanism that has yet to be identified.

How the Perception (Controlled) Pathway Influences the Action (Automatic) Pathway

Goodale and Milner (2004) report neurological cases in which there is dissociation between action and conscious perception. For example, patient D.F., who suffered

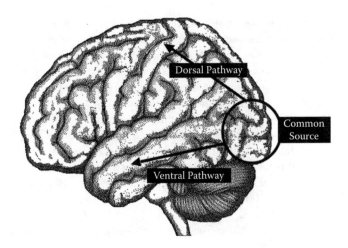

FIGURE 5.3 The perception and action pathways proposed by Milner and Goodale (1995).

from visual form agnosia, was incapable of reporting the orientation of a tilted slot (e.g., tilted 60 degrees), but could nonetheless negotiate the slot accurately when inserting an object into it. Along with other findings regarding the dichotomy of controlled versus automatic processes (Lieberman, 2007; Strack & Deutsch, 2004) and perception-action dissociations (see review in Westwood, 2009), this finding led to the view that there are distinct pathways for visual perception (situated ventrally in the brain) and action (situated dorsally) (Figure 5.3). Similarly, there is substantial evidence that emotional systems can be activated, and influence action, unconsciously. For instance, fear conditioning is believed to be mediated in part by modularized nuclei in the amygdala of the midbrain that receive polysensory information from afferent pathways different from those feeding the ventral perception pathway, which is associated with conscious processing and self-report (Lavond, Kim, & Thompson, 1993; LeDoux, 1996; Olsson & Phelps, 2004). Processing in both kinds of pathways occurs roughly in parallel (LeDoux, 1996). In addition, subliminal stimuli (Öhman & Mineka, 2001; Pessiglione et al., 2008) and the unconscious "suppressed image" during binocular rivalry (Williams, Morris, McGlone, Abbott, & Mattingley, 2004) can influence behavior and activate nuclei in the brain that are believed to be involved in emotional processing.

These discoveries inevitably lead one to an important question: If unconscious action pathways can influence the nature of a response to a stimulus, and, in some cases, can fully mediate the response without the need of conscious awareness, then what does the conscious pathway contribute to action? This recurrent question is beyond the scope of the present discussion (see review in Morsella, 2005). A second, perhaps more tractable puzzle pertains to the manner in which conscious processing can influence the unconscious action pathways (e.g., those involved in emotional processing, unconscious action production, or drive-related behaviors). This may occur when one is trying to intentionally stimulate an incentive system,

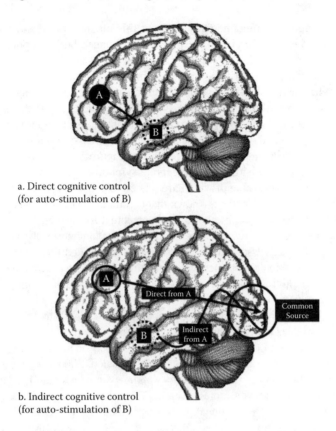

a. Direct cognitive control
(for auto-stimulation of B)

b. Indirect cognitive control
(for auto-stimulation of B)

FIGURE 5.4   (a) In the direct stimulation hypothesis, control regions of the frontal cortex can, through top-down processes, directly stimulate incentive or emotional neural systems (e.g., nuclei in the amygdala or hypothalamus). (b) In a model proposing that such activation is elicited through indirect cognitive control, control regions of the frontal cortex activate such systems only indirectly, through the "mandatory pathway" involving activation of certain perceptuo-semantic representations.

as when one is trying to make oneself hungry, thirsty, or sexually aroused. It seems that top-down processes are incapable of stimulating these drive-related systems directly (Figure 5.4a). As mentioned previously, intentional auto-stimulation seems to be achieved through indirect cognitive control. We now focus on the neuroanatomical pathway through which such indirect control may be achieved.

The Mandatory Pathway

Let us take the example of trying to make oneself hungry in the absence of food stimuli. (One could readily think of additional examples involving other basic drives, drives whose activation requires certain stimuli or releasers.) As is well known in method acting, in which actors actually make themselves angry, sad, or fearful in order to act angry, sad, or fearful, one way to make oneself hungry is to think about and imagine tasty food. In this manner, top-down processing actually activates, not the circuits responsible for hunger, but perceptual symbols (Barsalou, 1999, 2003, 2008; Farah, 2000; Kosslyn et al., 2006). This imagery then stimulates the appetitive system in a manner similar to the way that the corresponding external stimuli would. Neuroanatomically, activating the hunger system indirectly through perceptual symbols (Barsalou, 1999) makes a great deal of sense because low-level perceptual representations (whether visual, olfactory, auditory, or haptic) exist at an early stage of processing that happens to be shared by both action and perception pathways (Figure 5.4b; Goodale & Milner, 2004). In this and other situations, perceptual symbols are the common currency of many systems, only some of which are related to consciousness.

Consistent with this view, it is known that certain kinds of emotional states and emotional learning can occur only through perceptual-like representations and not through propositional representations such as those of language (Olsson & Phelps, 2004). For example, Olsson and Phelps (2004) demonstrated that, through vicarious classical conditioning, subjects could acquire a learned fear response toward a subliminal stimulus by observing someone else being shocked after being presented with the stimulus. However, telling subjects about the contingency between stimuli did not lead to this kind of vicarious conditioning. This suggests that the fear conditioning system does not understand language (at least not very well) but that it can process the meaning of basic perceptual events. Based on such observations and findings from research on *perceptual symbols* (Barsalou, 2003, 2008), we propose that the perceptual system is the *mandatory pathway* in which high-level top-down representations and linguistic representations are "cashed in" to function as releasers, releasers that can activate emotional processing and basic drives (Morselia, Lanska, Berger, & Gazzaley, in press). This "common currency" pathway furnishes a key by which top-down control could indirectly unlock and stimulate the action pathways of incentive and emotional systems (Figure 5.5) and perhaps of other systems as well.

How people learn to use this strategy of indirect control, and how they know that certain representations will activate certain systems, is an interesting question for metacognition research. It may be that high-level frontal cortex representations such as "make oneself hungry" (cf., Grafman & Krueger, in press) are already intimately associated with the lower-level perceptuo-semantic representations of food stimuli, because the latter constitute the semantics of the former (Barsalou, 2008; Pulvermuller, 2005). In this way, activation may simply flow backwards from highly abstract representations in frontal control regions of the brain to the perceptuo-semantic stages of processing that, by virtue of being the common source of many pathways, can influence multiple systems simultaneously.

It is important to note that this does not imply that top-down processes are incapable of turning off or otherwise disrupting emotional or incentive processes. It has been documented that the frontal cortex can directly inhibit activities of the amygdala (cf., Cunningham et al., 2004). In principle, there are important differences between the mechanisms required for activation and deactivation. Generally, for any system, deactivation can be instantiated in more ways than activation. There are often many ways to turn off or disrupt a process, but often

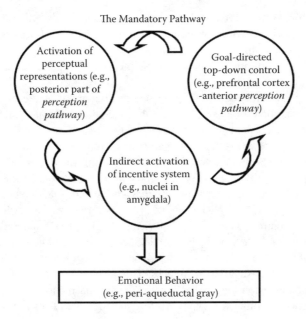

FIGURE 5.5   Process model: Indirect cognitive control.

few ways to initiate it. For the sake of illustration, there are many ways to termi-
nate the activities of a computer: One could unplug it, turn it off, or destroy the
internal hardware, but there is only one way to turn it on. Hence, we do not make
claims about deactivation, inhibition, or suppression; our claim is only about the
indirect ways in which we auto-stimulate systems that are otherwise encapsulated. Systems seem to be activated in a roundabout way using a mandatory pathway involving perceptuo–semantic representations. The architecture of this form
of indirect cognitive control is similar to that of the GFM.

OUT OF THE BLUE: SOURCES OF AUTOMATISMS

The least studied of the spontaneous actions mentioned thus far are automatisms.
We believe that this class of spontaneous action is scientifically informative
because it reveals aspects of what can be regarded as a simplistic and experimentally tractable form of nonreflexive action production. Although unintended
and often undesired, it is important to consider that automatisms are nevertheless
determined, but by causes that are not as transparent as those of reflexes or of
rational, intended goal-driven actions (e.g., opening the refrigerator when hungry).
Thus, unraveling the nature of these automatisms may lead to a better understanding of the mechanisms underlying larger-scale, nonreflexive, goal-driven actions
such as deciding, out-of-the-blue, to go for a walk, organize one's bookshelf, call
a friend, or have a snack. (For how the environment triggers habitual forms of
these behaviors, see Wood, Quinn, & Kashy, 2002.) The same cannot be said for

most laboratory tasks, which involve what may be construed as directly elicitable or reactive behaviors. Moreover, unlike reactive and reflexive behaviors, automatisms easily can be suppressed, but, interestingly, only after the intention of suppressing them is summoned to mind. Some theoretical approaches shed light on the potential causes of these phenomena.

For example, Kahneman (1973) proposed that automatisms are more likely to occur under conditions of low arousal, as when the mind is not in an attentive state, but bored and unoccupied. This point of view is based on the homeostatic notion that the cognitive apparatus strives to maintain an optimal level of arousal (see also the classic work by Berlyne, 1960). When below this threshold, arousal is increased by engaging in activities such as fiddling with objects or body parts. (For an account regarding how these task-irrelevant activities can actually facilitate certain cognitive tasks, see Olivers & Nieuwenhuis, 2005.) Alternatively, according to some models of self-control (Baumeister, Heatherton, & Tice, 1994) and action production (Levine, Morsella, & Bargh, 2007), these actions are more likely to occur under conditions of fatigue or high cognitive load, because it is more difficult to maintain their inhibition under such circumstances. This also appears to be the case in an interesting phenomenon long noted by ethologists, and incorporated into animal models of action planning, known as *displacement activity* (Tinbergen, 1952).

Displacement activity occurs when an animal, torn between two competing response tendencies (as in an approach-avoidance conflict; Miller, 1959), expresses a third, bizarre and unrelated response tendency, such as hopping or grooming. From this point of view, many nervous behaviors (e.g., fiddling with a pen while waiting at the dentist's office) are forms of displacement activity (e.g., stemming from the conflict between, say, health concerns and pain avoidance). In the laboratory, a situation well known to elicit response conflict occurs in the classic Stroop task (Stroop, 1935), in which subjects must name the colors in which words are written. On some trials, the name of the stimulus is different from the name that the subject must produce (e.g., the word red written in blue). This response conflict leads to increased error rates, response times (RT), and urges to err (Morsella, Gray, Levine, & Bargh, 2006), but it has yet to be demonstrated whether it can lead to displacement activity. Laboratory demonstrations revealing that such response conflicts in humans can actually facilitate the expression of task-unrelated actions (cf., Kim et al., 2005) would lend some initial support for the notion that displacement can lead to spontaneous action.

MEASURING AUTOMATISMS

Given the multidetermined nature of human action, it is likely the case that, compared to more persistent and prevalent causes (e.g., factors related to endocrinological, psychotropic, ideographic, or mood-related processes), immediate psychological factors such as cognitive load, low arousal, fatigue, and displacement activity account for only a fraction of automatisms. Nevertheless, the latter are of theoretical interest because, again, they may reveal how nonreflexive actions are brought to expression by the natural psychological characteristics of the immediate environment. Thus, we believe that the operations of these factors in the laboratory reflect how they influence spontaneous action in natural settings.

Considering the obscure and ephemeral nature of these phenomena, perhaps at this stage of understanding it is best to first obtain a rough estimate of the rate of occurrence of these actions in a laboratory setting and gain a general understanding of the conditions under which they are most likely to occur. Contrary to what one might expect, obtaining a reliable estimate of the average rate of occurrence of these automatisms is no small feat.

First, it is infeasible (if not impossible) to code all the behaviors that are exhibited by a given subject. For example, will one code fleeting eye movements, subthreshold muscular activations, or subtle postural shifts? Naturally, one can observe only a sample of all behaviors, and thus one must carefully select a subset of behaviors that is representative of all automatisms. Given their prominent role in classic automatisms (e.g., the Chevreul pendulum, dowsing, automatic writing, and Ouija boards), perhaps arm/hand/finger movements are the most representative.

Second, in terms of task instructions, it is of little value to ask subjects to "do nothing" in order to then observe and measure spontaneous behaviors. As was long ago proclaimed by Behaviorism, there is no such thing as a state of inaction or of "doing nothing" (Skinner, 1953): One is always acting, and being motionless or resting are simply forms of action. Thus, while awake, action production is always at play, in one form or another. Instructions to "do nothing" are therefore confusing to subjects, who eventually will find something to do (e.g., subvocally sing a song or count sheep). As well, it is also of little value to instruct subjects to be motionless, for such an aversive state is far different in nature from the mild activities of everyday life in which spontaneous action often occurs. Remaining motionless is far from simple, requiring tremendous endurance and motivation.

With these methodological and logistic constraints in mind, in a series of initial experiments we examined the rate and fluidity of automatisms that subjects exhibited while performing variants of the Stroop task (Stroop, 1935), a standard laboratory task. In this task, subjects name the colors in which stimulus words are written. When the word and color are incongruous (e.g., the word red presented in blue), response conflict leads to increased error rates and RTs (in Experiment 1, subjects simply viewed Stroop stimuli). When they are congruous (e.g., the word red presented in red), there is little or no interference (see review in MacLeod & MacDonald, 2000). These variants provided subjects with structured, clearly defined activities that, though far from challenging (as revealed in piloting, $n = 7$), presumably constrain behavior more so than vague instructions to the effect of "do nothing in particular" or "wait for the experimenter." In addition, the conflict condition of the Stroop paradigm allowed us to test specific predictions concerning displacement activity.

EXPERIMENT 1

Automatisms During the Passive Viewing of Stroop Stimuli

Beginning with the weakest manipulation, in Experiment 1, subjects previously trained to perform the Stroop task were instructed to simply look at (and not respond in any way to) Stroop stimuli while resting all of their fingers on a computer mouse. We refer to this as a simple *passive viewing* Stroop task. By not having subjects produce a verbal response during the test phase, all movements associated with the traditional Stroop response were diminished, if not eliminated. The number of mouse movements and clicks that subjects exhibited while performing this simple, low-arousal viewing task served as a measure of automatism production. We believe that, because of their varied motor repertoires, arm/hand/finger movements are the most informative and representative index of automatism generation.

Consistent with several theoretical orientations (Baumeister et al., 1994; Kahneman, 1973), our primary hypothesis was that automatism rate would increase as a function of cognitive load, fatigue, and boredom (i.e., low arousal). Thus, we predicted that the rate of automatisms would increase linearly as a function experimental block number, with the fewest automatisms occurring during the first blocks and the most during the last block. This prediction was based on the assumption that fatigue, load, and boredom presumably increase as a function of trial number. Importantly, not obtaining this effect, or obtaining an opposite pattern of results, would simultaneously cast doubt upon load/fatigue and arousal accounts and upon our general approach to the study of automatisms. In this regard, Experiment 1 was a critical initial inquiry into isolating the origins of automatisms.

Our second prediction was that, because of displacement, more automatisms would occur during the incongruent (conflict) rather than the congruent conditions. From this point of view, the computer mouse can be seen as a suitable (though quite unprovoking) target object that can afford displaced action to at least a minimal extent. Because subjects were instructed not to respond verbally or in any other way to Stroop stimuli, such a finding would provide further evidence that response conflicts can occur incidentally.

METHOD

Participants. Seventeen Yale University students participated for class credit or $8.

Procedure. Subjects were run individually in a two-part experiment, consisting of a training phase and a test phase. Training consisted of 72 practice Stroop trials having 24 congruent (e.g., the word red written in red), 24 incongruent (e.g., the word red written in blue), and 24 neutral (e.g., XXXX written in green) stimuli in random order. Eight common colors, correctly identified by all subjects, were used (red, orange, yellow, green, blue, purple, pink, and black). In the incongruent condition, targets (colors) and distracters (words) were re-paired systematically (e.g., if "red" was written in blue then "blue" was written in red).

Each trial of the training phase proceeded as follows. A ready prompt (a question mark, 48-point Helvetica font) appeared on the center of the screen until subjects indicated that they were ready to commence the trial by clicking the mouse button. Thereafter, a fixation point (+) was shown at the center of the screen for 1500 ms. It was followed by a blank screen spanning 700 ms, after which time a randomly selected Stroop stimulus appeared, remaining onscreen until the vocal response was made. Subjects were instructed to respond as quickly and as accurately as possible. After the response and an additional 700 ms, the next trial began. In this and the following experiments, stimulus presentation was controlled by PsyScope experimental software (Cohen, MacWhinney, Flatt, & Provost, 1993), and stimuli were presented on a white, 43-cm Apple eMac computer monitor (60 Hz), with a viewing distance of approximately 48 cm. All letter stimuli were presented in 48-point Helvetica font.

For the test phase of the experiments, subjects were instructed to no longer respond vocally but to simply look at the Stroop word stimuli. They were also told to rest their wrists on a wrist pad, place all of their fingers on a computer mouse (comfortably positioned 8 cm in front of the computer), and to avoid having any of their fingers touch the table. To diminish experimental demand, subjects were told the cover story that the study concerned visual attention. Lasting 28 min, the test phase consisted of 1680 trials. To facilitate measuring automatisms in terms of Stroop condition (congruent, incongruent, or neutral), the stimuli from the practice phase were presented in 15 blocks, with each block having 112 trials of the same Stroop condition. To diminish order effects, the 15 blocks were presented in random order. For example, for subject 1, block 1 may consist of 112 congruent trials followed by 112 incongruent trials; for subject 2, block 1 may consist of 112 incongruent trials followed by 112 congruent trials. Word stimuli appeared for 1000 ms. With some precision, the PsyScope software allowed us to record each movement and click of the mouse as a punctate event. The recording window began 200 ms after presentation of the stimulus word to diminish contamination from movements of the previous trial. We simply recorded whether a movement or click occurred or did not occur during the 800 ms recording window of each trial. During debriefing, all subjects reported that the task was comfortable and that they did not discern the true purpose of the study.

RESULTS

No data points were excluded from analysis. Subjects exhibited a substantial number of automatisms (mouse movements and clicks) during the test phase of the experiment (M = 374.59, SEM = 55.33). The mean proportion of trials on which automatisms occurred was .22 (SEM = .03). As predicted, this rate increased as a function of block number, F (4, 64) = 5.261, p = .001 (η_p^2 = .25) (Figure 5.6). We also examined the rate of automatisms as a function of Stroop condition and found that more automatisms tended to be exhibited during the presumably less stimulating neutral condition, F (2, 32) = 3.363, p = .0473, though more conservative tests reveal this difference is not significant (with Fischer's PLSD, ps > .05).

DISCUSSION

As predicted, there was a striking linear increase in the rate of automatisms as a function of block number. During the first block, automatisms occurred during roughly 14% of the trials; during the middle block, this rate increased to 22%;

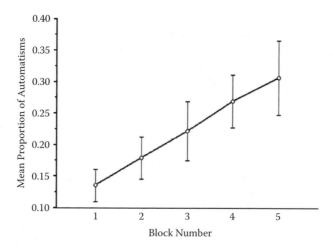

FIGURE 5.6   Mean proportion of automatisms as a function of block number, during a simple viewing task. Error bars indicate ± 1 *SEM*s.

and during the last block, the rate reached around 31%. This pattern of results is consistent with both arousal and load/fatigue accounts of automatism generation. However, though arousal and load/fatigue hypotheses can both account for the increase in automatisms as a function of block number, only an arousal hypothesis seems to account for the trend in which automatisms tended to be exhibited most during the neutral condition, which presumably was the least arousing condition of the three conditions. (It should be reiterated that this trend was not significant with more conservative, post-hoc tests.)

Contrary to our second prediction, there was no evidence consistent with the hypothesis that automatisms arose from displacement, perhaps because the over-all level of engagement and cognitive load of the task was minimal. Such a subtle manipulation (e.g., simply looking at the word red written in blue) may have been too weak to elicit the kinds of response conflict associated with displacement. Experiment 2 addresses whether the same pattern of results is obtained with a more arousing version of the task. In conclusion, as an explanatory variable, low arousal seems to be a more comprehensive predictor of automatisms than dis-placement or load/fatigue accounts, at least for this present variant of the Stroop.

EXPERIMENT 2

Automatisms During a Subvocal Stroop Task

To address the questions posed by Experiment 1, in Experiment 2 we obtained the same measure but with a more demanding and thus presumably more arousing task, in which Stroop-trained subjects were instructed to subvocally respond to Stroop stimuli (e.g., thinking "green" when red was written in a green hue). To diminish task-related movements, subjects were asked to sub-vocalize the response (i.e., to think but not utter the appropriate response). Because of the overall increase in the level of engagement of the task (and increased arousal), we predicted that the block-order effect and the neutral con-dition trend of Experiment 1 would be diminished. Second, we predicted that, because of displacement, more automatisms would be found in the conflict con-dition. We believed that, by increasing task-demands, and thus increasing load and response conflict, the computer mouse would more likely become a target of displaced action.

METHOD

Participants. Twenty-three Yale University students participated for class credit or $8.

Procedure. The procedures of the training and test phases were identical with those of Experiment 1 except that subjects were now instructed to subvocally respond to the Stroop stimuli. They were instructed, for example, to think "green" when confronted with red written in green. As well, due to the more demanding nature of the task and to logistical constraints, each of the 15 blocks now consisted of 80 instead of 112 trials, resulting in a total number of 1200 trials, spanning 20 min. Piloting ($n = 4$) revealed that subvocal response could be easily executed during the 1000 ms window of stimulus presentation. All subjects understood the instructions and found the task to be easy to perform. During debriefing, subjects reported that they did not discern the true purpose of the experiment.

RESULTS

Again, no data points were excluded from analysis. Subjects exhibited a substantial number of automatisms (mouse movements and clicks) during the test phase of the experiment ($M = 250.87$, $SEM = 31.56$). Replicating Experiment 1, the mean proportion of trials on which automatisms occurred was .21 ($SEM = .03$). As in Experiment 1, this rate tended to increase as a function of block number, but this time, the effect did not reach statistical significance, $F (4, 88) = 1.969$, $p = .1062$ ($\eta_p^2 = .08$). Unlike in Experiment 1, Stroop conditions did not yield an effect, $F (2, 44) = 0.681$, $p = .5115$, suggesting that, consistent with an arousal account, the increased cognitive demands and arousal level associated with the task diminished the resources necessary for generating automatisms.

A post hoc omnibus ANOVA applied to the rate data of both studies, with Stroop condition as a within-subjects factor and task (passive [Experiment 1] vs. subvocal [Experiment 2]) as a between-subjects factor, reveals a marginally non-significant main effect of Stroop condition, $F (2, 76) = 2.967$, $p = .0574$, but no main effect of task, $F (1, 38) = .111$, $p = .74$. Although the former seems to reflect the effect of the neutral condition in Experiment 1 (the largest difference found between the results of both studies), the interaction between task and Stroop con-dition was not statistically significant, $F (2, 76) = 1.930$, $p = .1522$ ($\eta_p^2 = .05$).

Discussion

Replicating Experiment 1, automatisms occurred on roughly 20% of the trials. However, as predicted and revealed by the substantially diminished effect size (η_p^2 decreased from .25 to .08), we failed to find the striking increase of automatism rate as a function of block number (although there was a trend, $p = .1062$). Naturally, it is difficult to draw conclusions from null findings. Nevertheless, the contrasting effects of both experiments are well accounted for by an arousal hypothesis: Having a more demanding task, this experimental session perhaps did not engender boredom/low-arousal, which increased block after block. The overall greater level of engagement and arousal may also explain the datum that, as predicted, the neutral condition no longer elicited more automatisms than the other Stroop conditions

Again, we failed to find any evidence consistent with the hypothesis that displacement can give rise to automatisms. This may be explained by the observation that displacement activity arises (or, at least, is detectable) only when there is the possibility of emitting a *reactive* action toward a suitable target for displacement (Dollard, Doob, Miller, Mowrer, & Sears, 1949; Lorenz, 1963; Tinbergen, 1952). Following this logic, reactive actions not involved in the response conflict (e.g., pressing a button when confronted with a probe) should "break through" more easily in the Stroop task.

In Experiment 3, subjects trained to perform the Stroop task were instructed to press a button (the space bar) upon detecting targets flanking word stimuli. As in Experiment 1, subjects were instructed to not make any naming responses whatsoever. Instead, they were instructed to just look at the center of the computer screen (where the words were presented) and respond only to the appearance of visual targets.* In accord with the notion of displacement activity, we predicted that RTs for detecting targets would be shorter for the conflict than the congruent Stroop conditions.

Experiment 3

Displacement Activity During a Passive Stroop Task

After Stroop training, in a dual-task paradigm, subjects performed the Stroop task along with another task—pressing the computer keyboard space bar in response to target stimuli ("flankers," a series of six hyphens flanking the word, e.g., "------red------") which appeared on each trial, 200 ms after the appearance of the word stimulus. A 200-ms pause between words and flankers was selected because it approximates the time at which Stroop conflict is hypothesized to be greatest

---

* In a pilot study ($n = 16$) in which participants were instructed to vocalize the response, we failed to reveal any significant effects ($ps > .60$), although RTs did tend to be shorter for the conflict condition (e.g., when the word red was written in blue, $M = 677.73$, $SEM = 49.47$) than for the congruent condition (e.g., when the word red was written in red, $M = 718.05$, $SEM = 67.10$). Lack of statistical significance may have resulted from the cumbersome, dual-task nature of the experiment, which yielded highly variable RTs and led some participants to report that the task was too confusing.

(Cohen, Dunbar, & McClelland, 1990). Moreover, we presented target stimuli on every trial in order to make the task as easy as possible and thus avoid artifacts resulting from higher-level, strategic processes. Flankers were sometimes presented during a Stroop conflict (e.g., the word red written in blue) and sometimes during no conflict (e.g., the word red written in red) or neutral (e.g., the letter string XXXX in red) conditions. In accordance with the notion of displacement activity, we predicted that RTs would be shorter for the conflict than for the congruent Stroop conditions.

METHOD

Participants. Twenty-two Yale University students participated for class credit or $8.

Procedure. Subjects were run individually in a three-part experiment, consisting of two training phases and one test phase. The first phase consisted of two blocks of 24 practice Stroop trials, each block presenting 8 congruent, 8 incongruent, and 8 neutral (XXXX) stimuli in random order. The neutral trials were not of theoretical interest, and were included only to diminish experimental demand and to increase the number of training trials without having to include additional, less easily identifiable colors. Again, eight common colors, correctly identified by all subjects, were used (red, orange, yellow, green, blue, purple, pink, and black).

Because test trials would now involve a cued response, technical aspects of the practice and test trials were different from those of the previous studies. Each trial of the practice and test phases proceeded as follows. A ready prompt (a question mark, 48-point Helvetica font) appeared on the center of the screen until subjects indicated that they were ready to commence the trial by uttering, "Go." Although it is customary for subjects to indicate their readiness by pressing a button, vocal responses were favored because we were again concerned that the initial button press would contaminate our manual dependent measure. After the response was detected by microphone, a fixation point (+) was shown at the center of the screen for 1500 ms. It was followed by a blank screen spanning 700 ms, after which time a randomly selected Stroop stimulus appeared, remaining on the screen until the vocal response was made. Subjects were instructed to respond as quickly and as accurately as possible. After the response and an additional 500 ms, the next trial began. As we learned from piloting (*n* = 4), the 500 ms between trials, plus the multiple pauses within trials, prevented subjects from entering a rhythm that could influence response speed and contaminate our measure.

After a short break, subjects were trained (15 trials) to respond to the flanker targets. Throughout all phases of the session, the flanker stimuli always appeared in the same position on the screen. During training, they were presented alone with empty space where word stimuli would appear in the subsequent test phase (e.g., ------ ------). We chose flankers as targets because they allow subjects to continue fixating in the center of the screen, where the word stimuli would appear. Subjects were instructed to respond by pressing the space bar with their index and middle fingers of their dominant hand as quickly and as accurately as possible every time the flankers appeared. After a break, subjects performed the test phase (24 trials), in which the same Stroop stimuli of the practice phase were randomly presented along with flanker stimuli. Subjects were instructed to fixate on the center of the screen and respond with a bar press to the flanker stimuli (the targets) and to disregard the word stimuli, that is, to not make any vocal responses whatsoever. The target appeared 200 ms after the onset of the word stimulus, and both stimuli remained on the screen until a response was made.

Subjects were periodically reminded to respond as quickly and as accurately as possible and to avoid becoming "trigger happy." They were unaware that the same behavior (pressing the space bar) would be elicited during each of the test trials. This was designed to minimize the influence of any decision-making processes that could contaminate our measure. We predicted that such a subtle manipulation would yield small but unambiguous effects.

RESULTS

Following Woodworth and Schlosberg (1954), RTs below 150 ms and above 2000 ms were excluded from analysis, resulting in the loss of 6.9% of the data set. Unfortunately, despite our efforts, the button-press task yielded many anticipatory errors. In any case, the same pattern of results was obtained with raw as with trimmed data, as noted in the following. Grand mean RT was 300.94 ms ($SEM = 11.03$). As shown in Figure 5.7, there was a main effect of condition, F $(2, 42) = 3.51$, $p = .039$ ($\eta_p^2 = .14$). Planned comparisons show a significant difference in RT between the congruent and incongruent conditions, $t (21) = 3.14$, $p = .005$ ($\eta_p^2 = .32$). The same pattern of results is encountered with square-root transformations of the data, $F (2, 42) = 4.00$, $p = .026$ ($\eta_p^2 = .16$). Because

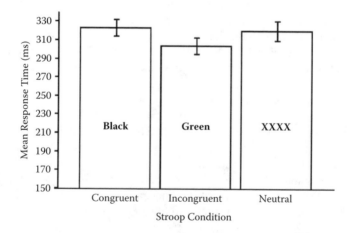

FIGURE 5.7 Mean button-press response time (ms) as a function of Stroop condition (congruent, incongruent, and neutral). For the sake of illustration, each bar presents the color black in the respective condition: "BLACK" written in black, "GREEN" in black, and "XXXX" in black. Error bars signify ± 1 *SEM*.

roughly 7% of the data was removed, it is worth noting that the same results were obtained with untrimmed, raw data, F (2, 42) = 3.70, p = .033 (η_p^2 = .15).

DISCUSSION

As predicted by the notion of displacement activity, it was found that RTs were shorter during the incongruent trials than during the congruent trials. The Stroop conditions affected behavior even though subjects were instructed not to respond in any way toward the word stimuli, suggesting that the incidental presence of the stimulus could nonetheless activate unconscious action plans that then competed for selection. Interestingly, this task, but not those of Experiments 1 and 2, was capable of eliciting behavior consistent with the notion of displacement activity. Still, it has yet to be demonstrated that, indeed, such an effect results from the action-related properties of the stimuli (e.g., as learned from Stroop training) and not from some other property. For example, it may well be the case that, for reasons independent of Stroop response conflict, an incongruous stimulus (e.g., the word red written in blue) somehow facilitates action production. We address this issue in the following experiment.

EXPERIMENT 4

Given the findings of Experiment 3, and because of logistical constraints, we decided in Experiment 4 to exclude the theoretically uninformative neutral condition and present only congruent and incongruent conditions. In addition, we now added a control condition in which the subjects exposed to the test stimuli were not previously trained to perform the Stroop task. Instead, these subjects received a sham training session in which they simply viewed the training stimuli. This condition was necessary to rule out the possibility that effects found with Stroop stimuli were due, not to the activation of acquired action plans, but to some other property of the stimuli (e.g., a perceptual or semantic property). For example, the results of Experiment 3 could be due, not to the activation of action plans, but to the fact that viewing discrepant stimuli (e.g., the word red written in blue) simply increases arousal and thus facilitates cued button-presses.

METHOD

Participants. Fifty-five Yale University students participated for class credit or $8.
Procedure. For "trained" subjects (n = 28), the procedures were the same as those of Experiment 3. They were run individually in a three-part experiment, consisting of two training phases and one test phase. The first phase consisted of 72 practice Stroop trials. (Again, the neutral trials were not of theoretical interest, and were included only to diminish experimental demand and to increase the number of training trials without having to include additional, less easily identifiable colors.) After a short break, subjects were trained (15 trials) to respond to

the flanker targets. After a break, subjects performed the test phase (48 trials), in which the same Stroop stimuli (minus the neutral stimuli) of the practice phase were randomly presented along with flanker stimuli. An equal number (24) of congruent and incongruent stimuli were presented in random order. Control subjects ($n = 27$) performed the same task without having received Stroop training. Instead, during the training session, these subjects were instructed to simply view the training stimuli.

RESULTS

Again, RTs below 150 ms and above 2000 ms were excluded from analysis, resulting in the loss of 13.26% of the data set. Similar to Experiment 3, the grand mean RT was 291.02 ($SEM = 6.55$). As predicted, there was an interaction between training and Stroop conditions $F (1, 53) = 5.994$, $p = .0177$ ($\eta_p^2 = .10$) (Table 5.1). Importantly, the same interaction was found with the raw, untrimmed data, $F (1, 53) = 7.150$, $p = .0099$ ($\eta_p^2 = .12$). Planned comparisons show a significant difference in RT between the congruent and incongruent conditions, $t (27) = 2.11$, $p = .0443$ ($\eta_p^2 = .14$), but only for trained subjects. Controls exhibited the reverse pattern, but this difference was insignificant, $t (26) = -1.761$, $p = .089$ ($\eta_p^2 = .11$). The same pattern of results is encountered with square-root transformations of the RT data, $F (1, 53) = 6.660$, $p = .0127$ ($\eta_p^2 = .11$). There were no main effects of training or Stroop condition, $ps > .28$.

DISCUSSION

As predicted by the notion of displacement activity, RTs were shorter during the conflict than congruent trials, but only for trained subjects. Interestingly, the Stroop conditions affected behavior even though subjects were instructed not to respond in any way toward the word stimuli. We also demonstrated that the effect is not obtained with subjects who lack Stroop training, which supports the view that the effect of Experiment 3 is due to the action-related properties of the stimuli and not to some other property. In conclusion, unlike the tasks of Experiments 1 and 2, the "reactive" tasks of Experiments 3 and 4 were capable of eliciting behavior consistent with the notion of displacement activity.

TABLE 5.1
Mean Response Time (ms) as a Function of Training Regimen and Stroop Condition

	Response Times			
	Trained Subjects		Control Subjects	
Stroop Condition	Mean	SEM	Mean	SEM
Congruent	287.53	9.59	290.49	9.66
Incongruent	280.46	9.03	305.57	10.83

CONCLUSION

Identifying why certain actions accompany cognitive tasks can serve as a portal through which to discover the general principles by which the mental apparatus reaches its cognitive goals (e.g., exert top-down control to suppress or enhance the activation of representations; cf., Gazzaley, Cooney, Rissman, & D'Esposito, 2005; Spivey, Richardson, & Dale, 2009). For example, seemingly functionless actions may serve as *additive movements* that sustain mental representations in working memory (e.g., during mental rotation or in a tip-of-the-tongue state) or as *subtractive movements* that diminish the influence of distracting information (cf., Gazzaley et al., 2005), as in gaze aversion (e.g., Glenberg et al., 1998). In some cases, actions may serve more of a modulatory function, rectifying suboptimal levels of arousal. They could also be byproducts of response conflict, as in the phenomenon of displacement activity, in which inhibition is not diffuse but seems to be representation-specific (see the following).

In our experiments, we focused only on automatisms, the least studied spontaneous behavior. Although these are only initial and tentative findings requiring further empirical corroboration, at this stage of understanding one can appreciate that, although the occurrence of a single automatism is a seemingly haphazard event, the general rate of occurrence of these actions is far from indeterminate. We sought to identify the function of these actions by eliminating hypotheses and contrasting situations in which the actions do and do not occur. We have found that, as predicted by diverse theoretical backgrounds, these automatisms can arise as a function of arousal and load/fatigue, and that their expression can be facilitated by response conflict, as suggested by the notion of displacement activity. In Experiment 1, we found a striking linear effect in which, consistent with arousal and load/fatigue accounts, the more trials performed the greater the rate of automatisms. During the first block, automatisms occurred during roughly 14% of the trials; during the middle block, this rate increased to 22%; and during the last block, the rate reached around 31%. However, the entire pattern of results (including the observation that, of the three conditions, the neutral condition yielded the most automatisms) was best explained by an arousal account of automatism generation. Consistent with this view, we failed to find the same pattern of results when arousal was increased by having subjects subvocally respond to Stroop stimuli (Experiment 2).

Demonstrating that low levels of arousal can lead to unintended, idiosyncratic actions, Experiments 1 and 2 add experimental support to the notion that "the idle mind is the devil's playground." From this point of view, levels of arousal, more than cognitive load or fatigue, may cause one to decide, out-of-the-blue, to go for a walk, organize one's bookshelf, call a friend, or have a snack. One limitation of these experiments was that we looked only at the limited arm/hand/finger behaviors detectable by computer mouse. With the proper technology and logistical resources, we could have probably observed muscular activity in other theoretically important but unrecorded regions (e.g., legs, eyes, and feet). Perhaps it was in these unrecorded regions where, via displacement activity, the Stroop conflict in Experiments 1 and 2 led to the production of automatisms. Nevertheless, we believe that, given their prominence in classic automatisms such as the Chevreul pendulum, dowsing, automatic writing, and Ouija boards (see review in Wegner, 2002, Chapter 4), arm/hand/finger movements are an informative index of the tendency to generate automatisms.

In Experiment 3, the dynamics among plans were explored by testing the etho-logical notion of displacement activity. These initial data reveal that an unrelated action may be facilitated during conflict in the Stroop paradigm (for converg-ing evidence, see Kim et al., 2005), at least under certain circumstances. An interesting alternative hypothesis is that the difference in RTs resulted not from displacement, but from the difficulty of inhibiting a naming response in the con-gruent condition, in which both the name and color of the stimulus elicit the same response, a level of provocation not encountered in the incongruent condition. However, unlike the displacement account, this alternative fails to explain how such inhibition affects the production of an act as easy to execute as our measure, and why such effects were not found in the other conditions, which required at least some degree of inhibition. Experiment 4 substantiated the claim that the displacement effect is due to the action-related properties of the stimuli and not to some other property.

We believe that the facilitation effect arose in part because of the effortlessness of the intended action (pressing the space bar on every trial). Had the performed task involved higher-level considerations, as in choice RT tasks, then perhaps we would have found pronounced interference rather than facilitation during con-flict. Indeed, in a task substantially more complicated than ours, Verbruggen, Liefooghe, and Vandierendonck (2004) found that subjects trained to inhibit the Stroop naming response upon detecting an unpredictable signal (a choice RT task) showed greater interference during the conflict than the congruent condition.

Interestingly, it seems that Stroop stimuli led to response conflict even though subjects were instructed not to respond to the stimuli in any way. This supports the hypothesis that, regardless of an actor's intentions, action plans can be unconsciously activated by nonfocal, incidental action-related stimuli (Levine et al., 2007), which is consistent with the general view that many of our behaviors occur "automati-cally," determined by causes far removed from our awareness (Bargh & Morsella, 2008). It has been demonstrated, for example, that people automatically imitate the postures, facial expressions, and speaking styles of others (Chartrand & Bargh, 1999; Giles, Coupland, & Coupland, 1991) and that perceptual stimuli (e.g., tools, office supplies, and other action-related objects) can automatically set us to physi-cally interact with the world (Chen & Bargh, 1999; Kay, Wheeler, Bargh, & Ross, 2004; Tucker & Ellis, 2001, 2004; see neuroimaging evidence in Grézes & Decety, 2002), suggesting that there is an automatic perception-behavior link from percep-tual processing to action formation (see review in Dijksterhuis & Bargh, 2001).

Displacement also suggests that the dynamics among activated plans are more complicated than that portrayed by accounts in which, during action selection, all nonselected plans are equally inhibited. The idea of displacement activity is one of selective, rather than diffuse, inhibition (cf., Gazzaley et al., 2005), for inhibition occurs among the most competitive plans but does not seem to affect less competitive ones, at least not to the same extent. Interestingly, the idea that multiple action plans are simultaneously activated during a task such as ours is supported by psychophysiological evidence showing that, in a Stroop-like task, response competition involves simultaneous activation of the brain areas associated with the target- and distracter-related responses (DeSoto, Fabiani, Geary, & Gratton, 2001). In terms of the real world, the result explains how unintended and deleterious behaviors such as aggressing, stereotyping, and failures in self-regulation would be more likely to break through during action conflicts, a hypothesis for which there is substantial evidence (e.g., Baumeister et al., 1994).

Corroborating Sperry's (1964) conclusion that, "In a machine, the output is usually more revealing of the internal organization than is the input" (p. 410), investigating how movements strategically influence arousal and cognition has revealed homeostatic-like mechanisms and forms of cognitive control that may have not been illuminated by probing solely into the nature of neural or self-reportable phenomena. It seems that automatisms help keep levels of arousal at optimal levels and lexical gestures can indirectly influence speech production by sustaining the activation of semantic representations in working memory. More generally, these kinds of findings reveal the mechanisms underlying indirect cognitive control. As in the research by Robert Krauss, movements have served as an excellent portal through which to study the mind/brain.

ACKNOWLEDGMENTS

This research was supported by grants from the National Institutes of Health to E. Morsella (F32-MH69083) and to J. Bargh (R01-MH60767). We gratefully acknowledge the advice and comments of Marcia Johnson, and the assistance of Stephen Krieger, Joanna Mattis, and Elizabeth Kennard. We thank Marcia Johnson and members of the Memory and Cognition Laboratory at Yale University for providing the space and equipment for running several of the studies.

REFERENCES

Alibali, M. W., Kita, S., & Yong, A. J. (2000). Gesture and the process of speech production: We think, therefore we gesture. *Language & Cognitive Processes*, *15*, 593–613.
Baddeley, A. D. (1986). *Working memory.* Oxford, England: Oxford University Press.
Bargh, J. A., & Morsella, E. (2008). The unconscious mind. *Perspectives on Psychological Science, 3*, 73–79.
Barsalou, L. W. (1999). Perceptual symbol systems. *Behavioral and Brain Sciences, 22,* 577–560.
Barsalou, L. W. (2003). Situated simulation in the human conceptual system. *Language and Cognitive Processes, 18,* 513–562.
Barsalou, L.W. (2008). Grounded cognition. *Annual Review of Psychology, 59,* 617–645.
Baumeister, R. F., Heatherton, T. F., & Tice, D. M. (1994). *Losing control: How and why people fail at self-regulation.* San Diego, CA: Academic Press.

Beattie, G. W. (1980). A further investigation of the cognitive interference hypothesis of gaze patterns during conversation. *British Journal of Social Psychology, 20,* 243–248.

Beattie, G. W., & Coughlan, J. (1999). An experimental investigation of the role of iconic gestures in lexical access using the tip-of-the tongue phenomenon. *British Journal of Psychology, 90,* 35–56.

Beattie, G. W., & Shovelton, H. (2000). Iconic hand gestures and the predictability of words in context in spontaneous speech. *British Journal of Psychology, 91,* 473–491.

Berlyne, D. E. (1960). *Conflict, arousal, and curiosity.* New York: McGraw Hill.

Borghi, A. M., Glenberg, A. M., & Kaschak, M. P. (2004). Putting words in perspective. *Memory & Cognition, 32,* 863–873.

Botvinick, M. (2007). Conflict monitoring and decision making: Reconciling two perspectives on anterior cingulate function. *Cognitive, Affective and Behavioral Neuroscience, 7,* 356–366.

Brooks, L. R. (1968). Spatial and verbal components of the act of recall. *Canadian Journal of Psychology, 22,* 349–368.

Brooks, L. R. (1970). An extension of the conflict between visualization and reading. *Quarterly Journal of Experimental Psychology, 22,* 91–96.

Buchsbaum, B. R., & D'Esposito, M. (2008). The search for the phonological store: From loop to convolution. *Journal of Cognitive Neuroscience, 20,* 762–778.

Burgess, N., & Hitch, G. J. (1999). Memory for serial order: A network model of the phonological loop and its timing. *Psychological Review, 106,* 551–581.

Butterworth, B. (1978). Maxims for studying conversations. *Semiotica, 24,* 317–339.

Butterworth, B., & Hadar, U. (1989). Gesture, speech and computational stages: A reply to McNeill. *Psychological Review, 96,* 168–174.

Carpenter, W. B. (1874). *Principles of mental physiology.* New York: Appleton.

Chartrand, T. L., & Bargh, J. A. (1999). The chameleon effect: The perception-behavior link and social interaction. *Journal of Personality and Social Psychology, 76,* 893–910.

Chen, M., & Bargh, J. A. (1999). Consequences of automatic evaluation: Immediate behavioral predispositions to approach or avoid the stimulus. *Personality and Social Psychology Bulletin, 25,* 215–224.

Chiu, C-y., Hong, Y-y., & Krauss, R. M. (unpublished). Gaze direction and fluency in conversational speech. University of Hong Kong. (Available as downloadable pdf file at: http://www.columbia.edu/~rmk7/PDF/Gaze.pdf)

Cohen, J. D., Dunbar, K., & McClelland, J. L. (1990). On the control of automatic processes: A parallel distributed processing account of the Stroop effect. *Psychological Review, 97,* 332–361.

Cohen, J. D., MacWhinney, B., Flatt, M., & Provost, J. (1993). PsyScope: A new graphic interactive environment for designing psychology experiments. *Behavior Research Methods, Instruments, & Computers, 25,* 257–271.

Cunningham, W. A., Johnson, M. K., Raye, C. L., Gatenby, J. C., Gore, J. C., & Banaji, M. R. (2004). Separable neural components in the processing of Black and White Faces. *Psychological Science, 15,* 806–813.

De Laguna, G. (1927). *Speech: Its function and development.* New Haven, CT: Yale University Press.

DeSoto, M. C., Fabiani, M., Geary, D. C., & Gratton, G. (2001). When in doubt, do it both ways: Brain evidence of the simultaneous activation of conflicting responses in a spatial Stroop task. *Journal of Cognitive Neuroscience 13,* 523–536.

Dijksterhuis, A., & Bargh, J. A. (2001). The perception-behavior expressway: Automatic effects of social perception on social behavior. In M. P. Zanna (Ed.), *Advances in experimental social psychology, (33,* 1–40). San Deigo, CA: Academic Press.

Dobrogaev, S. M. (1929). Ucnenie o reflekse v problemakh iazykovedeniia [Observations on reflexes and issues in language study]. *Iazykovedenie i Materializm,* 105–173.

Dollard, J., Doob, L. W., Miller, N. E., Mowrer, O . H., & Sears, R. R. (1949). *Frustration and aggression.* New Haven, CT: Yale University Press.

Ekman, P., & Friesen, W. V. (1972) Hand movements. *Journal of Communication, 22,* 353–374.

Farah, M. J. (2000). The neural bases of mental imagery. In M. S. Gazzaniga (Ed.), *The cognitive neurosciences* (2nd ed., pp. 965 – 974). Cambridge, MA: MIT Press.

Frick-Horbury, D., & Guttentag, R. E. (1998). The effects of restricting hand gesture production on lexical retrieval and free recall. *American Journal of Psychology, 111,* 43–62.

Gazzaley, A., Cooney, J. W., Rissman, J., & D'Esposito, M. (2005). Top-down suppression deficit underlies working memory impairment in normal aging. *Nature Neuroscience, 8,* 1298–1300.

Giles, H., Coupland, J., & Coupland, N. (1991). *Contexts of accommodation: Developments in applied sociolinguistics.* New York: Cambridge University Press.

Glenberg, A. M. (1997). What memory is for. *Behavioral and Brain Sciences, 20,* 1–55.

Glenberg, A. M., Schroeder, J. L., & Robertson, D. A. (1998). Averting the gaze disengages the environment and facilitates remembering. *Memory & Cognition, 26,* 651–658.

Goldin-Meadow, S., Nusbaum, H., Kelly, S. D., & Wagner, S. (2001). Explaining math: Gesture lightens the load. *Psychological Science, 12,* 516–522.

Goldin-Meadow, S., & Wagner, S. M. (2005). How our hands help us learn. *Trends in Cognitive Sciences, 9,* 234–241.

Goodale, M., & Milner, D. (2004). *Sight unseen: An exploration of conscious and unconscious vision.* New York: Oxford University Press.

Grafman, J., & Krueger, F. (2009). The prefrontal cortex stores structured event complexes that are & the representational basis for cognitively derived actions. In E. Morsella, J. A. Bargh, and P. M. Gollwitzer (Eds.), *Oxford handbook of human action.* New York: Oxford University Press.

Graham, T. A. (1999). The role of gesture in children learning to count. *Journal of Experimental Child Psychology, 74,* 333–355.

Grézes, J., & Decety, J. (2002). Does visual perception of object afford action? Evidence from a neuroimaging study. *Neuropsycholgia, 40,* 212–222.

Harnad, S. (1990). The symbol grounding problem. *Physica D, 42,* 335–346.

Hebb, D. O. (1968). Concerning imagery. *Psychological Review, 75,* 466–477.

Hommel, B., Müsseler, J., Aschersleben, G., & Prinz, W. (2001). The theory of event coding (TEC): A framework for perception and action planning. *Behavioral and Brain Sciences, 24,* 849–937.

Hostetter, A. B., & Alibali, M. W. (2008). Visible embodiment: Gesture as simulated action. *Psychonomic Bulletin & Review, 15,* 495–514.

Hull, C. L. (1943). *Principles of behavior.* New York: Appleton-Century.

Kahneman, D. (1973). *Attention and effort.* Englewood Cliffs, NJ: Prentice Hall.

Kay, A. C., Wheeler, S. C., Bargh, J. A., & Ross, L. (2004). Material priming: The influence of mundane physical objects on situational construal and competitive behavioral choice. *Organizational Behavior and Human Decision Processes, 95,* 83–96.

Kendon, A. (1980). Gesticulation and speech: Two aspects of the process of utterance. In M. R. Key (Ed.), *Relationship of verbal and nonverbal communication* (pp. 207–226). The Hague: Mouton.

Kendon, A. (1983). Gesture and speech: How they interact. In J. M. Weimann & R. P. Harrison (Eds.), *Nonverbal interaction* (pp. 13–45). Beverly Hills, CA: Sage.

Kendon, A. (1994). Do gestures communicate? A review. *Research on Language and Social Interaction, 27,* 175–200.

Kim., S.-Y., Kim, M.-S., & Chun, M. M. (2005). Concurrent working memory load can reduce distraction. *Proceedings of the National Academy of Sciences, USA, 102,* 16524–16529.

Kosslyn, S. M., Ganis, G., & Thompson, W. L. (2003). Mental imagery: Against the nihilistic hypothesis. *Trends in Cognitive Science, 7,* 109–111.

Krauss, R. M. (1998). Why do we gesture when we speak? *Current Directions in Psychological Science, 7,* 54–59.

Krauss, R. M., Chen, Y., & Gottesman, R. F. (2000). Lexical gestures and lexical access: A process model. In D. McNeill (Ed.), *Language and gesture* (pp. 261–283). Cambridge, UK: Cambridge University Press.

Krauss, R. M., & Hadar, U. (1999). The role of speech-related arm/hand gestures in word retrieval. In R. Campbell & L. Messing (Eds.), *Gesture, speech, and sign* (pp. 93–116). Oxford, UK: Oxford University Press.

Laeng, B., & Teodorescu, D.-S. (2002). Eye scanpaths during visual imagery reenact those of perception of the same visual scene. *Cognitive Science, 26,* 207–231.

Lavond, D. G., Kim, J. J., & Thompson, R. F. (1993). Mammalian brain substrates of aversive classical conditioning. *Annual Review of Psychology, 44,* 317–342.

Lawrence, B. M., Myerson, J., Oonk, H. M., & Abrams, R. A. (2001). The effects of eye and limb movements on working memory. *Memory, 9,* 433–444.

LeDoux, J. E. (1996). The emotional brain: The mysterious underpinnings of emotional life. New York: Simon & Schuster.

Levine, L. R., Morsella, E., & Bargh, J. A. (2007). The perversity of inanimate objects: Stimulus control by incidental musical notation. *Social Cognition, 25,* 265–280.

Lieberman, M. D. (2007). The X- and C-systems: The neural basis of automatic and controlled social cognition. In E. Harmon-Jones & P. Winkelman (Eds.), *Fundamentals of social neuroscience* (pp. 290–315). New York: Guilford.

Logie, R. H. (1995). *Visuo-spatial working memory.* Hove, UK: Lawrence Erlbaum Associates.

Lorenz, K. (1963). *On aggression.* New York: Harcourt, Brace, & World.

MacLeod, C. M., & MacDonald, P. A. (2000). Interdimensional interference in the Stroop effect: Uncovering the cognitive and neural anatomy of attention. *Trends in Cognitive Sciences, 4,* 383–391.

McNeill, D., Cassell, J., & McCullough, K.-E. 1994. Communicative effects of speech-mismatched gestures. *Language and Social Interaction, 27,* 223–237.

Mead, G. H. (1934). *Mind, self, and society.* Chicago: University of Chicago Press.

Miller, N. E. (1959). Liberalization of basic S-R concepts: Extensions to conflict behavior, motivation, and social learning. In S. Koch (Ed.), *Psychology: A study of science, Vol. 2* (pp. 196–292). New York: McGraw-Hill.

Milner A. D., & Goodale, M. A. (1995). *The visual brain in action.* New York: Oxford University Press.

Morsella, E. (2002). The motor components of semantic representation. (Doctoral dissertation, Columbia University, 2002). *Dissertation Abstracts International: Section B: the Sciences & Engineering, 63 (4-B).* (University Microfilms No. AAI3048195).

Morsella, E. (2005). The function of phenomenal states: Supramodular interaction theory. *Psychological Review, 112,* 1000–1021.

Morsella, E., Bargh, J. A., & Gollwitzer, P. M. (2009). *Oxford handbook of human action.* New York: Oxford University Press.

Morsella, E., Gray, J. R., Levine, L. R., & Bargh, J. A. (2006). *On the function of consciousness: The subjective experience of incompatible intentions.* Poster presented at the Annual Convention of the American Psychological Society, New York.

Morsella, E., & Krauss, R. M. (1999, October). *Electromyography of arm during the lexical retrieval of abstract and concrete words.* Poster presented at the annual convention of the Society for Psychophysiology, Granada, Spain. Psychophysiology, 36, S82–S82.

Morsella, E., & Krauss, R. M. (2004). The role of gestures in spatial working memory and speech. *The American Journal of Psychology, 117,* 411–424.

Morsella, E., & Krauss, R. M. (2005). Muscular activity in the arm during lexical retrieval: Implications for gesture-speech theories. *Journal of Psycholinguistic Research, 34,* 415–427.

Morsella, E., Lanska, M., Berger, C. C., & Gazzaley, A. (in press). Indirect cognitive control through top-down activation of perceptual symbols. *European Journal of Social Psychology.*

Öhman, A., & Mineka, S. (2001). Fears, phobias, and preparedness: Toward an evolved module of fear and fear learning. *Psychological Review, 108,* 483–522.

Olivers, C. N. L., & Nieuwenhuis, S. (2005). The beneficial effect of concurrent task-irrelevant mental activity on temporal attention. *Psychological Science, 16,* 265–269.

Olsson, A., & Phelps, E. A. (2004). Learned fear of "unseen" faces after Pavlovian, observational, and instructed fear. *Psychological Science, 15,* 822–828.

Pessiglione, M., Petrovic, P., Daunizeau, J., Palminteri, S., Dolan, R. J., & Frith, C. D. (2008). Subliminal instrumental conditioning demonstrated in the human brain. *Neuron, 59,* 561–567.

Pine, K. J., Bird, H., & Kirk, E. (2007). The effect of prohibiting gesture on children's lexical retrieval ability. *Developmental Science, 10,* 747–754.

Pulvermuller, F. (2005). Brain mechanisms linking language and action. *Nature Reviews Neuroscience, 6,* 576–582.

Rauscher, F. H., Krauss, R. M., & Chen, Y. (1996). Gesture, speech, and lexical access: The role of lexical movements in the processing of speech. *Psychological Science, 7,* 226–231.

Rose, M., & Douglas, J. (2001). The differential facilitatory effects of gesture and visualisation processes on object naming in aphasia. *Aphasiology, 15,* 977–990.

Rose, M., Douglas, J., & Matyas, T. (2002). The comparative effectiveness of gesture and verbal treatments for a specific phonologic naming impairment. *Aphasiology, 16,* 1001–1030.

Skinner, B. F. (1953). *Science and human behavior.* New York: Macmillan.

Sousa-Poze, J. F., Rohrberg, R., & Mercure, A. (1979). Effects of type of information (abstract concrete) and field dependence on asymmetry of hand movements during speech. *Perceptual and Motor Skills, 48,* 1323–1330.

Sperry, R. W. (1964). Neurology and the mind-brain problem. In R. L. Isaacson (Ed.), *Basic readings in neuropsychology* (pp. 403–429). New York: Harper & Row.

Spivey, M., Richardson, D., & Dale, R. (in press). The movement of eye and hand as a window into language and cognition. In E. Morsella, J. A. Bargh, & P. M. Gollwitzer (Eds.), *Oxford handbook of human action* (pp. 225–249). New York: Oxford University Press.

Strack, F., & Deutsch, R. (2004). Reflective and impulsive determinants of social behavior. *Personality and Social Psychology Bulletin, 8,* 220–247.

Stroop, J. R. (1935). Studies of interference in serial verbal reactions. *Journal of Experimental Psychology, 18,* 643–662.

Tinbergen, N. (1952). 'Derived' activities: Their causation, biological significance, origin and emancipation during evolution. *Quarterly Review of Biology, 27,* 1–32.

Tucker, M., & Ellis, R. (2001). The potentiation of grasp types during visual object categorization. *Visual Cognition, 8,* 769–800.

Tucker, M., & Ellis, R. (2004). Action priming by briefly presented objects. *Acta Psychologica, 116*, 185–203.

Verbruggen, F., Liefooghe, B., & Vandierendonck, A. (2004). The interaction between stop signal inhibition and distracter interference in the flanker and Stroop task. *Acta Psychologica, 116*, 21–37.

Washburn, M. F. (1928). Emotion and thought: a motor theory of their relation. In C. Murchison (Ed.), *Feelings and emotions: The Wittenberg Symposium* (pp. 99–145). Worcester, MA: Clark University Press.

Wegner, D. M. (2002). *The illusion of conscious will.* Cambridge, MA: The MIT Press.

Werner, H., & Kaplan, B. (1963). *Symbol formation.* New York: Wiley.

Westwood, D. A. (2009). The visual control of object manipulation. In E. Morsella, J. A. Bargh, and P. M. Gollwitzer (Eds.), *Oxford handbook of human action.* New York: Oxford University Press.

Williams, M. A., Morris, A. P., McGlone, F., Abbott, D. F., & Mattingley, J. B. (2004). Amygdala responses to fearful and happy facial expressions under conditions of binocular suppression. *The Journal of Neuroscience, 24,* 2898–2904.

Wood, W., Quinn, J., & Kashy, D. (2002). Habits in everyday life: Thought, emotion, and action. *Journal of Personality and Social Psychology, 83,* 1281–1297.

Woodworth, R. S., & Schlosberg, H. (1954). *Experimental psychology* (2nd ed.). New York: Holt, Rinehart & Winston.

Section II

Human Communication

6 What Robots Could Teach Us About Perspective Taking

Cristen Torrey, Susan R. Fussell, and Sara Kiesler

A distinctly social ability that underlies shared meaning, empathy, and cooperation is taking the perspective of another person during conversation. Research on communication has explored the manner in which human speakers account for their listeners' perspectives and adjust their communications in their attempts to be understood (e.g., Clark & Wilkes-Gibbs, 1986; Fussell & Krauss, 1992; Krauss & Fussell, 1991; Krauss, Vivekananthan, & Weinheimer, 1968). Speakers attend to their listeners' group memberships and likely areas of expertise as they construct their messages (e.g., Clark & Marshall, 1981; Fussell & Krauss, 1992; Hupet, Chantraine, & Neff, 1993; Isaacs & Clark, 1987). Speakers attend to what their partners can see, that is, their spatial perspective within the environment (e.g., Gergle, Kraut, & Fussell, 2004b; Kraut, Miller, & Siegel, 1996; Lockridge & Brennan, 2002; Schober, 1993). In addition, speakers attend to the verbal and nonverbal responses of their listeners to assess whether their message is comprehended and to make appropriate repairs and adjustments (e.g., Clark & Wilkes-Gibbs, 1986; Krauss & Bricker, 1966; Krauss & Weinheimer, 1964, 1966). These adjustments produce communication that is more effective, whether in the context of a single message (e.g., Fussell & Krauss, 1989) or over the course of an ongoing conversation (Kraut, Lewis, & Swezey, 1982; Schober & Clark, 1989).

There now exists considerable evidence on the information people use in perspective taking (for a recent review, see Schober & Brennan, 2003), but we know very little about failures in perspective taking and how conversationalists cope with inaccurate or inadequate perspective taking. We suggest that the specific nature of perspective taking in effective communication becomes particularly visible in conversations between humans and machines. Currently, the most common experience people have conversing with a machine is when they make a phone call to a customer service department and are greeted by an automated representative. These computer-driven speakers communicate with limited, if any, perspective-taking abilities. These speakers have no sense for the caller's familiarity with the task in question or with the number of times the caller has already been forced to listen to the complete set of instructions. Nearly everyone has a frustrating story to tell about these automated helpers. Many of these frustrations can be traced to an absence of perspective-taking skill on the part of the machine. These automated conversational partners do not have any sense for their listeners.

It seems likely that our conversations with machines might benefit from their use of perspective-taking strategies. Yet it is not at all clear how automated help systems, computer agents, or robots will be able to take the individual perspectives of their listeners. In ongoing research, we are exploring perspective taking between humans and automated conversational partners, particularly in the embodied form of humanoid robots. Because machines are literal, they must be told precisely how perspective taking should unfold. This necessity highlights some gaps in our understanding of perspective taking, especially when it must be created or repaired.

When attempting to implement perspective-taking theories in a robotic form, we need to elaborate the details of the theory in a precise, computational manner. For example, if the robot predicts that the listener does not know a referent, we must specify the number of additional words of description that the robot should add. Thus far, theory informed by previous research underspecifies the answer to this and similarly specific questions about the process of perspective taking. Because of these challenges, we believe that conversational robots offer a unique opportunity to investigate the role of perspective taking in effective conversation in a controlled manner and to observe the consequences of poor perspective taking. In this chapter, we begin by describing empirical studies exploring the presence and consequences of perspective taking in human-robot communication. We then describe our attempts to implement perspective-taking strategies with robotic conversational partners. We conclude by posing some issues still to be explored in understanding conversational perspective-taking behavior.

ROBOTS AS CONVERSATIONAL PARTNERS

Research on humanoid robotic machines has made impressive progress. Part of the motivation behind the development of humanoid robots is the ease with which people relate to machines socially when these machines give anthropomorphic cues such as humanlike form (Powers & Kiesler, 2006) and speech (Nass & Lee, 2001). Many roboticists argue that robots with human form and language will be more effective communicators than machine-like robots because they will evoke familiar social responses in the humans with whom they interact. If these robots can live up to the expectations their social forms create, then getting information from them and working alongside them should be easier as well (Scassellati, 2004).

We are pursuing perspective taking as a feature in the development of intelligent human-robot communication. We believe perspective taking may be particularly important for robots interacting with a varied group of individuals in the role of an advisor, instructor, or guide. Robots in roles such as these may give tours in a museum, guide people in airports or shopping malls, tutor students, or answer questions in an information kiosk. As they interact with people of different backgrounds and levels of expertise, it may be advantageous for such robots to have the capacity to adjust their communication using perspective-taking strategies. Our initial approach to understanding perspective taking between humans and

robots begins by asking two questions designed to understand the appropriateness of the perspective-taking approach for human-robot communication. First,
do human speakers assume the robot has a perspective? Second, if robots were
able to take their human listeners' perspective, would listeners benefit?

Do Speakers Take a Robot's Perspective?

We have found that people do make assumptions about the knowledge a robot
has, using the same sorts of cues that people use when making assumptions about
one another's perspectives. In one study, participants were asked to estimate the
likelihood that a robot would recognize different landmarks (Lee, Kiesler, Lau,
& Chiu, 2005). The landmarks shown were familiar to residents of Hong Kong,
familiar to residents of New York, familiar to both, or familiar to neither. When
the robot was introduced as a research project of a New York university, participants estimated that the robot was more likely to recognize New York landmarks.
When the robot was introduced as a research project of a Hong Kong university,
participants estimated that the robot was more likely to know Hong Kong landmarks. This experiment suggested that people estimate a robot's knowledge differently based on the robot's "nationality," in much the same way as they do with
other people (Fussell & Krauss, 1991; Isaacs & Clark, 1987).

The landmarks experiment tested people's predictions about what the robot
was likely to know based on where the robot was built. If people predict that
the robot is unlikely to know something, we would expect that prediction to
result in more descriptive messages (Fussell & Krauss, 1992). In a new experiment, we tested whether participants would make assumptions about a robot's
"gender" from its voice and appearance and tested whether these assumptions
would translate into changes in participants' communicative behavior (Powers,
Kramer, Lim, Kuo, Lee, & Kiesler, 2005). Participants were asked to instruct
a humanoid robot in the modern rules of dating. The gender of the robot was
manipulated using the color of the robot's plastic lips (red or grey) and its voice
pitch (higher or lower). Participants were told that the robot was gathering information to become a dating counselor. The robot asked participants a series of
questions about what typically happens on dates. For example, the robot asked
participants how to set up a date, who should do the planning for the date,
and whether either member of the couple should buy new clothes for the date.
Overall, participants used a greater number of words when describing dating to
a male robot, suggesting that the male robot was perceived to have less knowledge of dating norms than the female robot. Further, male participants said more
to the female robot than the male robot while female participants said more to
the male robot than the female robot. We suggest that participants were using
their own knowledge as a guide in predicting what the robot knew (Fussell &
Krauss, 1992; Nickerson, 1999). When the participants' and the robot's gender
overlapped, the participants may have perceived that there was less need for
descriptive detail. In this study, we found that participants constructed different

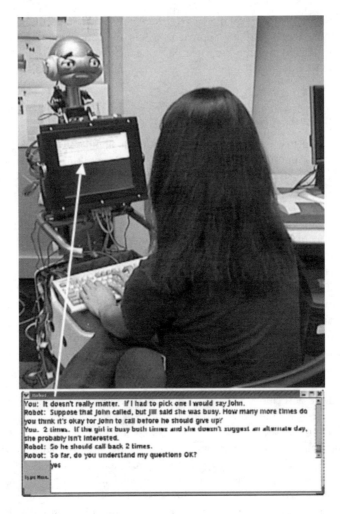

FIGURE 6.1 Interacting with a talking robot about dating. (Adapted from Powers et al., 2005.)

messages depending on the robot's gender (and the stereotypes that go with it), as well as their own similarity to the robot (Figure 6.1 and Figure 6.2).

Do Listeners Benefit From a Perspective-Taking Robot?

The previous work provided some evidence that speakers were considering the robot's perspective and adjusting their messages accordingly. In subsequent research, we considered whether there were advantages to having robots take their listeners' perspectives and adjust messages to listeners' expertise (Torrey, Powers, Marge, Fussell, & Kiesler, 2006). In human–human communication, messages designed specifically for a listener are understood more easily than messages created for

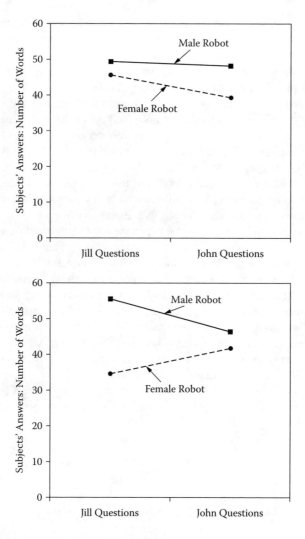

FIGURE 6.2 Number of words participants used in answering a male or female robot's questions about a woman (Jill) or a man (John) in a dating scenario. (From Powers et al., 2005.)

someone else or a generic listener (Fussell & Krauss, 1989; Krauss et al., 1968; Kraut et al., 1982; Schober & Clark, 1989). In this study, we explored the benefits and consequences of adaptive communication on conversational efficiency, and we used a postconversation questionnaire to investigate listeners' perceptions of the robot, the task, and the conversation. We were particularly interested in the extent to which appropriate perspective-taking behavior improved social relations with the robot. Prior research on the maintenance of "face" in conversation suggests that speakers may insult their listeners by ignoring their needs (e.g., Goffman, 1955;

Holtgraves, 2002), but we are not aware of any empirical communication research that has tested the impact of the appropriateness of a speaker's perspective-taking communication on the listener's impressions.

We asked participants in a laboratory study to find and select ten cooking tools from sets of pictures on a computer monitor. A robot directed them to find each tool in turn and responded to any questions participants had about the tool, its size, for example, or its shape. Participants who signed up for the study were pre-tested for cooking expertise by completing a short quiz on cooking methods. We used their knowledge of cooking methods to inform the robot's behavior because pre-testing showed that this knowledge is highly correlated with people's knowledge of cooking tools. Thus, the robot could use the information that the participant knew how to sauté, for example, to infer that the participant also had some knowledge about whisks and silicone spatulas. We selected participants so that half were "experts," meaning they got a perfect score on the pre-test, and half were "novices," meaning they scored less than 50% correct on the pre-test. These participants interacted either with a robot whose perspective-taking communication was designed for experts ("Now, we need a paring knife") or a robot whose perspective-taking communication was designed for novices ("Now, we need a paring knife. It is usually the smallest knife in the set. It has a short, pointed blade that is smooth, not jagged."). Participants were told they could ask the robot for help. We measured the number of questions participants asked the robot, their task performance, and used questionnaire measures to investigate participants' perceptions of the robot, the task, and their communication with the robot (Figure 6.3).

Our results showed that novice users were affected disproportionately by a lack of information in the robot's directions. When the robot introduced the tool

FIGURE 6.3   Our robot as a cooking assistant, programmed with knowledge of cooking tools. (From Torrey et al., 2006.)

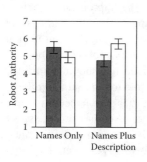 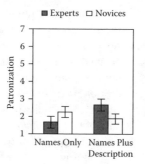 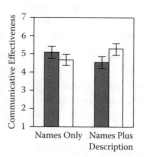

FIGURE 6.4 Experts and novices evaluate the robot more positively when the dialogue is adaptive to their information needs. (From Torrey et al., 2006.)

by its proper name alone, novices asked twice as many clarifying questions as did experts. These questions extended the amount of time novices spent completing the task, but surprisingly it did not influence any of the questionnaire measures. The extra time novices spent on the task and experts' unneeded interaction with the robot did not negatively affect their perception of the robot as a conversational partner, as we had supposed it might. We surmised that participants did not care if their task performance was inefficient, and that participants might have even enjoyed conversing with the robot. Therefore, in a follow-up experiment, we offered a small monetary bonus to participants if they managed to complete the task quickly. When participants were particularly motivated to work quickly, the robot offering unnecessary descriptions was rated as less effective, less authoritative, and more patronizing. Expert participants found the robot to be more effective, more authoritative, and less patronizing when the robot used only names of tools as a guide rather than extra descriptions. These experiments suggest that while all participants benefited from an appropriate level of detail in the robot's communication, it was only participants with a particular demand on their time who evaluated the robot negatively if it did not have good perspective-taking abilities (Figure 6.4).

BUILDING A PERSPECTIVE-TAKING ROBOT

Our results suggest that people assume a robot has a perspective, and they adjust for it. Participants in the cooking tool study, however, did not seem to have a strong expectation that the robot should adjust to their perspective, even though they performed better when their level of expertise was accommodated. The idea of "least collaborative effort" has been proposed to describe the joint endeavor that human speakers engage in when they communicate (Clark & Wilkes-Gibbs, 1986). Although effort expended in a conversation need not be distributed perfectly, we generally assume that both parties in a conversation share the effort to create joint meaning. In a conversation between peers, both parties are making adjustments to communicate effectively, efficiently, and respectfully. When people and robots communicate, the appropriate distribution of effort is not as clear. One could argue that humans, being more flexible than computers, should bear responsibility for adjusting their communication to be understood. On the other hand, one could argue that robots are built to assist in the achievement of human goals, and their design should minimize human effort. Under this assumption, if robots were able to read human minds, so much the better. Our previous work demonstrates that people seem to have an automatic tendency to take the robot's perspective, and yet they do not expect perspective taking from a robot in a reciprocal way. Based on our participants' improved performance when the robot was using a form of perspective taking, we believe it may be worth the effort to develop perspective-taking strategies that can be used by robots. This is particularly true when robots are providing instruction, directions, or other types of information and may interact with people of varying levels of expertise.

But how can perspective-taking strategies be practically implemented on a robot? One possibility is a user modeling approach. By user modeling, we mean that the robot has a model, or knowledge, of an individual's expertise or attitude. This approach requires that the robot have probabilistic knowledge of how expertise is distributed in the population. Then, when interacting with an individual, the robot, based on initial information, could make assumptions about the listener's position in the distribution and what the listener is likely to know. The pre-test we used in the cooking tools experiment is a crude example of this approach. By pre-testing participants, the robot gathered information about an individual's level of expertise; the robot could then use these assumptions to plan its communication about further tools.

However, extensive planning of utterances to address listeners' perspectives may not be necessary. An alternative (or supplementary) approach involves the robot offering a small amount of information, for example, the proper name of a tool, and then watching carefully for signals that the name is accepted by the listener. For instance, the listener may provide a backchannel utterance like "mm-hmm" or "uh-huh" that signals acceptance. The robot might also attend to task activity, so that if the listener's expected action was not taken in a timely manner, the robot could automatically initiate a repair. These two approaches are by no means the only ways of building perspective-taking abilities into a robot, nor are the two approaches mutually exclusive. There is no reason why a robot might not use both approaches simultaneously. In the sections that follow, we discuss how these two approaches to perspective taking might be developed on a conversational robot.

Adjusting a Probabilistic Model

In our previous experiment with a cooking tool selection task, we inferred our participants' knowledge of cooking tools by quizzing them about several cooking methods. By gauging their knowledge of cooking methods, we could infer their likely expertise on cooking tools. People who know how to poach an egg are also likely to know the names of quite a number of cooking tools. This general approach could be expanded into a more complete user model for use by a robot, specific to the cooking domain. When a person demonstrated knowledge of the word "poach" while conversing with the robot, the robot would calculate the likelihood that the person has other cooking knowledge based on the distribution of such knowledge in the population. In that case, the robot could be confident that the person also knew how to sauté, for example, and it would not need to elaborate on such a direction. A user model, as just described, would require a model of how domain knowledge is distributed in the population, most likely obtained through surveys. This distribution would need to be created for different domains and for different groups of people with whom the robot might interact.

To be feasible, this general approach would require the specification of numerous details. With what sort of model does the robot begin? Is there an efficient order when introducing information, such that the robot models the listener in the quickest possible way? Does the robot adjust its user model based on performance cues only? On the other hand, should the robot also adjust based on affective cues such as a frustrated inflection in the listeners' voice? What are the specific features that make the robot's communication appropriate for listeners at different levels of expertise? There are no specific guidelines from which we can draw theories of human–human communication, but future work with robots offers a unique opportunity to investigate the application of these research questions. With robots, questions about perspective taking can be investigated in controlled ways where the robot interacts in precisely the same way with each participant.

REACTING TO GROUNDING CUES

Even when they have little knowledge of others, speakers can adjust to the requirements of their listeners by paying close attention to the effect of their communication (Clark & Wilkes-Gibbs, 1986). Rather than expending effort up front in constructing the precisely appropriate utterance for a listener, a speaker may make a reasonable attempt. Speakers need not wait for the listener to make explicit requests to make a repair; in fact, they seem to prefer to initiate the repair themselves (Sacks, Schegloff, & Jefferson, 1974). Speakers might use numerous cues to confirm that their utterance is accepted or as evidence that a repair is necessary. Speakers attend to their listeners' verbal responses, including backchannel communications or lack thereof. If a listener uses an "uh-uh" or "ok" to confirm each step of a direction, when that backchannel communication is absent, the speaker may attempt a repair (Gergle, Kraut, & Fussell, 2004b). If the speaker can see the listener's activities, the speaker can watch to see if the listener makes the expected movements and repair if those movements are not made (Brennan, 2004; Gergle et al., 2004b). By attending to these verbal and nonverbal communicative elements, speakers can initiate repairs before listeners have to ask questions or make explicit requests for a repair.

We attempted this approach to perspective-taking behavior in another experiment using the cooking tool selection task explained previously. We implemented two ways the robot could have awareness of the listeners' activity, that is, through gaze awareness and task activity awareness. The manipulation of gaze awareness we used in this experiment made use of an eye contact sensor that could roughly indicate whether the participant was looking at the computer monitor on which the task was displayed. Our model of gaze behavior followed an empirical model proposed by Nakano, Reinstein, Stocky, and Cassell (2003). In their study, Nakano et al. observed that speakers attended to their listeners' gaze when a new referent was introduced. If the listener's gaze moved to the referred object, then that object was grounded in the conversation. However, if the listener continued to gaze at the speaker, the speaker understood that elaboration was required. In the context of the cooking tool selection task, the robot assumed participants were working on the task and needed no help when they were looking at the monitor that displayed the pictures of the cooking tools. When participants were not looking at the monitor, the robot assumed they were looking back at the robot to ask a question or to re-read the directions written on the screen. When the robot became aware that the participant was not attending to the monitor, the robot offered an additional unit of information to help the participant make his or her selection. For example, the robot asked the participant to select the paring knife, and if the participant looked back at the robot without selecting a tool the robot said, "The blade is smooth, not jagged." In addition to gaze awareness, we also manipulated task activity awareness. From pre-testing, we knew that participants who knew the correct cooking tool could find and select it within 4 sec. We therefore gave the robot a simple timer, set to 4 sec, such that if, after being directed to choose a tool, the participant had not made a selection in that amount of time, the robot offered an additional unit of information. This approach assumes that when participants have not made a selection in a given time period, they do not recognize the name of the tool and require further elaboration (Figure 6.5).

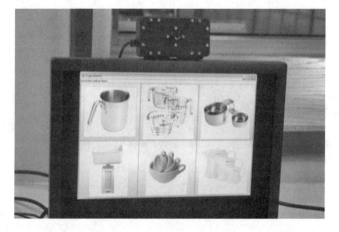

FIGURE 6.5   A small eye contact sensor was mounted on top of the monitor where the cooking tools are displayed to detect whether the participant is looking in the direction of the monitor. (From Torrey et al., 2007.)

We explored these two types of awareness in preliminary experimental treatments that contrasted a robot's use of gaze awareness, both gaze and task activity awareness, and neither form of awareness (Torrey, Powers, Fussell, & Kiesler, 2007). Participants interacting with a robot with both forms of awareness asked fewer questions than did participants interacting with a robot with neither form of awareness. However, these awareness strategies did not improve participants' task accuracy or their time on the task. Participants made the same number of mistakes regardless. Clearly, a robot's simply having a perspective-taking strategy is insufficient to improve shared meaning. One question, in particular, is whether the specific help given by the robot to participants was appropriate to their needs. The robot had a list of additional information, to be given out one piece at a time, but these elaborations were not associated with the mistake the participant had made previously or, for example, where on the screen the participant's mouse had been hovering. It may not be enough to consider only that the listener is not taking action and needs more information. An important aspect of a truly intelligent, perspective-taking robot would be the ability to choose the specific kind of help that is necessary for each individual at a particular point in time. (Recall your experiences with an automated telephone help system. The most sophisticated of these can understand that you need more help but they frequently offer the wrong kind of help.) A perspective-taking robot may need to account for not only when a listener needs help, but also what specific bit of information the listener needs, and further, how that information should be phrased.

CONCLUSION

Our research on perspective taking in human-robot interaction shows many similarities between this process and perspective taking in interpersonal communication. People make assumptions about what robot partners know, based on their attributes, and these assumptions guide how they formulate their messages. People are also sensitive to how well their robotic partner considers their own perspective. Overall, the field of human-robot interaction has benefited from the vast body of prior research on human perspective taking.

While attempting to develop a perspective-taking robot from existing theory, however, we have encountered a number of aspects of perspective taking that are underspecified in our current theories of human perspective-taking behavior. What are the cues a robot might best use to make assumptions about a listener's perspective? Group membership and its related expertise have interesting effects on the way speakers produce messages. However, how do speakers recognize expertise by virtue of group membership in their listeners? Is speakers' recognition of expertise an all-or-nothing decision (in the way we have implemented it)? Given the speed and naturalness of conversation, it seems likely that many interactions begin that way. In addition, once the speaker has decided upon the listener's expertise, how, precisely, does he or she provide the requisite level of detail in a message? Should cooking tools, for example, be described for less knowledgeable listeners in terms of shape, size, color, usage, or other features?

How much information should be provided in each utterance, before pausing for feedback from the addressee?

Despite the challenges in developing perspective-taking behavior at the level of detail required by a computer program, the use of a conversational robot in testing these decisions is a unique opportunity. When we investigate these issues with a conversational robot, the robot's behavior can be strictly controlled. For example, it is possible to create a robot that provides specific types of information to addressees, or does not follow conventions of eye gaze, interruption, elaboration, and repair. It is an interesting opportunity to test features of communication that humans are not likely to do on command in the laboratory, such as ignore the listeners' perspective. We know that errors in perspective taking do occur, and clever techniques using confederate speakers have been developed to study such errors on the addressees' side (e.g., Keysar, Barr, Balin, & Brauner, 2000). With robotic speakers, we can more thoroughly investigate the communicative and affective consequences of various kinds of perspective-taking strategies and errors, thereby contributing to our theoretical understanding of the mechanisms of the perspective-taking process.

The consequences of inadequate or inaccurate perspective-taking assumptions are important to consider, both practically and theoretically. For the near future, robots are unlikely to be perfect conversational partners, and it is important to understand how poor perspective-taking abilities might affect human performance and impressions of robots. Affective reactions to poor perspective taking are particularly intriguing and understudied in prior human communication literature. For example, what degree of error (e.g., talking to a full professor as if he or she were an undergraduate vs. an assistant professor), and how many errors are necessary before the listener reacts emotionally, for example, by feeling insulted, disliking the speaker, or getting angry? With robot speakers, we can investigate these issues by manipulating communication while keeping the speakers' other characteristics carefully controlled.

In conclusion, we have attempted to show how the fields of human communication and human-robot interaction can shape and inform one another in such a way that both fields are advanced. The human research on perspective taking has fostered productive research on how we should design humanoid robots to converse in social settings; at the same time, the research on robot perspective taking has generated important questions for basic theory and, in addition, offers special opportunities for answering these questions.

ACKNOWLEDGMENTS

The authors are grateful for assistance provided by our many collaborators over the years: Sau-lai Lee, Ivy Yee-man Lau, Chi-Yue Chiu, Aaron Powers, Adam Kramer, Shirlene Lim, Jean Kuo, Matthew Marge, Hau-Yu Wong, and the members of the Project on People and Robots. This research was supported by National Science Foundation ITR #IIS-0121426, HSD #IIS-0624275, and IGERT #DGE-0333420.

REFERENCES

Brennan, S. E. (2004). How conversation is shaped by visual and spoken evidence. In J. Trueswell & M. Tanenhaus (Eds.), World situated language use: Psycholinguistic, linguistic and computational perspectives on bridging the product and action traditions. Cambridge, MA: The MIT Press.

Clark. H. H., & Marshall, C. E. (1981). Definite reference and mutual knowledge. In A. K. Joshi, B. L. Webber, & I. A. Sag (Eds.), *Elements of discourse understanding* (pp. 10–63). Cambridge, England: Cambridge University Press.

Clark, H. H., & Wilkes-Gibbs, D. (1986). Referring as a collaborative process. *Cognition, 22*, 1–39.

Fussell, S. R., & Krauss, R. M. (1989). Understanding friends and strangers: The effects of audience design on message comprehension. *European Journal of Social Psychology, 21*, 445–454.

Fussell, S. R., & Krauss, R. M. (1991). Accuracy and bias in estimates of others' knowledge. *European Journal of Social Psychology, 21*, 445–454.

Fussell, S. R., & Krauss, R. M. (1992). Coordination of knowledge in communication: Effects of speakers' assumptions about what others know. *Journal of Personality and Social Psychology, 62*, 378–391.

Gergle, D., Kraut, R. E., & Fussell, S. R. (2004a). Language efficiency and visual technology: Minimizing collaborative effort with visual information. *Journal of Language and Social Psychology, 23,* 491–517.

Gergle, D., Kraut, R. E., & Fussell, S. R. (2004b). Action as language in a shared visual space. *Proceedings of the Annual Conference on Computer-Supported Cooperative Work (CSCW 2004)* (pp. 487–496). New York: ACM Press.

Goffman, E. (1955). On face-work: An analysis of ritual elements in social interaction. *Psychiatry, 19*, 213–231.

Holtgraves, T. (2002) Face management and politeness. In T. Holtgraves (Ed.), *Language as social action: Social psychology and language* (pp. 37–63). Mahwah, NJ: Lawrence Erlbaum Associates.

Hupet, M., Chantraine, Y., & Neff, F. (1993). References in conversation between young and old normal adults. *Psychology and Aging, 8,* 339–346.

Isaacs, E. A., & Clark, H. H. (1987). References in conversation between experts and novices. *Journal of Experimental Psychology: General, 116*, 26–37.

Keysar, B., Barr, D. J., Balin, J. A., & Brauner, J. S. (2000). Taking perspective in conversation: The role of mutual knowledge in comprehension. *Psychological Science, 11,* 32–38.

Krauss, R. M., & Bricker, P. D. (1966). Effects of transmission delay and access delay on the efficiency of verbal communication. *Journal of the Acoustical Society of America, 41*, 286–292.

Krauss, R. M., & Fussell, S. R. (1991). Perspective-taking in communication: Representations of others' knowledge in reference. *Social Cognition, 9*, 2–24.

Krauss, R. M., Vivekananthan, P. S., & Weinheimer, S., (1968). "Inner speech" and "external speech": Characteristics and communication effectiveness of socially and nonsocially encoded messages. *Journal of Personality and Social Psychology, 9*, 295–300.

Krauss, R. M., & Weinheimer, S. (1964). Changes in the length of reference phrases as a function of social interaction: A preliminary study. *Psychonomic Science, 1,* 113–114.

Krauss, R. M., & Weinheimer, S. (1966). Concurrent feedback, confirmation and the encoding of referents in verbal communication. *Journal of Personality and Social Psychology, 4,* 343–346.

Kraut, R. E., Lewis, S. H., & Swezey, L. (1982). Listener responsiveness and the coordination of conversation. *Journal of Personality and Social Psychology, 43,* 718–731.

Kraut, R. E., Miller, M. D., & Siegel, J. (1996). Collaboration in performance of physical tasks: Effects on outcomes and communication. *Proceedings of CSCW'96* (pp. 57–66). New York: ACM Press.

Lee, S., Kiesler, S., Lau, I. Y., & Chiu, C. (2005). Human mental models of humanoid robots. *Proceedings of the 2005 IEEE International Conference on Robotics and Automation (ICRA '05).* Barcelona, April 18–22, 2767–2772.

Lockridge, C. B., & Brennan, S. E. (2002). Addressees' needs influence speakers' early syntactic choices. *Psychonomic Bulletin and Review, 9,* 550–557.

Nakano, Y., Reinstein, G., Stocky, T., & Cassell, J. (2003). Towards a model of face-to-face grounding. *Proceedings of the Annual Meeting of the Association for Computational Linguistics.* July 7–12, Sapporo, Japan, 553–561.

Nass, C., & Lee, K. M. (2001). Does computer-synthesized speech manifest personality? Experimental tests of recognition, similarity-attraction, and consistency-attraction. *Journal of Experimental Psychology: Applied, 7,* 171–181.

Nickerson, R. S. (1999). How we know—and sometimes misjudge—what others know: Imputing one's own knowledge to others. *Psychological Bulletin, 125,* 737–759.

Powers, A., & Kiesler, S. (2006). The advisor robot: Tracing people's mental model from a robot's physical attributes. *Conference on Human-Robot Interaction 2006.* Salt Lake City, UT, March 1–3, 218–225.

Powers, A., Kramer, A., Lim, S., Kuo, J., Lee, S., & Kiesler, S. (2005). Eliciting information from people with a gendered humanoid robot. *Proceedings of the 2005 IEEE International Workshop on Robots and Human Interative Communication (RO-MAN 05).* Nashville, TN, Aug. 2005, 158–163.

Sacks, H., Schegloff, E., & Jefferson, G. (1974). A simplest systematics for the organization of turn-taking for conversation. *Language, 50*(4), 696–735.

Scassellati, B. (2004). Theory of mind for a humanoid robot. *Autonomous Robots, 12,* 13–24.

Schober, M. F. (1993). Spatial perspective-taking in conversation. *Cognition, 47,* 1–24.

Schober, M. F., & Brennan, S. E. (2003). Processes of interactive spoken discourse: The role of the partner. In A. Graesser, M. Gernsbacher, & S. Goldman (Eds.), *The handbook of discourse processes* (pp. 123–164). Mahwah, NJ: Lawrence Erlbaum Associates.

Schober, M. F., & Clark, H. H. (1989). Understanding by addressees and overhearers. *Cognitive Psychology, 21,* 211–232.

Torrey, C., Powers, A., Fussell, S. R., & Kiesler, S. (2007). Exploring adaptive dialogue based on a robot's awareness of human gaze and task progress. *Proceedings of the Conference on Human Robot Interaction* (HRI '07). New York: ACM Press.

Torrey, C., Powers, A., Marge, M., Fussell, S. R., & Kiesler, S. (2006). Effects of adaptive robot dialogue on information exchange and social relations. *Proceedings of the Conference on Human Robot Interaction* (HRI '06). New York: ACM Press.

7 Does Being Together for Years Help Comprehension?

Michael F. Schober and Laura L. Carstensen

People in long-term relationships are said to be able to communicate volumes with a single word or glance because they can rely on shared knowledge and experiences. Does this shared background also improve communication about unfamiliar things? In an experiment, 96 people (old, middle-aged, and young, matched for education) conversed with their spouses or with opposite-sex strangers to match unfamiliar geometric shapes and photographs of unfamiliar children. People were less accurate, less confident, less efficient, and less likely to entrain (use the same descriptions) with their partners for the unfamiliar shapes than for the photographs of children. Older pairs were almost as accurate as younger pairs, but they were less efficient and less likely to entrain. Although married couples were more confident that they had understood each other, there was little evidence that they were more accurate, efficient, or likely to entrain than were the strangers. In this chapter, we discuss how this suggests that people in long-term relationships may not learn much about each other's communicative habits beyond the content of their shared experiences.

INTRODUCTION

Conversations between people who know each other are different from conversations between strangers. Intimates can use terms that other people cannot understand (Clark & Schaefer, 1987; Fleming & Darley, 1991) by referring to experiences or events they alone have shared. They use what has been called an "implicit" style (Hornstein, 1985), seeming to communicate volumes with one small phrase or utterance. They ask each other fewer questions (Kent, Davis, & Shapiro, 1981), they use abbreviated expressions and ellipses, and they shift topics rapidly without explicit transitions (Hornstein, 1985).

How can they do this? Part of the answer is in what has been called their *common ground* (Clark & Marshall, 1981): the knowledge, beliefs, and assumptions that two parties share (and believe that they share). People can take as their common ground what they perceive and experience together (physical co-presence), what they talk about together (linguistic co-presence), and what they can infer is common knowledge within the various communities they know they belong to (community co-membership) (Clark & Carlson, 1981). It is presumably because friends share substantial common ground that they refer to mutually known people and events, and to each other's lives, more often than strangers do (Planalp, 1993). Common ground explains how friends can make references that only the two of them understand, and that deceive or mislead overhearers and conversational bystanders (Clark & Schaefer, 1987; Fleming & Darley, 1991).

Much remains unknown about the individual and interactive processes involved in common ground, although there has been substantial theorizing and argumentation (for reviews, see Krauss & Fussell, 1996; Pickering & Garrod, 2004; Schober & Brennan, 2003). Issues under dispute include the precise nature of the mental representations involved and how they connect with other kinds of memory (e.g., Horton & Gerrig, 2005), the degree to which interlocutors' representations are as aligned as they appear (e.g., Schober, 2005), what affects partner adaptation and its time course (e.g., Keysar, Barr, & Horton, 1998; Metzing & Brennan, 2003), and what aspects of language use are affected (e.g., Schober & Brennan, 2003). For purposes of experimental rigor, controlled studies have, most often focused on how strangers build common ground. This means we end up knowing notably less about the long-term common ground that builds over years of knowing an interlocutor: how fine-grained and detailed it is and how it affects speaking style and conversation.

Clearly long-term conversational partners share a great deal of declarative knowledge, and so it makes sense that they will talk differently about things they both know about than they would about those topics with strangers. In addition, one might hypothesize, long-term conversational partners may have other resources that strangers don't. They may come to know their partner's *linguistic* habits—which syntactic forms or wordings the partner is liable to use, or whether the partner is verbose or concise. They may also come to know about each other's *interactive* habits—what kinds of evidence of understanding they are liable to give each other. This could include (tacit or explicit) knowledge of how attentive the partner is, whether the partner prefers to complete utterances or to be interrupted the moment he or she is understood, and whether the partner's *uh-huh*s tend to be signs of understanding or requests for more information.

If long-term experience with a conversational partner brings this kind of knowledge, then long-term conversational partners should understand each other better than comparable strangers do even when talking about something that is not part of their previously shared experiences and perceptions. In the study we describe here (see also Bortfeld, Leon, Bloom, Schober, & Brennan, 2001, for other analyses of the data set), we compared long-term partners' and strangers' accuracy and efficiency of understanding in task-oriented conversations about novel stimuli on which none of them shared experience. If the long-term partners understand each other better than the strangers do, this would suggest that they have knowledge about each other's interactive habits beyond the content of their shared experiences.

In the study, we focused on one kind of long-term conversational partner: married couples. For many adults, the marital relationship represents the most enduring intimate relationship in life; and indeed research on long-term marriage paints a positive picture of the developmental course of these relationships in later life. Marital satisfaction, studied longitudinally, increases after retirement (Guilford & Bengtson, 1979). Older couples report fewer conflicts and less severe conflicts than middle-aged and younger couples do (Levenson, Carstensen, & Gottman, 1993). Moreover, observational research examining couples while they resolve emotionally charged conflicts reveals that older couples express less negative emotion and more positive emotion to one another when they converse about these "hot" topics (Carstensen, Gottman, & Levenson, 1995).

Of course, marital conflicts and everyday conversation between spouses centers around issues that are well rehearsed, perhaps even scripted. Thus, these studies tell us little about the facility with which older couples deal with new material. When conversing about new topics, knowledge of the communicative habits of one's partner may improve understanding or attunement, but it could just as easily hinder understanding. Levenson et al. (1993), for example, found that older couples ranked "communication" at the top of a list of potential conflicts (even though the mean rating of conflict severity was lower than for middle-aged couples). It is possible that people who know each other well will avoid topics, phrasings, or references they know could cause offense, causing them to speak more circuitously or cautiously, and less effectively. They might extend discussion beyond what is essential for understanding or slip into unprofitable conversational routines or off-the-topic arguments.

Another issue the current study addresses is whether the length of time that partners have been together influences understanding. We compared understanding in married couples who had been together for three different lengths of time: only a few years, about 25 years, and over 40 years. The different groups were also of different ages because of the relative scarcity (and nonrepresentativeness) of recently married older people who matched other selection criteria. This means that in this study, age was perfectly confounded with length of relationship, and any differences among the three groups could be explained by age, cohort, or length of relationship. To help distinguish between relationship length and age/cohort, we compared interactions between spouses to interactions with age-matched strangers. To further ensure comparability, strangers were also married people, speaking with partners who were not their spouses. Thus, any differences across the three groups that are the same for married couples, and strangers can reasonably be attributed to age or cohort as opposed to relationship length.

Previous Research

Relationship and Conversational Reference

Little previous research has directly addressed whether knowledge of communicative habits affects understanding, because in most studies of intimates the conversation is about topics on which they already share some common ground. Thus, the observed differences in intimates' and strangers' conversations could result entirely from the content-based knowledge they share, rather than from any additional knowledge of each other's linguistic and conversational habits. However, two laboratory studies come closer to addressing the issue. One study (Fussell & Krauss, 1989) examined how friends wrote descriptions for each other of abstract line drawings about which they did not share previous common ground. Friends understood each other's written descriptions of abstract line drawings a bit better than strangers did, but the differences were small. Contrary to Fussell and Krauss's expectations, friends' messages did not differ from the strangers' in length or on any of their other measures. The reported closeness of the friendships, number of shared interests, similarity of backgrounds, and length of acquaintance did not predict friends' accuracy of understanding.

The lack of strong findings in the study is hard to interpret. First, subjects wrote the descriptions rather than interacted conversationally, and so the friends might not have been able to use metaconversational knowledge about each other that could have made differences between friends and strangers larger. Second, the subjects did not know each other well; most had known each other less than six months, and a few did not even know their partners' last names. Perhaps developing the metacommunicative knowledge that might show an advantage in understanding for intimates does not develop in brief acquaintanceships.

Another study (Boyle, Anderson, & Newlands, 1994) compared conversational descriptions of locations on unfamiliar maps by friends and strangers. Friends, who had known each other for two years on average, performed marginally better on the task than strangers did. Their conversations differed in some ways: unlike in the Fussell and Krauss (1989) study, friends took *more* words and turns, but they interrupted each other marginally less often than strangers did and had less overlapping speech. These results give a mixed picture. The task performance results marginally support the notion that experience with a partner brings advantages to understanding beyond those brought by discussing topics that are part of common ground, but the word counts suggest that friends are *less* efficient than strangers, perhaps because they have other (social) goals beyond efficient task performance. Because length of acquaintance was not factored in, it is unclear whether the effects were stronger among friends who knew each other better.

Age and Conversational Reference

On conversational tasks, older adults are known to perform differently than young adults in laboratory settings; in one study (Gould, Trevithick, & Dixon, 1991), for example, old adults engaged in non-task-relevant discussion notably more than young adults did. By some accounts, linguistic capabilities and performance decline with age (e.g., Emery, 1986; Kemper, 1988). Older adults, for example, may be less able to adjust their utterances for different partners (Horton & Spieler, 2007). However, by other accounts the changes, if any, are small and subtle (Salthouse, 1991). In general, the many studies on language performance in aging vary so much in their methodologies and their corresponding results that it is hard to predict exactly what sorts of age-related changes might come into play in the conversational setting in which we are interested.

One exception is Hupet, Chantraine, and Nef's (1993) directly relevant comparison of how young and old pairs of strangers referred to unfamiliar figures in task-oriented laboratory conversations. In this study, old pairs (mean age 70 years) spoke differently than the young pairs (mean age 24 years) did. Not only did the old pairs use more words and turns per reference, but also their language was more complicated. It had greater lexical variety, longer utterances, more relative clauses, more right-branching clauses, and greater mean length of subordinate clauses (for related results, see Gould & Dixon, 1993; Horton & Spieler, 2007; Kogan & Jordan, 1989). Old pairs were less likely to consider previously shared information. In describing stimuli that their partners had already described, partners in old pairs used the same term as their partners had only 28% of the time, while the young speakers used the same terms 55% of the time. Old pairs were also less likely than young pairs to use definite references like "the little man kneeling down," which assume prior shared knowledge, and they were more likely to use indefinite ("a little man kneeling down") and completely new descriptions of already-described stimuli. Based on their pretesting of their participants, Hupet et al. (1993) ruled out that these differences resulted from working-memory capacity differences or specifically linguistic deficits in aging; rather, they suggest, old people either are more likely to forget what their partners said before (a memory capacity hypothesis), or they may have stored irrelevant information and private thoughts along with what their partners said before because of inefficient inhibitory mechanisms (a memory content hypothesis).

The current study extends the Hupet et al. (1993) study in two ways. First, we examined married couples of three different age ranges rather than two (we include middle-aged couples). Thus, we could determine whether Hupet et al.'s age-related changes in referring are linear over the life span. Second, we manipulated the novel topics under discussion. In the Hupet et al. study, participants described unfamiliar abstract geometric shapes (following Krauss & Weinheimer, 1966), and the old participants were relatively poor at using the same terms their partners used. This may be because speakers do not already have words for abstract shapes, or perhaps such figures are unusually hard to process or remember. We suspect that speakers may be better at using shared descriptions if the unfamiliar topic is more similar to things about which they ordinarily talk. Therefore, in the current study participants described not only abstract shapes but also photographs of unfamiliar children. This should tap into the more common and concrete pastime of discussing other people's appearances and identities and might allow participants to refer to shared declarative knowledge.

METHOD

Participants. Ninety-six married college-graduate adults (48 mixed-sex pairs) participated in the study for $25.00 payment. Sixteen pairs were young adults (mean age of 28.8 years, SD 2.2 years, ranging from 24 to 33) who had been married for a mean of 3.75 years (SD 1.7 years). Sixteen were middle in age (mean age 47.9 years, SD 3.4 years, ranging from 42 to 56), married for a mean of 25.2 years (SD 3.1 years). Sixteen were old (mean age 67.1 years, SD 2.7 years, ranging from 63 to 72), married for a mean of 42.6 years (SD 2.8 years). All were native speakers of American English. To maximize comparability across the age groups, all pairs were contacted through the Stanford Alumni Association, so at least one member of each pair was a Stanford University graduate; all non-Stanford alumni were graduates of Bay Area colleges. The sample was highly educated; the groups did not differ in years of post-high-school education, averaging 5.38 (young), 6.13 (middle), and 5.38 (old) years. People with notable hearing loss were disqualified.

So that we could further assess comparability across the age groups, participants completed several tasks in the laboratory in addition to the experimental task. Cognitive abilities were assessed using a test of verbal fluency (animal naming), as well as the Digit Symbol subtest of the Wechsler Adult Intelligence Scale-Revised (1981). In addition, health status was screened using the Wahler Health Symptoms Inventory (1983), which surveys the type and frequency of physical complaints people experience in everyday life. Participants in all age groups did not differ in the number of animals generated, $F(2, 93) = 0.10$, n.s., nor in physical health symptoms, $F(2, 93) = 0.35$, n.s. The usual age difference in digit symbol performance (Lindenberger, Mayr, & Baltes, 1993) was observed; old adults completed reliably fewer digit substitutions (52.7) than middle-aged adults (64.6), who completed reliably fewer than young adults (71.0), linear trend $F(1, 95) = 57.73$, $p < .0001$. However, aside from this (expectable) difference, the age groups were reasonably well-matched, although, no doubt, all subsamples were positively biased relative to the population in terms of education, physical health, and verbal fluency.

Ratings of marital satisfaction differed across groups; middle-aged partners rated themselves as reliably less satisfied with their marriages than the young couples ($F(1, 95) = 5.50$, $p < .03$) and the old couples ($F(1, 95) = 8.99$, $p < .005$). This finding is consistent with the larger literature on marital quality: middle age is the period characterized by lowest levels of marital satisfaction (Carstensen, Graff, Levenson, & Gottman, 1996). Young couples rated their marriages as reliably less traditional than the middle-aged couples, who rated their marriages as less traditional than the old couples, linear trend $F(1, 95) = 19.97$, $p < .0001$. However, the different age groups did not differ in their ratings of how egalitarian their marriages were.

Stimuli. One set of stimuli consisted of sixteen abstract geometric figures, originally from or modified from the Chinese game of Tangram (Elffers, 1976), taken from Schober and Clark's (1989) study of referring (see Figure 7.1). These figures are similar to those used as stimuli in Hupet et al. (1993). A second set of stimuli comprised sixteen black-and-white photographs of children, taken at a private school in Mexico (see Figure 7.2 for examples).

Procedure. Ninety-six participants performed a matching task in mixed-sex pairs, either with their spouse (24 pairs) or with a married stranger of the same

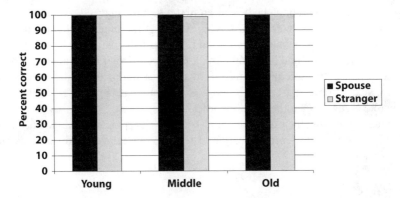

FIGURE 7.1 Accuracy on matching task for photographs of children (both rounds).

age group (24 pairs). Two married couples who had not met each other were brought into the lab at the same time. Participants performed the matching task either with their spouse or with the opposite-sex partner from the other couple. The task was audio- and videotaped, for subsequent transcription and coding.

In the task, one person, the *director*, viewed an array of 12 figures (or photos) selected from the full set of 16 (this was so that participants could not use a process of elimination to perform the task). The partner, designated the *matcher*, on the other side of a visual barrier, saw the full set of 16 figures (or photos) in no particular order. The director's task was to get the matcher to arrange the figures in the same order as in the director's array. The director and matcher could say anything they liked to each other to complete the task, so long as they matched the figures in sequential order following the director's array.

Each pair performed the matching task four times. In two rounds, they matched the photographs of children, and in two rounds they matched Tangram

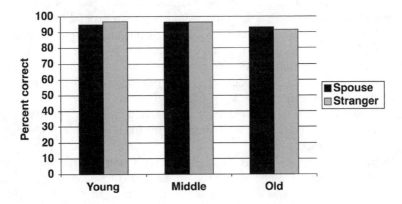

FIGURE 7.2 Accuracy on matching task for Tangram figures (both rounds).

figures; half the pairs matched children first and half matched Tangram figures first. Partners always switched task roles after the first round, so that the director in Round 1 became the matcher in Round 2. In half the pairs, the female partner was the first director and in the other half, the male partner was the first director. In each round, the director's stimuli were arranged in one of six different preselected random orders; after the round was over, an experimenter rearranged the director's figures in another random order.

After completing the experimental task in pairs, participants individually completed the set of tests described earlier. They also rated the experimental task for its difficulty.

RESULTS

We focus on four main measures of understanding, compiled from videotapes of the matcher's hand movements and from transcriptions of the audiotaped conversations: (1) accuracy at the matching task, (2) confidence of understanding, (3) efficiency of communication, and (4) the likelihood that partners used the same terms to describe the same figures. This last measure has been called *entrainment* (Brennan & Clark, 1996; Garrod & Anderson, 1987).

Accuracy. All pairs were highly accurate at the matching task. By the time they had completed the task, accuracy was virtually perfect for the photographs of children (see Figure 7.1). Accuracy was also extremely high for the Tangram figures, although it was reliably poorer than for the photos, $F(1, 42) = 20.54$, $p < .001$ (see Figure 7.2). As the figures show, married couples were just as accurate as strangers were, $F(1, 42) = 0.00$, n.s., and pairs of all age groups were equally accurate, $F(2, 42) = 1.78$, n.s. This was true for both sets of stimuli, interaction of marital status × stimulus type, $F(1, 42) = 0.00$, n.s.; interaction of age × stimulus type, $F(2, 42) = 1.61$, n.s.

A more stringent test of accuracy of understanding is the extent to which participants made any matching errors during the task, whether or not the errors were subsequently repaired. These rates show almost the same patterns as the final accuracy data. All pairs made fewer errors for the photos than for the Tangrams, $F(2, 42) = 37.88$, $p < .001$. But married couples were no more accurate than strangers were, $F(1, 42) = 1.86$, n.s., and no more accurate for photos than for Tangrams, interaction of marital status × stimulus type $F(1, 42) = 2.24$, n.s. Overall, younger pairs made fewer errors than middle-aged pairs did, who made fewer errors than older pairs did, linear trend $F(1, 42) = 4.17$, $p < .05$. This was largely because of errors on the Tangram figures, where older pairs were more likely to have made errors than younger pairs were, linear trend on the interaction of age × stimulus type $F(1, 42) = 4.15$, $p < .05$.

Overall, the accuracy results show that people found the Tangram figures harder to match than the photos of children, and that older people made more errors than younger people did on the Tangram figures, but this did not differ according to their marital status. Accuracy in general was extremely high; this makes sense given the nature of the task, and it is consistent with the results of other studies of referential communication. Pairs are highly accurate because they can speak for as long as it takes to understand each other.

Confidence. One measure of confidence of understanding their partners is how often matchers changed their minds during the task, replacing a figure they had already placed on the array. All pairs were more confident in matching the photos of children than in matching the Tangram figures, $F(1, 42) = 15.22$, $p < .001$. Married couples were marginally more confident than strangers (that is, they changed their minds less often), $F(2, 42) = 3.05$, $p < .10$; this was marginally more true for the Tangram figures than for the child photos, interaction of marital status × stimulus type $F(1, 42) = 3.31$, $p < .10$. In addition, more of the strangers changed their minds at least once (17 of 24 pairs) than did married couples (9 of 24). Pairs of all age groups did not differ in confidence, $F(2, 42) = 0.76$, n.s., and this did not differ for photos and Tangram figures, interaction of age × stimulus type $F(1, 42) = 0.46$, n.s.

Another measure of confidence is how easy or hard people rated the task after the experiment. All participants rated the matching task as more difficult with the Tangram figures (3.54 on a 7-point scale) than with the child figures (1.72), $F(1, 90) = 222.37$, $p < .001$. The ratings for participants who spoke with their spouse did not differ overall from the ratings for participants who spoke with strangers, $F(1, 90) = 1.32$, n.s. However, participants who spoke with their spouse rated the Tangram figures as easier to match than did participants who spoke with strangers, interaction of marital status × stimulus type $F(1, 90) = 5.24$, $p < .03$. Ratings did not differ for different age groups, $F(2, 90) = 1.11$, n.s. nor for photos and Tangram figures across the different age groups, interaction of age × stimulus type $F(2, 90) = 0.02$, n.s.

The confidence results suggest that married couples were marginally more confident that they had understood each other than were strangers, even though their accuracy was no better. Everyone found the Tangram figures more difficult than the child figures; this is consistent with the accuracy data.

Efficiency of communication. Since accuracy was essentially at ceiling, one measure of efficiency is the time it took to complete the matching task. Although the means hint that married couples completed the task more quickly than did strangers, 1354 vs. 1409 sec, these differences were not at all reliable, $F(1, 42) = 0.10$, n.s., nor did this differ across the different ages, interaction of marital status × age $F(2, 42) = 0.22$, n.s. Young pairs completed the task reliably more quickly (1035 sec) than did middle-aged pairs (1431 sec), who completed the task more quickly than old pairs (1677), linear trend $F(1, 42) = 8.90$, $p < .005$.

Another measure of efficiency is the number of words it took for pairs to accomplish the task. This may be the more appropriate measure because old people are more likely to speak and process information slowly (e.g., Birren & Fisher, 1992; see also Light & Burke, 1988), and so time may be artificially inflated for older participants. All pairs were substantially more efficient in matching the photos (1120 words) than the Tangrams (2834 words), $F(1, 42) = 139.62$, $p < .0001$. Married couples again were not reliably more efficient than strangers, 1919 vs. 2036 words, $F(1, 42) = 0.33$, n.s., and this did not differ for photos and Tangrams, interaction of marital status × stimulus type $F(1, 42) = 0.93$, n.s. Older pairs were less efficient than younger couples, linear trend $F(1, 42) = 7.07$, $p < .02$. This was

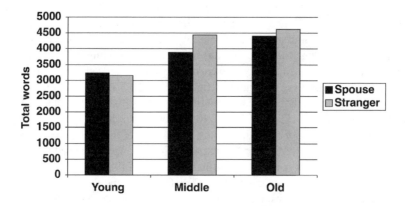

FIGURE 7.3 Efficiency: Word counts to complete task (all rounds).

true whether partners were married or strangers, interaction of age × marital status $F(2, 42) = 0.21$, n.s. (see Figure 7.3). Young pairs were more efficient (1593 words) than middle-aged pairs (2082 words), who were more efficient than old pairs (2256 words), linear trend $F(1, 42) = 5.73$, $p < .03$.

One more measure that is relevant to the issue of comprehension efficiency is the extent to which pairs were able to speed up their descriptions the second time they discussed the photos or Tangrams. We measured this by taking the ratio of the number of words the pair uttered in the second round of the task to the number of words in the first round. Here there were virtually no reliable differences for the different stimulus types and ages. For example, married couples seemed to improve their efficiency somewhat more than strangers did, averaging .63 as many words in the second round as in the first, compared to the strangers' .74, but this difference only approached reliability, $F(1, 42) = 2.68$, $p = .109$.* And although the means suggest that older pairs improved their efficiency less than young pairs (.63, .66, .76, respectively), these differences were not at all reliable, $F(2, 42) = 1.41$, n.s.

Therefore, married couples did not seem to be reliably more (or less) efficient than strangers on this task. One possibility is that these word counts are not a sensitive enough measure of efficiency. Married couples in one laboratory experiment have been shown to engage more and more over time in non-task-related discussion, compared to strangers (see Gould, Kurzman, & Dixon, 1994). However, this does not account for the lack of reliable differences here; the amount of non-task-related discussion in this study was negligible. When we coded for the rare off-task discussion and removed those words from the word counts, the adjusted word counts show the same pattern of results. In any case, the possible differences between married couples and strangers are small enough to be undetectable with this sample size, even though differences from age group and topic were detectable.

---

* It only made sense to examine improved efficiency for the second round compared with the first, rather than over all four rounds, because the topic (Tangrams or children) changed after two rounds.

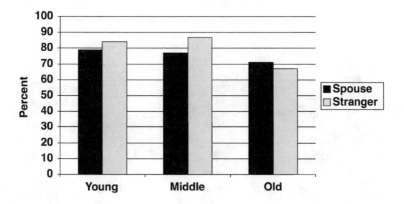

FIGURE 7.4 Entrainment (likelihood of using same description as partner did), photographs of children.

Entrainment. The extent to which people use the same terms has been argued to index whether they have reached a shared perspective (e.g., Bortfeld & Brennan, 1997; Brennan & Clark, 1996; Garrod & Anderson, 1987; Schober, 1998). Because lexical equivalence can be coded in various ways, we used two different criteria to determine how often a director used the same words in Round 2 as his or her partner already had in Round 1 to describe the same figure. Under the strict criterion, only verbatim descriptions were counted as the same; these included shortened versions of the Round 1 descriptions, as when "A geisha walking to the right, or kneeling—it has a square corner in the lower left-hand side" was re-described as "the geisha," or when "A girl with a dirty white shirt and an insignia on the right—she's pointing" was re-described as "the pointer with the insignia." We also included descriptions with only minor variations, like "the guy biting his lip" for "thin boy biting his lip." Under a more lenient criterion, descriptions that included at least one previous term but that also might include additional descriptors were counted as the same. Under this criterion, for example, "our 'I' with the arm waving to the left" was counted the same as the original "lower 'I' with a left arm going up to the left, with a pointy bottom." Similarly, we included "the guy that looks like a goofball—he has a cartoon on his shirt" as the same as the original "a boy with a very wide grin leaning toward the camera and a cartoon on his T-shirt—it says 'Greetings'." Both criteria produced the identical pattern of results; here we report the results using the more lenient criterion.

Overall, people were much more likely to entrain on descriptions of children (94%) than on descriptions of Tangrams (78%), F(1, 38) = 44.43, p < .001* (see Figure 7.4 and Figure 7.5). This differed by age group, linear trend on the interaction of age × stimulus type, F(1, 38) = 6.05, p < .02; older pairs entrained far less

---

* The degrees of freedom in all these analyses reflect the fact that partial data from four cases were unrecoverable due to technical errors at the time of coding.

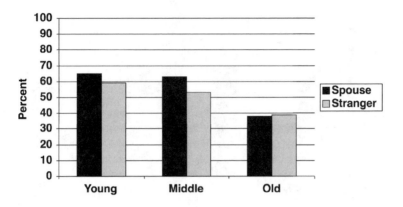

FIGURE 7.5   Entrainment (likelihood of using same description as partner did), Tangram figures.

for Tangrams than for photos. Married couples were no more likely to use the same expressions than strangers were, 86% vs. 87%, F(1, 38) = 0.32, n.s.; this was true for Tangrams and photos, interaction of marital status × stimulus type F(1, 38) = 0.95, n.s. But members of younger pairs were more likely to entrain on the same expressions than older pairs were, linear trend F(1, 38) = 9.67, p < .005; overall, younger pairs entrained 92% of the time, middle-aged pairs entrained 86% of the time, and old pairs entrained 82% of the time. This was not affected by whether partners were married or not, interaction of age × marital status, F(2,38) = 0.19, n.s.

The entrainment rates in this study are higher than are those in the Hupet et al. (1993) study, but the difference is actually small under the more stringent criterion for lexical equivalence (entrainment rates for Tangram figures of 62% [young], 59% [middle], and 44% [old] in our study compared to 55% [young] and 28% [old] in the Hupet et al. study). However, note that the pattern of entrainment is the same—old pairs entrained much less than did young pairs. Whether old people entrained less because they disagreed with their partner's earlier description or because they did not remember the earlier description is unclear from our data, but given the generally high accuracy rate, it probably is not because they had failed to understand the earlier description.

A complementary measure of entrainment is how often a director in Round 2 would introduce a radically different description than his or her partner had used to describe the same figure in Round 1, as in this example:

First description: "A futuristic windmill. Like a large triangle and then it has these two funny little triangles up at the top and a square in between."
Partner's description: "A donkey sitting. It's a triangle with a flat bottom and a straight line up and then a head with two ears on top of it."

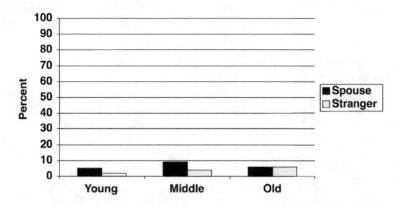

FIGURE 7.6 Likelihood of using radically different description than partner did, photographs of children.

As Figure 7.6 and Figure 7.7 show, the same general pattern emerges as for use of the same expressions. In all pairs, speakers were more likely to use completely different expressions for Tangrams than for children, $F(1, 38) = 45.36$, $p < .001$. Older pairs were more likely to use different expressions than younger pairs were, linear trend $F(1, 38) = 10.80$, $p < .003$. But long-term relationship didn't seem to make a difference; although the means hint at a possible difference, marital partners were not reliably less likely to use different expressions than strangers were, $F(1, 38) = 0.15$, n.s. This was true across all ages, interaction of age × marital status, $F(2, 38) = 0.28$, n.s.

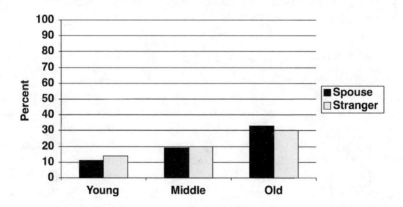

FIGURE 7.7 Likelihood of using radically different description than partner did, Tangram figure.

We expected that married couples might rely on description strategies that referred to their own common ground, as in this example from one of our old couples describing a photograph of a child:*

Director (D): The next one looks like a dead ringer for Ben.
Matcher (M): Oh, my gosh.
D: And, uh...
M: [laughs]
D: He, he also has a T-shirt. And uh, he has uh... Mickey Mouse on the front of the T-shirt, that ought to be easy.
M: Wait a minute! [laughs] have to study this. Okay. Now. I see two T-shirts. Or three T-shirts of boys with Mickey Mouse on them.
D: Uh-huh.
M: So:
D: This one says "Mickey."
M: They all say "Mickey"!
D: They all say "Mickey," and this one has sort of a, uh, Indian or Aztec's design below Mickey's head.
M: Okay, and he's kind of ... the little boy is kind of grinning.
D: Yeah, looks like Ben.
M: And looks like Ben.
D: Don't you think he looks like Ben?
M: Yeah, I guess he ... guess he looks like Ben in *his*
D: *Why* sure.
M: And and Mickey's above the Aztec design?
D: That's correct
M: Okay.

Note that such a description strategy does not necessarily increase efficiency; here describing the figure as "looking like Ben" may well have complicated matters. In any case, such examples were rare. Overall, married couples really did not seem to use different strategies in this task than strangers did.

DISCUSSION

All four measures of understanding show a similar pattern. First, the nature of the novel topic under discussion mattered enormously. When people discussed the photos of unfamiliar children, they understood each other more accurately, with greater confidence, and with greater efficiency, and they were more likely to use the same terms as their partner had used. They were less accurate, less confident, and less efficient when discussing abstract geometric shapes (and less fluent, as reported in Bortfeld et al., 2001). This was true for all age groups and no different for married couples and strangers.

Second, older pairs were as confident and almost as accurate as younger pairs, but they were less efficient and less likely to use the same terms as their partner

---

* In this excerpt, pauses are represented by periods surrounded by spaces (...), and overlapping speech is enclosed within asterisks. Lengthened sounds are followed by a colon.

had used. The efficiency and entrainment results replicate Hupet et al.'s (1993) findings, and they extend them to include middle-aged pairs (see also Kogan & Jordan, 1989; Shewan & Henderson, 1988). On most measures where there were age differences, middle-aged pairs fell between young and old pairs. This suggests that age-related changes in referential communication may be continuous over the life-span.

Most centrally for our current purposes, on virtually every measure partners with long-term relationships were not reliably more accurate or efficient in talking about unfamiliar things than were strangers, and they were not reliably more likely to adopt their partner's expressions. However, married couples did seem to be more confident that they understood each other. This suggests that people who have known each other a long time may not actually have learned as much about how the other talks about or understands *new* things as they think (for a related result, see Ryder, 1968). Certainly, any possible comprehension advantage from long-term relationship is dwarfed by other variables like age and topic.

These results are, of course, not the final word on this topic. First, our sample population was extremely well educated and high functioning; whether the results would extend to less educated or more poorly functioning couples is unclear. Second, it would be useful to further de-confound age and length of relationship by observing middle-aged and old couples who have only been together briefly, as well as same-sex long-term couples. Third, in our sample, middle-aged couples reported being less satisfied in their marriages than the young or old couples did. To the extent that marital satisfaction reflects good communication between the partners, our three age groups may have been less than perfectly comparable. However, the linear as opposed to curvilinear patterns in the results speak against this explanation.

So does being together for years improve comprehension? Our findings suggest that the years will have their effects—and, at least on this task, not particularly good ones—and that those effects will be the same with one's spouse as with a stranger. However, we are *not* suggesting that married couples routinely fail to understand each other any better than strangers do. Many, if not most, discussions by long-term partners probably involve shared experiences, from which they can draw on their perceptual, linguistic, or community common ground. Even when they talk about novel topics, those topics are probably more like discussing photographs of children, for which accuracy, efficiency, and rates of entrainment were quite high, than like describing abstract geometric shapes. So the confidence that married couples often feel that they accurately and efficiently understand each other's shorthand phrases and cues is not misplaced. However, our results suggest that this confidence should not, perhaps, extend as far as it does.

ACKNOWLEDGMENTS

This research was supported by NIA Grant R01-8816 to Laura Carstensen and NSF grant IRI9402167 to Michael Schober. Selected results were presented at the 38th Annual Meeting of the Psychonomic Society, Philadelphia, PA. We thank Susan Brennan for comments on an earlier version of this paper. We also thank Susan Charles,

Donald Christensen, and Tom George for helping with data collection, and we thank Jon Bloom, Daphne Leahy, Silvia Leon, Alex Russell, Marcy Russo, Randall Sowder, and Patty Watts for help with transcription and coding of conversations.

Correspondence should be addressed to Michael F. Schober, Office of the Dean, New School for Social Research, 6 E. 16th St., 10th floor, New York, NY 10003; schober@newschool.edu.

REFERENCES

Birren, J. E., & Fisher, L. M. (1992). Aging and slowing of behavior: Consequences for cognition and survival. *Nebraska Symposium on Motivation 1991, 39*, 1–37.

Bortfeld, H., & Brennan, S. E. (1997). Use and acquisition of idiomatic expressions in referring by native and non-native speakers. *Discourse Processes, 23*(2), 119–147.

Bortfeld, H., Leon, S. D., Bloom, J. E., Schober, M. F., & Brennan, S.E. (2001). Disfluency rates in conversation: Effects of age, relationship, topic, role, and gender. *Language and Speech, 44*, 123–149.

Boyle, E. A., Anderson, A. H., & Newlands, A. (1994). The effects of visibility on dialogue and performance in a cooperative problem solving task. *Language and Speech, 37,*1–20.

Brennan, S.E., & Clark, H. H. (1996). Conceptual pacts and lexical choice in conversation. *Journal of Experimental Psychology: Learning, Memory and Cognition, 22*, 1482–1493.

Carstensen, L. L., Gottman, J. M., & Levenson, R. W. (1995). Emotional behavior in long-term marriage. *Psychology and Aging, 10*, 140–149.

Carstensen, L. L., Graff, J., Levenson, R. W., & Gottman, J. M. (1996). Affect in intimate relationships: The developmental course of marriage. In C. Magai & S. McFadden (Eds.), *Handbook of emotion, adult development and aging* (pp. 227–247). Orlando, FL: Academic Press.

Clark, H. H., & Carlson, T. B. (1981). Context for comprehension. In J. Long & A. Baddeley (Eds.), *Attention and performance IX* (pp. 313–330). Hillsdale, NJ: Lawrence Erlbaum Associates.

Clark, H. H., & Marshall, C. R. (1981). Definite reference and mutual knowledge. In A. K. Joshi, B. L. Webber, & I. A. Sag (Eds.), *Elements of discourse understanding* (pp. 10–63). Cambridge: Cambridge University Press.

Clark, H. H., & Schaefer, E. F. (1987). Concealing one's meaning from overhearers. *Journal of Memory and Language, 26*, 209–225.

Elffers, J. (1976). *Tangram: The ancient Chinese shapes game.* New York: McGraw-Hill.

Emery, O. B. (1986). Linguistic decrement in normal aging. *Language & Communication, 6*, 47–64.

Fleming, J. H., & Darley, J. M. (1991). Mixed messages: The multiple audience problem and strategic communication. *Social Cognition, 9*, 25–46.

Fussell, S. E., & Krauss, R. M. (1989). Understanding friends and strangers: The effects of audience design on message comprehension. *European Journal of Social Psychology, 19*, 509–525.

Garrod, S., & Anderson, A. (1987). Saying what you mean in dialogue: A study in conceptual and semantic coordination. *Cognition, 27*, 181–218.

Guilford, R., & Bengtson, V. (1979). Measuring marital satisfaction in three generations: Positive and negative dimensions. *Journal of Marriage and the Family, 39*, 387–398.

Gould, O., Kurzman, D., & Dixon, R. A. (1994). Communication during prose recall conversations by young and old dyads. *Discourse Processes, 17,* 149–165.

Gould, O. N., & Dixon, R. A. (1993). How we spent our vacation: Collaborative storytelling by young and old adults. *Psychology and Aging, 8,* 10–17.

Gould, O. N., Trevithick, L., & Dixon, R. A. (1991). Adult age differences in elaborations produced during prose recall. *Psychology and Aging, 6,* 93–99.

Hornstein, G. A. (1985). Intimacy in conversational style as a function of the degree of closeness between members of a dyad. *Journal of Personality and Social Psychology, 44,* 671–681.

Horton, W. S., & Gerrig, R. (2005). Conversational common ground and memory processes in language production. *Discourse Processes, 40,* 1–35.

Horton, W. S., & Spieler, D. H. (2007). Age-related differences in communication and audience design. *Psychology and Aging, 22,* 281–290.

Hupet, M., Chantraine, Y., & Nef, F. (1993). References in conversation between young and old normal adults. *Psychology and Aging, 8,* 339–346.

Kemper, S. (1988). Geriatric psycholinguistics: Syntactic limitations of oral and written language. In L. L. Light & D. M. Burke (Eds.), *Language, memory and aging* (pp. 50–76). Cambridge, UK: Cambridge University Press.

Kent, G. G., Davis, J. D., & Shapiro, D. A. (1981). Effect of mutual acquaintance on the construction of conversation. *Journal of Experimental Social Psychology, 17,* 197–209.

Keysar, B., Barr, D. J., & Horton, W. S. (1998). The egocentric basis of language use: Insights from a processing approach. *Current Directions in Psychological Science, 7,* 46–50.

Kogan, N., & Jordan, T. (1989). Social communication within and between elderly and middle-aged cohorts. In M. A. Luszcz & T. Nettelbeck (Eds.), *Psychological development: Perspectives across the life-span* (pp. 409–415). Amsterdam, North-Holland: Elsevier.

Krauss, R. M., & Fussell, S. R. (1996). Social psychological models of interpersonal communication. In E. T. Higgins & A. Kruglanski (Eds.), *Social psychology: Handbook of basic principles* (pp. 655–701). New York: Guilford Press.

Krauss, R., & Weinheimer, S. (1966). Concurrent feedback, confirmation, and the encoding of referents in verbal communication. *Journal of Personality and Social Psychology, 4,* 343–346.

Levenson, R. W., Carstensen, L. L., & Gottman, J. M. (1993). Long-term marriage: Age, gender, and satisfaction. *Psychology and Aging, 8,* 301–313.

Light, L. L., & Burke, D. M. (1988). *Language, memory and aging.* Cambridge, UK: Cambridge University Press.

Lindenberger, U., Mayr, U., & Baltes, P. (1993). Speed and intelligence in old age. *Psychology and Aging, 8,* 207–220.

Metzing, C., & Brennan, S. E. (2003). When conceptual pacts are broken: Partner-specific effects in the comprehension of referring expressions. *Journal of Memory and Language, 49,* 201–213.

Pickering, M. J., & Garrod, S. (2004). Toward a mechanistic psychology of dialogue. *Behavioral and Brain Sciences, 27,* 169–190.

Planalp, S. (1993). Friends' and acquaintances' conversations II: Coded differences. *Journal of Social and Personal Relationships, 10,* 339–354.

Ryder, R. G. (1968). Husband-wife dyads versus married strangers. *Family Process, 7,* 233–238.

Salthouse, T. A. (1991). *Theoretical perspectives on cognitive aging.* Hillsdale, NJ: Lawrence Erlbaum Associates.

Schober, M. F. (1998). Different kinds of conversational perspective-taking. In S. R. Fussell & R. J. Kreuz (Eds.), *Social and cognitive psychological approaches to interpersonal communication* (pp. 145–174). Mahwah, NJ: Lawrence Erlbaum Associates.

Schober, M. F. (2005). Conceptual alignment in conversation. In B. F. Malle & S. D. Hodges (Eds.), *Other minds: How humans bridge the divide between self and others* (pp. 239–252). New York: Guilford Press.

Schober, M. F., & Brennan, S. E. (2003). Processes of interactive spoken discourse: The role of the partner. In A. C. Graesser, M. A. Gernsbacher, & S. R. Goldman (Eds.), *Handbook of discourse processes* (pp. 123–164). Mahwah, NJ: Lawrence Erlbaum Associates.

Schober, M. F., & Clark, H. H. (1989). Understanding by addressees and overhearers. *Cognitive Psychology, 21,* 211–232.

Shewan, C. M., & Henderson, V. L. (1988). Analysis of spontaneous language in the older normal population. *Journal of Communication Disorders, 21,* 139–154.

Wahler, H. J. (1983). *Wahler physical symptoms inventory.* Los Angeles, CA: Western Psychological Services.

Wechsler, D. (1981). *Manual for the Wechsler Adult Intelligence Scale—Revised.* New York: Psychological Corporation.

8 A Communication Perspective to the Emergence of a Brand Culture

Shirley Y. Y. Cheng and Chi-yue Chiu

Think ...Think Different...

"IBM think"; "Apple think different." Apple adopted the *Think Different* slogan in the late 1990s, probably as a play on the venerable *IBM Think* motto, to define the essence of Apple users, one of the strongest brand communities in the world. The *Think Different* campaign enlisted well-known personalities including Albert Einstein, Thomas Edison, and Frank Lloyd Wright as the identity-defining icons of the Apple culture.* In 2002, the ill-fated *Apple Switch* Campaign, which featured famous Apple switchers like Tony Hawk, Will Ferrell, and Yo-yo Ma, replaced the *Think Different* campaign, when Apple believed that PC users were ready to be converted.

Culture influences behaviors, but how does a culture start? Decades of (cross-)cultural research have provided numerous examples of culture's influence on behaviors (for reviews, see Chiu & Hong, 2006, 2007; Lehman, Chiu, & Schaller, 2004). However, the question of how a culture begins is still awaiting answers from social psychology.

---

* Einstein, Edison, and Wright had never used an Apple computer; the computer in the background of the Robert Krauss photo is a Macintosh.

Does social psychology have the methodological equipment to approach this question? On the surface, it seems that when it comes to the question of how a culture starts, social psychologists must defer to historians. Upon further probing, although inventing a world culture in a research laboratory is still far beyond our psychological imagination, simulating a novel brand culture (like the Apple culture) in a social psychology experiment may still be within our reach. Such experimental simulation studies could be informative because they may help us identify some facilitative conditions for culture formation in general. Recently, to explore the promises and limits of this research strategy, we have turned our laboratory into a culture incubator. In this chapter, we present the preliminary results from our culture simulation research. The key variables we examined in this research are minority status and serial reproductive communication of narratives about in-group members. We posit that the confluence of these factors has facilitative effects on the formation of a brand culture.

BRAND CULTURES AND WORLD CULTURES: SOME CRITICAL COMMONALITIES

As mentioned, current research in (cross-) cultural psychology has focused on the psychological and behavioral differences between national or ethnic groups. In this research, culture is often treated as the foundational self-schema or modal values of a national or ethnic group. We think this treatment of culture is overly restrictive; we prefer to define culture as a set of loosely organized knowledge (including the declarative and procedure knowledge, as well as motivational predilections) produced and reproduced by a network of interconnected individuals (Chiu & Chen, 2004; Chiu & Hong, 2005, 2006, 2007). According to our definition of culture, religious and brand communities are also cultural groups because members of these communities collectively construct and reproduce shared knowledge through formal and informal interactions.

Buddhism, Communism, Confucianism, and Christianity are very different world cultures, but there are several critical commonalities in how they started:

1. When they started, they were minority religions or ideologies.
2. The founding members of these religious/ideological communities believed that members of their communities shared similar positive characteristics.
3. These founding leaders were aware and proud of their group's marginal status and were eager to convert the nonbelievers.
4. There were numerous tales, legends, and myths circulating in the communities about the religion/ideology, as well as its leaders and practitioners.

Interestingly, these characteristics are found in the early stage of many intellectual movements, political revolutions, and terrorist groups.

Brand cultures and world cultures are dissimilar in many respects, but their developmental histories also share the critical commonalities just described. A brand community refers to a collection of consumers who are strongly bound together by a common brand choice/preference. Members of a brand community are often strangers to each other and they seldom interact. Despite these, ethnographic studies (Muñiz & O'Guinn, 2001) have shown that these communities have powerful cultures, replete with complex rituals, traditions, and behavioral expectations. Members of a brand community tend to perceive their group to share similar positive traits, identify themselves as members of a community, are aware and proud of being consumers in a niche market, and feel that they have the mission to convert the nonusers. Take Apple users, the most widely researched brand community, as an example. Loyal Apple users often refer to themselves as Apple devotees or Mac people. When Apple devotees talk about themselves publicly in their Web sites, they often acknowledge their minority status (e.g., "We Mac people do strange things."—an Apple devotee in London) and compare themselves to a religious group (e.g., "I guess a lot of Macintosh users are either evangelists or are defensive simply because they believe the Macintosh system is superior to Windows. Since 90% of computer users don't realize this, there's a feeling they need to be shown the light."—another Apple devotee in Toronto) (Evans, 2005).

In addition, numerous brand stories echoing these themes are circulated among Apple users. One ethnographic study (Muniz & Schau, 2005) has examined how the users of Apple Newton, a PDA product, reacted after Apple had abandoned the product. Despite the community's perilous position, the community survived for some time, and its members continued to share brand stories or tales with several common motifs. These motifs reinforced the idea that Newton, like Jesus, with its miraculous performance, would resurrect from its death, triumph over competing technologies, and would convert the unbelievers.

In short, brand communities seem to possess the psychological characteristics of major world cultures at their embryonic stage of development. Thus, studying how brand communities arise may shed some light on the social psychological processes that support the formation of new cultures.

CONDITIONS THAT ENABLE THE EMERGENCE OF A BRAND CULTURE

Why do people form brand communities and cultures? One explanation focuses on the mystical experiences belonging to a brand community can confer. For example, Muñiz and Schau (2005) maintain that

A common aspect of brand communities could be the potential for transcendent and magico-religious experiences. The capacity for magic and mysticism may be one factor that attracts people to form communities around these brands, as well as the quality that facilitates the transformative, liberatory, and emancipatory aspects of consumptions sometimes enacted in them. (p. 746)

The emergence of a novel brand culture is a poorly understood process. Thus, it is not surprising that some writers have characterized it in such mystical terms. However, we propose that a brand culture may emerge as an outcome of some ordinary social psychological processes. Specifically, we contend that consumers of an unpopular but desirable brand (henceforth referred to as a *niche brand*) are motivated to perceive their consumer group as sharing certain positive attributes and to talk about these shared attributes when they communicate with users of the same brand. Furthermore, these effects are enhanced as the messages are reproduced in serial communications. When most users of the brand believe that other members also believe in the sharedness of the positive characteristics, this belief will become part of the shared reality (Echterhoff, Higgins, & Groll, 2005; Hardin & Higgins, 1996) in the emerging brand culture.* The proposed model is illustrated in Figure 8.1. This model is consistent with the observations reviewed previously; that is, brand communities are characterized by heightened awareness of the brand's minority status and by the wide circulation of identity-defining narratives in the community. In the following sections, we will review the model's component processes and the results of the studies we have conducted to test the model.

AWARENESS OF MINORITY STATUS

This proposed model is consistent with the optimal distinctiveness theory (Brewer, 1991). According to this theory, individuals have both the need to seek social connectedness and the need to differentiate the self from others. Seeking connectedness and distinctiveness are two opposing motivations—an activity that satisfies one need is likely to frustrate the other. Thus, when managing relationships with their in-group, individuals are inclined to find a strategy that would optimize the likelihood of achieving connectedness and distinctiveness. That is, people are inclined to search for an optimal strategy that would confer a sense of connectedness and at the same time allows them to be recognized as a distinctive person.

According to the optimal distinctiveness theory, in any given situation, the relative strength of the needs for connectedness and distinctiveness depends on, among other factors, the extent to which the two needs have been fulfilled (Chiu & Hong, 1999; Pickett, Booner, & Coleman, 2002; Pickett & Brewer, 2001). As illustrated in Figure 8.2, the size of one's in-group is a determining factor of the relative strength of the needs for distinctiveness and connectedness. Membership in a small, inclusive group fulfills the need for distinctiveness but does not confer a sense of connectedness. According to the theory of optimal distinctiveness, fulfillment of the need for distinctiveness would elicit a desire for connectedness, which can be satisfied by elevating the level of perceived in-group similarity with

---

* Recent studies have shown that culture is not just the modal characteristics of a cultural group; also important are the shared beliefs about the group's modal characteristics. For example, in a collectivist culture, most people are collectivistic. Furthermore, most people expect that other people in the culture are collectivistic (Wan, Chiu, Peng, & Tam, 2007; Wan et al., 2007).

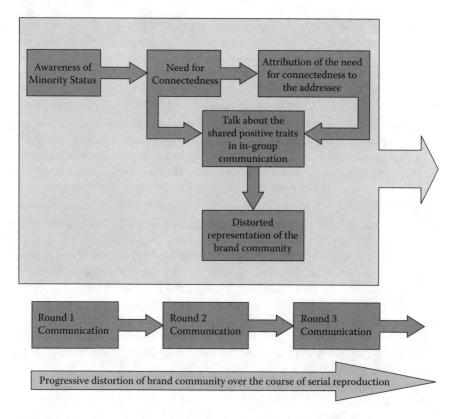

FIGURE 8.1   A communication model of the emergence of a brand culture.

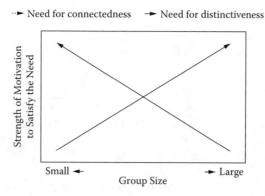

FIGURE 8.2   Group size and the relative strength of the need for connectedness and distinctiveness.

respect to a certain attribute. Applying this theory to the brand community context, when consumers of a niche brand are aware of their minority status, they are motivated to perceive other users of the same brand as sharing certain positive traits and to talk about these shared traits in in-group communication. Returning to the example of Mac devotees, Robert Fulford (1997), a columnist, has commented that Mac users' devotion to the brand community identity is an expression of a highly distinctive consumer group's craving for connection:

> You can't go there (Graceland) without being changed somehow. It's not the house, it's not Presley himself, it's the strangers you see going through, people from Japan or Sweden or almost everywhere. It's their need. *They are hungry for something, for connection. Some find it at Graceland, others on the screen of their Macintosh* (emphasis added).

In contrast, people in a group of considerable size would feel that they are connected to a large group; however, being a member of a large group does not satisfy the need for distinctiveness. In the consumer context, users of a popular brand feel that they belong to a large consumer group; their need for connectedness has been satisfied but the need to differentiate themselves from other in-group members has not. Consequently, they are motivated to perceive high levels of diversity in the in-group and not talk about the group's shared characteristics. Back to the example of Mac devotees versus PC users, this line of reasoning suggests that PC users may be more concerned about maintaining personal uniqueness than feeling connected. Thus, it may not be a coincidence that Umberto Eco (1994), an Italian novelist, would compare Mac users to Catholics and PC users to Protestants, arguing that the Macintosh tells the faithful that everyone has a right to salvation, whereas the Microsoft system used in PCs "allows free interpretation of the scripture, demands difficult personal decisions ... and takes for granted the idea that not all can reach salvation. To make the system work, you need to interpret the program yourself."

COMMUNICATION AND SHARED KNOWLEDGE

Culture is a network of *shared* knowledge, and people construct shared knowledge through communication (Chiu, Krauss, & Lee, 1999; Krauss & Chiu, 1998). Not surprisingly, communication is given a major role in many theories of cultural evolution (Breakwell, 1993; Bruner, 1990; Latané, 1996; Lau, Lee, & Chiu, 2004; Moscovici, 1988; Sperber, 1996). Although each of these theories has a unique slant, they share the assumption that ideas that are more frequently reproduced in communication are more likely to become a part of culture.

Not all ideas have the same likelihood of being selected for communicative reproduction. For example, ideas that are consistent (vs. inconsistent) with the shared reality in the culture have been shown to have a higher chance of being reproduced in communication (Berger & Heath, 2005; Kashima, 2000; Lyons & Kashima, 2003; Norenzayan, Atran, Faulkner, & Schaller, 2006). Other ideas that have a relatively high chance of being passed on are those that carry either surprisingly positive or surprisingly negative news (Heath, 1996) and those that have the ability to evoke emotions like anger, fear, or disgust (Health, Bell, & Sternberg, 2001; Sinaceur, Heath, & Cole, 2005). All these suggest that the characteristics or psychological effects of an idea determine how likely it will be reproduced in communication.

As we proposed in the last section, how likely a message concerning the shared characteristic of a group will be reproduced also depends on the communicators' current concerns. Consumers of a niche brand have a desire for connectedness and are therefore motivated to talk about the shared positive characteristics of their group, whereas consumers of a popular brand may be less likely to do so because of their craving for distinctiveness.

Dynamic Social Impact Theory

There are several explanations why communication would facilitate the development of shared cognitions. The dynamic social impact theory (Latané, 1996) holds that people who live closer to each other have more opportunities to influence and be influenced by others. In a neighborhood, minority opinion holders tend to receive more persuasive communications from the majority opinion holders than do majority opinion holders from the minority opinion holders. Thus, minority opinion holders are more likely to be converted than are majority opinion holders. These interpersonal processes give rise to local clustering of opinions—people living in the same neighborhood would become more similar in their opinions.

However, the dynamic impact theory does not explain how brand cultures emerge. The theory maintains that the same interpersonal processes would lead to spatial clustering of minority opinions, shielding minority opinion holders from majority influence. Although the theory can explain why minority cultures may survive majority influence, it does not explain why almost all consumer brands with a strong brand culture are minority brands (Muñiz & O'Guinn, 2001).

Coordination of Perspectives

Another theory of communication and shared knowledge construction focuses on the cognitive consequences of the collaborative processes in interpersonal communication (Lau, Chiu, & Lee, 2001). According to this theory, shared knowledge between the communicators emerges naturally as communicators spontaneously coordinate their perspectives in interpersonal communication. Communication is a collaborative process. When formulating communicative messages, the speaker would spontaneously assess the addressee's knowledge (Fussell & Krauss, 1992) to form mutually acceptable referring expressions. For example, when describing a landmark to a listener who is unfamiliar with it, the speaker expects the listener not to know the landmark's name. In this context, the speaker would have a lowered tendency to name the landmark and an increased likelihood of describing its physical appearance (Lau, Chiu, & Hong, 2001).

Returning to the example of brand culture, when consumers of a niche brand talk about their brand community with another user of the same brand, they are not only motivated by the need for connectedness to attribute shared positive traits to the community, they are also inclined to simulate the psychological states of other brand users by projecting their own need for connectedness to them. As a result, they are likely to talk about the brand users' shared positive traits.

Saying Is Believing

Furthermore, after the speaker has formulated a communicative message, they may start to believe in what they have said (Chiu, Krauss, & Lau, 1998). For example, after being induced to talk about certain characteristic traits of Apple users, the speaker may believe more firmly that most Apple users possess these traits. There is now considerable evidence for this "saying is believing" effect (Higgins & McCann, 1984; Higgins, McCann, & Fondacaro, 1982; McCann, Higgins, & Fondacaro, 1991). For example, in one study, the participants were asked to describe some ambiguous behaviors of a stimulus person to a listener. When the participants were led to believe that the listener had a positive (or negative) attitude toward the stimulus person, they formulated relatively positive (or negative) descriptions of the behaviors. More important, the speakers' subsequent memory representations of the stimulus person were distorted to be consistent with the valence of the descriptions.

Chiu et al. (1998) attributed this "saying is believing" effect to recoding interference (Schooler & Engstler-Schooler, 1990). When a communicator uses language to describe a state of affairs, a verbal representation of it is created. This verbal representation may overshadow the perceptual representation or a pre-existing verbal representation of the same state of affairs. As a result, the memory representation of the state of affairs is distorted in the direction of the verbal descriptions. The verbal overshadowing effect is particularly prominent for stimuli that are difficult to verbalize.

Serial Reproduction Effect

The "saying is believing" effect is strengthened after every reproduction of the message. That is, when the message is reproduced over the course of a serial communication chain, the representation of the referent will spread to new individuals, and its contents will become progressively more distorted. Consequently, there will be progressive shrinkage in the amount of variability in the way the referent is described and cognitively represented. In line with this idea, it has been shown that in a serial production of a story containing both stereotype-consistent and stereotype-inconsistent behavioral information about a football player, stereotype-consistent information tends to be retained over the course of the reproduction chain, whereas stereotype-inconsistent information is progressively screened out. As a result, the representation of the football player becomes increasingly more similar to what one would expect a football player to be like (Kashima, 2000; Lyons & Kashima, 2001).

Furthermore, both the "saying is believing" and serial reproduction effects are particularly prominent when the communicator expects the communicated representation to be widely shared in the community (Echterhoff et al., 2005; Lyons & Kashima, 2003).

Emergence of Brand Cultures

How can the emergence of a new brand culture be accounted for? In Figure 8.1, we present a model that integrates the ideas reviewed previously to address this question. There are two reasons why consumers of a niche brand are motivated to talk about the brand users' shared positive traits in in-group communication. First, being aware of their minority status, they seek connectedness. Second, they attribute a similar motive to the addressee. Having described the shared positive traits in their consumer group, their memory representation of the group is distorted in the direction of the descriptions. Finally, over the course of the serial reproduction chain, the biases in the representation spread to other brand users and become progressively stronger. Consequently, most brand users believe that other brand users possess the positive traits and a brand culture is created.

The proposed model seems plausible. However, can it be tested in a social psychology experiment? We have just started a two-stage research program to test this model. In the first stage, we seek to demonstrate that when the optimal conditions (awareness of the minority status of the consumer group to which one belongs, opportunities of in-group communication) are present, a novel brand culture would emerge over the course of the serial communication chain. In the second stage, we remove these conditions to test how necessary they are for the emergence of a brand culture. In the next sections, we will review the results from this program of studies.

EXPERIMENTAL EVIDENCE

OVERVIEW OF THE EXPERIMENTAL PARADIGM

Figure 8.3 presents the experimental paradigm we developed to simulate the emergence of a brand culture. We hypothesize that a brand culture is most likely to emerge when the consumers are aware of their minority status and have the opportunity to spread narratives of in-group members to other in-group members. To test this hypothesis, we manipulated the participants' majority and minority status

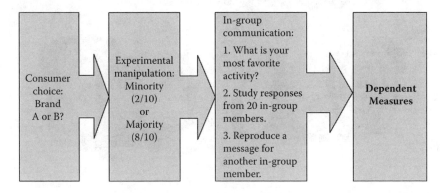

FIGURE 8.3   The basic experimental paradigm.

and provided them with an opportunity to spread narratives of in-group members to another in-group member in a communication task before they responded to a set of dependent measures that assessed the extent to which the participants would attribute shared essence to their in-group members. Specifically, in the experiment, the participant was presented with two novel brands of messenger bags, instructed to choose one of the two bags, read about the behaviors of 20 other participants who had made the same choice (from now on referred to as the *stimulus group*), and wrote an essay to communicate his or her impression of the group to the next participant who chose the same brand (hereafter referred to as the *addressee*).

CONSUMER CHOICE AND MANIPULATION OF MAJORITY/MINORITY STATUS

To elaborate, to examine the effect of minority status awareness on the emergence of brand culture, we randomly assigned undergraduate students to the majority or minority brand condition. We did so by presenting to them two messenger bags of two unfamiliar European brands (see Figure 8.4). Both brands are not available for purchase in the U.S. market, and our pilot study results showed that the two brands were equally attractive to the undergraduates. In addition, no pilot study participants had heard of the two brands. The participant was told that as a token of appreciation for their participation, he or she would have a 10% chance of winning the chosen messenger bag in a lottery.

After the participant had made the choice, he or she was randomly assigned to one of the two experimental conditions. In the minority brand condition, irrespective of the participant's choice, the experimenter made the following "incidental" remark in front of the participant: "This is a unique choice; about *two out of ten* participants chose this bag." Next, the experimenter asked the participant to write down his or her name on a list of "other participants who had chosen the same brand as the participant did." There were only a few hand-written names on the list. In the majority brand condition, the experimenter made the following "incidental" remark: "This is a popular choice; about *eight out of ten* participants chose this bag." Next, the participant wrote down his or her name on a much longer list of "other participants who had chosen the same brand."

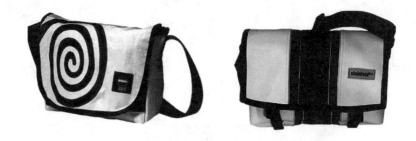

FIGURE 8.4   Pictures of the messenger bags used in the experiments.

These procedures allow us to isolate the effect of minority status awareness on the emergence of brand cultures. In real life situations, deciding between majority and minority brands is a consumer *choice*. Thus, although minority (vs. majority) brands typically have a stronger brand culture, it is unclear whether this association is due to the effects of minority brand status, the actual differences between the brands, or a self-selection bias. For example, Apple users have a stronger brand culture than do PC users. This may happen because of certain distinctive features of Apple products or certain characteristics of the consumers who prefer Apple products. Such interpretive ambiguity is not an issue in our experiments because irrespective of the participants' actual choice, they were randomly assigned to the minority or majority brand.

THE COMMUNICATION TASK

Next, a communication task was introduced to offer the participant an opportunity to spread narratives of in-group members to another in-group member. The task required the participant to describe the favorite activities of the stimulus group to the addressee. To increase the cover story's credibility, the experimenter asked the participant to write down his or her most favorite activity on a piece of paper. Next, the participant was shown 20 handwritten answers from "20 previous participants who had chosen the same brand." The participant was given 5 min to study these activities and form an overall impression of the stimulus group. The participant was encouraged to visualize the group members' appearances, preferences, personality, attitudes, and values.

The same 20 activities were presented to the participants in the two experimental conditions. The activities were preselected to include activities that varied widely in the level of openness to experience. We chose openness because a pretest with undergraduate students from the same student population showed that openness is regarded as a desirable trait. The mean desirability rating was 6.13 on a 7-point scale ($SD = 0.72$; with 7 = extremely desirable); over 80% of the pretest participants chose 6 or above on the scale.

In another pretest, we had another sample from the same student population read each activity and rate the level of openness of a person who enjoyed the activity. The results showed that on a scale ranging from 1 to 9, the mean level of openness associated with the 20 activities was 6.75 (range = 5.56 to 8.19); the mean level of openness of the 20 activities was moderately open. An example of the low-openness activities is "Watch football and eat pizza with friends" (openness score = 5.56) and an example of the high-openness activity is "Learn a new hobby" (openness score = 8.19).

After completing a 10-min filler task included to clear the participant's short-term memory of the activities, the participant were asked to write a 150-word essay to describe the stimulus group. The participant was reminded that the essay would be presented to the next participant who made the same brand choice, and the participant was encouraged to include concrete behavioral information, and tried to describe as many activities as possible. The instructions of the writing task were as follows:

The narrative should be an ESSAY of around 150 words. Try your best to include the concrete behavioral information you have read about those participants. In your writing, *try to include as much information and describe as many of those participants as possible.* This will help the next student form a more vivid impression of these participants as a whole.

Because all participants studied the same activities, how they described these activities to the next participants reflects the biasing effects of the majority/minority brand manipulation.

Two independent coders classified each essay into one of the two categories: essays that described a global impression of the stimulus group or essays that described diverse activities of individuals and/or subgroups. Essays that described a global impression were further classified into two categories depending on whether openness to experience was a major component of the global impression.

As expected, compared to participants in the majority brand condition, those in the minority brand condition were more likely to characterize the stimulus group as a *group* of open individuals. In contrast, the essays produced by the majority brand participants tended to emphasize the diversity of the activities. The following example essays illustrate this striking difference.

Minority brand essay:

Many of the participants seemed to enjoy trying new and sometimes more unusual activities. One participant enjoyed writing music while another enjoyed discovering new recipes. Also, I noticed a few participants interested in spending time with friends and even analyzing a friend's issues and creating the best advice.... Overall, many of the participants seemed to enjoy time with friends and in some cases trying or creating new things....

Majority brand essay:

This group of students seems to be very diverse in personalities. Some students seem to be very adventurous and outgoing. They like to try new foods, or watch foreign films. I picture these students wanting to travel and learn more about other cultures. They are probably smart and/or goal oriented....

PERCEPTION OF THE STIMULUS GROUP

After the communication task, to assess the extent to which the participants attributed shared essence to their in-group, we had the participant rate the stimulus group on five personality traits (openness, extraversion, emotional stability, agreeableness, and conscientiousness), the perceived homogeneity of the group members to each other, and the desirability of openness as a personal quality.

Consistent with the predictions of our model, although all participants received the same behavioral information, the minority brand participants perceived the stimulus group to be more open than did the majority brand participants. The minority brand participants also attributed greater homogeneity to the in-group than did the majority brand participants. Moreover, the two conditions did not differ in the perceived desirability of openness. Although participants in both conditions perceived openness to be a desirable trait, minority (vs. majority) brand participants were more likely to attribute openness to their group. Furthermore, participants in the two conditions did not differ in other personality ratings (e.g., extraversion, agreeableness), indicating that the minority (vs. majority) brand participants were not more prone to generalized dispositional thinking. Instead, as we propose, the minority brand participants seemed particularly prepared to pick up behavioral signals of their group's shared positive traits. When many (but not all) in-group members engaged in activities that signaled openness, the minority brand participants readily picked up the signals and used them to form a global impression of the group. They communicated this impression in their essay and rated the group as a group of open individuals.

REPLICATION OF THE BASIC RESULTS

We replicated these results in a recently completed study. Using a new sample, we again found that compared to majority brand participants, minority brand participants attributed higher levels of openness to the stimulus group. Some new measures were included in the replication study to examine the effects of minority status awareness and serial reproduction on the participants' social motivations and group identification. First, after the communication task, the participants rated how important it was for them to feel connected and distinctive. These measures allowed us to assess whether our assumptions about the participants' motivation to optimize connectedness and distinctiveness is correct. As expected, compared to each other, minority brand participants valued connectedness more, whereas the majority brand participants valued distinctiveness more.

Finally, also after the communication task, we assessed the participants' strength of identification with the stimulus group (the extent to which they thought they and the stimulus group belonged to the same group and the extent to which they perceived themselves to be similar to the stimulus group). Again as expected, minority brand participants exhibited stronger identification with the stimulus group than did majority brand participants. These results provide initial support to our proposed model of brand culture emergence.

SERIAL REPRODUCTION

We had completed another experiment that tested the effect of serial reproduction on the crystallization of brand culture. The procedures of this experiment were identical to those in the previous experiment, but with one exception. Instead of reading activity descriptions prepared by the researchers, the participants read and reproduced the essays written by the participants of the same condition in the previous experiment. That is, participants in the minority (majority) brand condition read the essays written by the participants in the minority (majority) brand condition in the previous experiment.

As in the previous experiment, participants in the minority brand condition rated the stimulus group as more open than did participants in the majority brand condition. Furthermore, compared to the majority brand participants, minority

brand participants believed more strongly that the stimulus group was homog-
enous and cohesive. The minority (vs. majority) brand participants also perceived
the stimulus group to be more trustworthy. Again, the two experimental conditions did not differ in the ratings of other personality traits or in the perceived
desirability of openness.

In short, a brand culture emerges when most brand users believe that other
brand users possess some common qualities (Wan et al., 2007). Our preliminary
results suggest that awareness of minority status and serial reproduction of brand
stories can facilitate the emergence of a novel brand culture.

BOUNDARIES OF THE EFFECTS

The program of research described previously has just entered Stage 2. The goal of
Stage 2 studies is to identify the boundaries of the effects discovered in the first stage
of the investigation. For example, we have completed two experiments to determine
whether the participant needs to be a brand user for the minority status and serial reproduction effects to occur. In one experiment, when the participants were not required
to make a brand choice at the beginning of the experiment, the perceptual biases
described previously disappeared, indicating that being a member of the minority
group is necessary for our effects to take place. Another experiment was conducted
to determine whether describing in-group activities is necessary for the perceptual
bias to occur. If in-group communication is a necessary condition for the perceptual
bias, the bias will emerge only when the participants perform the communication task
before rating the group. Thus, we manipulated the order of the dependent measures.
Half of the participants described the activities first and the remaining half performed
the ratings first. In this experiment, in-group communication was found to be a critical factor for the occurrence of the perceptual bias—the bias was obtained only when
the participants described the communication task first.

In a third experiment, we tested whether serial reproduction effects would
occur only when the story reproducer perceived the narratives to be a part of the
shared reality (Lyons & Kashima, 2003). In the experiment, the participants read
an essay of one previous participant (as opposed to the essays written by all participants) in the same experimental condition. Although the essays in the minority
brand condition (vs. those in the majority brand condition) contained more references to the openness of the group, the minority brand participants were not more
likely than the majority brand participants to attribute openness to the stimulus
group, probably because the participants attributed the contents of the essay to the
essay writer's idiosyncratic opinions.

CONCLUSIONS AND FUTURE DIRECTIONS

We begin with the assumption that similar social psychological processes underlie the emergence of a brand culture and that of a religious or ideological tradition. For example, the Acts of Apostles in the Bible tells the stories of how
the twelve apostles started the early Christian ministry after Jesus' resurrection.

These stories were circulated when Christianity was still a minority religion in the Roman Empire. Thus, we tried to simulate the emergence of a brand culture in the research laboratory. Our preliminary results showed that both awareness of minority status and serial reproduction of brand stories facilitate the emergence of shared beliefs about the sharedness of a certain positive quality in an in-group. Such shared beliefs are major constituents of a brand culture.

It is tempting to extrapolate from these findings that awareness of minority status and serial reproduction of in-group stories also facilitates the emergence of a religious or ideological tradition. However, before we make such generalizations, it is prudent to demonstrate that the two social psychological factors discussed in the present chapter also facilitate the emergence of a new religious/ideological culture. In a recently completed study, we have obtained some encouraging results. In this study, we had participants choose a position on an unfamiliar but controversial philosophical issue: "Does the feeling of disgust arise from sensory perception or in the mind's taste buds?" or in more concrete terms, "If you had to choose, would you rather eat poo-flavored chocolate or chocolate-flavored poo?" After the participants had indicated their choice, they were randomly assigned to the majority or minority condition. They read and talked about the behaviors of individuals who had made the same choice and rated these individuals' levels of morality and sociality. The results showed that compared to those in the majority condition, participants in the minority condition attributed higher levels of morality and sociability to the individuals about whom they had read. They also had a greater tendency to perceive these individuals as a group. These results suggest that our model may account for the emergence of a new ideological culture.

As mentioned, social psychologists have stayed away from studying the emergence of culture partly because social psychology does not seem to have the methods to address this question. We hope that even if the preliminary results reviewed in the present chapter have not explained how a culture emerges, they will convince the readers that social psychology may be able to provide an intelligent answer to this very challenging research question.

Of course, it would be naïve to believe that awareness of minority status and serial reproduction of brand stories are sufficient to start and maintain a brand culture. Institutional practices also play an important role in maintaining and reinforcing a brand culture. Returning to the example of Apple culture, Apple, Inc. has wittingly crafted a cultural identity for Apple users. During the *Think Different* Campaign, the following identity-defining message was broadcast frequently in the media to reinforce the idea that Apple users belong to a highly select group of "crazy," open, rebellious, and creative individuals.

Here's to the crazy ones.
The misfits.
The rebels.
The troublemakers.
The round pegs in the square holes.
The ones who see things differently.

They're not fond of rules.
And they have no respect for the status quo.
You can praise them, disagree with them, quote them, disbelieve them, glorify or vilify them.
About the only thing you can't do is ignore them.
Because they change things.
They invent. They imagine. They heal.
They explore. They create. They inspire.
They push the human race forward.
Maybe they have to be crazy.
How else can you stare at an empty canvas and see a work of art?
Or sit in silence and hear a song that's never been written?
Or gaze at a red planet and see a laboratory on wheels?
We make tools for these kinds of people.
While some see them as the crazy ones, we see genius.
Because the people who are crazy enough to think they can change the world, are the ones who do.

When will institutionalized practices become important in the crystallization, maintenance, and spread of a brand culture? How do these practices interact with the basic social psychological factors we consider in the present chapter to determine the future of a brand community? Furthermore, as a brand culture becomes more successful (e.g., when a large number of PC users switch to Apple), Apple will gradually lose its minority status and become a less identity-signaling brand (Berger & Heath, 2007). When this happens, the Apple culture may start to disintegrate, unless the culture is already externalized in many institutional practices. These are some exciting issues for social psychologists seeking new research challenges.

ACKNOWLEDGMENTS

We owe tribute to Bob Krauss for being courageous enough and "crazy" enough to break the ground, show us the way, and to push the discipline forward. As we explore the new territories in this investigation, we are delighted and encouraged to find that Bob has already been there and has paved the paths leading to our discovery.

We also wish to thank Janet Chan, Charis Kwan, Lisa Lam, Lacey O'Donnell, and Joon-hooh Sung for their assistance in running the experiments presented in this chapter.

Correspondence concerning this chapter should be sent to Shirley Cheng or Chi-yue Chiu, Department of Psychology, University of Illinois, Psychology Building, 603 East Daniel Street, Champaign, IL 61820. E-mail: ycheng2@uiuc.edu or cychiu@uiuc.edu.

REFERENCES

Berger, J. A., & Heath, C. (2005). Idea habitats: How the prevalence of environmental cues influences the success of ideas. *Cognitive Science, 29,* 195–221.
Berger, J. A., & Heath, C. (2007). Where consumers diverge from others: Identity-signaling and product domains. *Journal of Consumer Research, 34,* 121–134.

Breakwell, G. M. (1993). Integrating paradigms, methodological implications. In G. M. Breakwell & D. V. Canter (Eds.), *Empirical approaches to social representations* (pp. 184–201). Oxford, UK: Clarendon Press.

Brewer, M. B. (1991). The social self: On being the same and different at the same time. *Personality and Social Psychology Bulletin, 17*, 475–482.

Bruner, J. (1990). *Act of meaning*. Cambridge, MA: Harvard University Press.

Chiu, C-y., & Chen, J. (2004). Symbols and interactions: Application of the CCC model to culture, language, and social identity. In S-h. Ng, C. Candlin, & C-y. Chiu (Eds.), *Language matters: Communication, culture, and social identity*. Hong Kong: City University of Hong Kong Press.

Chiu, C-y., & Hong, Y. (1999). Social identification in a political transition: The role of implicit beliefs. *International Journal of Intercultural Relations, 23*, 297–318.

Chiu, C-y., & Hong, Y. (2005). Cultural competence: Dynamic processes. In A. Elliot & C. S. Dweck (Eds.), *Handbook of motivation and competence* (pp. 489–505). New York: Guilford.

Chiu, C-y., & Hong, Y-y. (2006). *Social psychology of culture*. New York: Psychology Press.

Chiu, C-y., & Hong, Y-y. (2007). Cultural processes: Basic principles. In E. T. Higgins & A. E. Kruglanski (Eds.), *Social psychology: Handbook of basic principles*. New York: Guilford.

Chiu, C-y., Krauss, R. M., & Lau, I. (1998). Some cognitive consequences of communication. In S. R. Fussell & R. J. Kreuz (Eds.), *Social and cognitive approaches to interpersonal communication* (pp. 259–276). Mahwah, NJ: Lawrence Erlbaum Associates.

Chiu, C-y., Krauss, R. M., & Lee, S. L. (1999). Communication and social cognition: A post-Whorfian approach. In T. Sugiman, M. Karasawa, J. H. Liu, & C. Ward (Eds.), *Progress in Asian social psychology* (Vol. 2, pp. 127–143). Seoul, Korea: Kyoyook-Kwahak-Sa Publishing.

Echterhoff, G., Higgins, E. T., & Groll, S. (2005). Audience-tuning effects on memory: The role of shared reality. *Journal of Personality and Social Psychology, 89*, 257–276.

Eco, U. (1994, September 30). The holy war: Mac vs. DOS. *Expresso*. http//umbertoeco-readers.blogspot.com/2007/11/holy-ear-mac-vs-dos.html.

Evans, S. (2005, April 21). Apple a day keeps the music at play. *BBC News*.

Fulford, R. (1997, August 13). Apple devotees. *Globe and Mail*.

Fussell, S. R., & Krauss, R. M. (1992). Coordination of knowledge in communication: Effects of speakers' assumptions about others' knowledge. *Journal of Personality and Social Psychology, 62*, 378–391.

Hardin, C., & Higgins, E. T. (1996). Shared reality: How social verification makes the subject objectives. In R. M. Sorentino & E. T. Higgins (Eds.), *Handbook of motivation and cognition* (Vol. 3, pp. 28–84). New York: Guilford.

Heath, C. (1996). Do people prefer to pass along good or bad news? Valence and relevance as predictors of transmission propensity. *Organizational Behavior and Human Decision Processes, 68*, 79–94.

Heath, C., Bell, C., & Sternberg, E. (2001). Emotional selection in memes: The case of urban legends. *Journal of Personality and Social Psychology, 81*, 1028–1041.

Higgins, E. T., & McCann, C. D. (1984). Social encoding and subsequent attitudes, impressions and memory: 'Context-driven' and motivational aspects of processing. *Journal of Personality and Social Psychology, 47*, 26–39.

Higgins, E. T., McCann, C. D., & Fondacaro, R. (1982). The "communication game": Goal-directed encoding and cognitive consequences. *Social Cognition, 1*, 21–37.

Kashima, Y. (2000). Maintaining cultural stereotype in the serial reproduction of narratives. *Personality and Social Psychology Bulletin, 26*, 594–604.

Krauss, R. M., & Chiu, C-y. (1998). Language and social psychology. In D. Gilbert, S. Fiske-Emory, & G. Lindzey (Eds.), *Handbook of social psychology* (4th ed., Vol. 2, pp. 41–88). New York: Guilford.

Latané, B. (1996). Dynamic social impact: The creation of culture through communication. *Journal of Communication, 46,* 13–25.

Lau, I. Y-M., Chiu, C-y., & Hong, Y. (2001). I know what you know: Assumptions about others' knowledge and their effects on message construction. *Social Cognition, 19,* 587–600.

Lau, I. Y-M., Chiu, C-y., & Lee, S-L. (2001). Communication and shared reality: Implications for the psychological foundations of culture. *Social Cognition, 19,* 350–371.

Lau, I. Y-M., Lee, S. L., & Chiu, C-y. (2004). Language, cognition, and reality: Constructing shared meanings through communication. In M. Schaller & C. Crandall (Eds.), *The psychological foundations of culture* (pp.77–100). Mahwah, NJ: Lawrence Erlbaum Associates.

Lehman, D., Chiu, C., & Schaller, M. (2004). Culture and psychology. *Annual Review of Psychology,* 55, 689–714.

Lyons, A., & Kashima, Y. (2001). The reproduction of culture: Communication processes tend to maintain cultural stereotypes. *Social Cognition, 19,* 372–394.

Lyons, A., & Kashima, Y. (2003). How are stereotypes maintained through communication? The influence of stereotype sharedness. *Journal of Personality and Social Psychology, 85,* 989–1005.

McCann, C. D., Higgins, E. T., & Fondacaro, R. A. (1991). Primacy and recency in communication and self-persuasion: How successive audiences and multiple encodings influence subsequent judgments. *Social Cognition, 9,* 47–66.

Moscovici, S. (1988). Notes towards a description of social representations. *European Journal of Social Psychology, 18,* 211–250.

Muñiz, A. M. Jr., & O'Guinn, T. C. (2001). Brand community. *Journal of Consumer Research, 27,* 412–432.

Muñiz, A. M. Jr., & Schau, H. J. (2005). Religiosity in the abandoned Apple Newton brand community. *Journal of Consumer Research, 31,* 737–747.

Norenzayan, A., Atran, S., Faulkner, J., & Schaller, M. (2006). Memory and mystery: The cultural selection of minimally counterintuitive narratives. *Cognitive Science, 30,* 1–23.

Pickett, C. L., Bonner, B. L., & Coleman, J. M. (2002). Motivated self-stereotyping: Heightened assimilation and differentiation needs result in increased levels of positive and negative self-stereotyping. *Journal of Personality and Social Psychology, 82,* 543–562.

Pickett, C. L., & Brewer, M. B. (2001). Assimilation and differentiation needs as motivational determinants of perceived ingroup and outgroup homogeneity. *Journal of Experimental Social Psychology, 37,* 341–348.

Schooler, J. W., & Engstler-Schooler, T. Y. (1990). Visual overshadowing of visual memories: Some things are better left unsaid. *Cognitive Psychology, 22,* 36–71.

Sinaceur, M., Heath, C., & Cole, S. (2005). Emotional and deliberative reactions to a public crisis. *Psychological Science, 16,* 247–254.

Sperber, D. (1996). *Explaining culture: A naturalistic approach.* Oxford, UK; Cambridge MA: Blackwell.

Wan, C., Chiu, C-y., Peng, S., & Tam, K-p. (2007). Measuring cultures through intersubjective norms: Implications for predicting relative identification with two or more cultures. *Journal of Cross-Cultural Psychology, 38,* 213–226.

Wan, C., Chiu, C-y., Tam, K., Lee, S., Lau, I. Y., & Peng, S. (2007). Perceived cultural importance and actual self-importance of values in cultural identification. *Journal of Personality and Social Psychology, 92,* 337–354.

9 Mind Merging

David McNeill, Susan Duncan, Amy Franklin,
James Goss, Irene Kimbara, Fey Parrill,
Haleema Welji, Lei Chen, Mary Harper,
Francis Quek, Travis Rose, and Ronald Tuttle

In this chapter, we focus on highly multimodal depictions of multiparty meetings (U.S. Air Force war gaming sessions). The data we code are eclectic—chains of linguistic co-reference, gaze deployments, "F-formations" (a category from Kendon, 1990), and parses of turn management, floor control, coalition formation, and conflict. The concept of a hyperphrase ties all the threads together; the idea of a growth point is the ultimate theoretical unit to which it is all tethered, with the hyperphrase describing various surface ways that growth points, the cognitive units communication aims to share, materialize during ongoing inter-actions. The project is relevant to a comment Krauss and Pardo (2004) made regarding a behavioral and brain sciences (BBS) contribution by Pickering and Garrod (2004), namely, that while communication plausibly involves the align-ment of speakers and their cognitive states, a move to reduce this to mechanistic priming excludes the reflective processes in dialogue.

INTRODUCTION

Our emphasis in this chapter is on floor control in multiparty discourse. The approach is broadly psycholinguistic, a perspective that includes turn management, turn exchange, and coordination; how to recognize the dominant speaker even when he or she is not speaking; and a theory of all this. The data to be examined comprise multimodal depictions of five-party meetings (U.S. Air Force war gaming sessions).

Multiparty discourse can be studied in various ways, for example, as signals of turn-taking intentions, marking the next "projected" turn unit and its content, and others. We adopt a perspective that emphasizes how speakers coordinate their *individual cognitive states* as they exchange turns while acknowledging and maintaining *the dominant speaker's status*. This goal is similar to Pickering and Garrod's (2004) interactive alignment account of dialogue, but we add gesture, gaze, posture, F-formations (Kendon, 1990), and several levels of co-referential chains—all to be explained in the following. We adopt a theoretical position agreeing with their portrayal of dialogue as "alignment" and of this alignment as automatic, in the sense of not draining mental resources, but not the type of "mechanistic" (priming) account of it they advocate (cf., Krauss & Pardo, 2004 for other qualms). The theory we are following is described in the next section. Alignment in this theory is nonmechanistic, does not single out priming, and regards conversational signaling (cf., papers in Ochs, Schegloff, & Thompson, 1996) as providing a synchrony of individual cognitive states, or "growth points." The role of gesture in all this is to produce converging imagery as well as speech as a means of socially constructed mutual cognition. Our aim is to analyze this cognitive "reflective" process (from Krauss & Pardo, 2004).

THEORETICAL BACKGROUND

THE GROWTH POINT

A growth point (GP) is a mental package that combines both linguistic categorical and imagistic components. Combining such semiotic opposites, the GP is inherently multimodal and creates a condition of instability, the resolution of which propels thought and speech forward. The GP concept, while theoretical, is empirically grounded. GPs are inferred from the totality of communication events with special focus on speech–gesture synchrony and co-expressivity (cf., McNeill, 2005 for extensive discussion). It is called a growth point because it is meant to be the initial pulse of thinking for and while speaking, out of which a dynamic process of organization emerges. It is thinking for speaking in the sense of Dan Slobin (1987)—the adjustment of one's thought to fit the affordances provided by the language one is using; it is thinking while speaking in a dynamic sense, that thought and language, as they unfold, are inseparable processes. GPs are brief such dynamic processes, during which idea units take form. If two individuals share GPs, they can be said to "inhabit" the same state of cognitive being and this, in the theoretical picture being considered, is what communication aims to achieve, at least in part. The concept of inhabitance was expressed by Merleau-Ponty (1962) in the following way: "Language certainly has inner content, but this is not self-subsistent and self-conscious thought. What then does language express, if it does not express thoughts? It presents or rather it *is* the subject's taking up of a position in the world of his meanings" (p. 193; emphasis in the original). The GP is a unit of this process of "taking up a position in the world of meanings." In this model, an analysis of conversation should bring out how alignments of inhabitance come about and, as this is taking place, how the participants maintain the overall conversational milieu.

THE HYPERPHRASE

A second theoretical idea—the "hyperphrase"—is crucial for analyzing these alignments and maintenances, and how they are attained in complex multiparty meetings. A hyperphrase is a nexus of converging, interweaving processes that cannot be completely untangled. We approach the hyperphrase through a multimodal structure comprising verbal and nonverbal (gaze, gesture) data.

To illustrate the concept, we shall examine one such phrase from a National Science Foundation sponsored project carried out jointly by Quek, Harper, and McNeill (the "Wombats study"). This hyperphrase implies a communicative pulse structured on the verbal, gestural, and gaze levels simultaneously. The hyperphrase began part way into the verbal text (# is an audible breath pause, / is a silent pause, * is a self-interruption; F_0 groups are indicated with underlining, and gaze is in italics):

> *we're gonna go over to # thirty-five 'cause / they're ah* / they're from the neigh borhood they know what's going on #"*.

The critical aspect indicating a hyperphrase is that gaze turned to the listener in the middle of a linguistic clause and remained there over the rest of the selection. This stretch of speech was also accompanied by multiple occurrences of a single gesture type whereby the right hand with its fingers spread moved up and down over the deictic zero point of the spatialized content of speech (see Table 9.1). The speaker and listener in this experiment had before them a model village with actual objects on a surface; as the speaker described what was to be done, her right hand constantly shifted locations, hovering over different spots on the board (in the example, it was over two houses with readable numbers 35 and 36). Considering the two non-verbal features, gaze and gesture, together with the lexical content of the speech, this stretch of speech is a *single production pulse* organized thematically around the idea unit, "the people from the neighborhood in thirty-five." This would plausibly be the unpacking of a GP. Such a hyperphrase brings together several linguistic clauses. It spans a self-interruption and repair, and spans nine F_0 groups. The F_0 groups subdivide the thematic cohesion of the hyperphrase, but the recurrence of similar gesture strokes compensates for this oversegmentation. For example, the F_0 break between "what's" and "going on" is spanned by a single gesture down stroke. It is unlikely that a topic shift occurred within this gesture. Thus, the hyperphrase is a production domain in which linguistic clauses, prosody, and speech repair all play out, each on its own timescale, and are held together as the hyperphrase nexus.

Thus, we have two major theoretical ideas with which to approach the topic of multiparty discourse—the GP and the hyperphrase. The GP is the theoretical unit of

TABLE 9.1
Illustrating a Hyperphrase

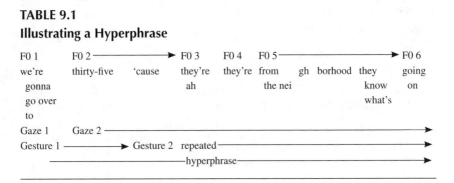

the speaker's state of cognitive being. The hyperphrase is a package of multimodal information that presents a GP. Through hyperphrases GPs can be shared. Multiple speakers can contribute to the same hyperphrases and growth points. Speaker 2 synchronizes growth points with Speaker 1 by utilizing various turn-taking "signals" to achieve synchrony. This hypothesis assumes that conversationalists align GPs— Speaker 2 emits signals in a hyperphrase until he or she senses alignment, and then allows an exchange of the speaking turn. The signals can be seen as bringing one state of cognitive being into alignment with another, with the hyperphrase package managing the coordination. We do not suppose that all turn exchanges are so organized, but we see evidence, in multiparty discourse, that much of it is.

The repeated gesture in the example seems to serve as a metric to "regiment the flow" of the discourse in a cohesive/coherent text-segment, to use a concept introduced by Silverstein (1993). A "configuration of indexicals" across modalities in the hyperphrase shows mutual indexicality that is pointing toward one GP. The hyperphrase is an "indexical structure" of a "textual event" in Silverstein's parlance.

THE VACE PROJECT*

The aim of our research project under the Video Analysis and Content Extraction (VACE) program is to understand, across a wide multimodal front, interpersonal interactions during meetings of approximately five to six individuals, U.S. Air Force officers taking part in military gaming exercises at the Air Force Institute of Technology (AFIT), at the Wright Patterson Air Force Base, in Dayton, OH. The participants represent various military specialties. The commanding officer for the gaming session is always in position E. The task of this particular meeting was to figure out how a captured "alien missile head" (which in fact looked rather like a coffee thermos with fins) functioned. The session lasted approximately 42 minutes. The examples to be studied are extracted from the latter half of this period. Figure 9.1 shows the meeting room and camera configuration.

We give some general statistics for gesture (pointing) and gaze during the entire meeting, including notes on some coding difficulties in the case of gaze, and then analyze two focus segments, concentrating on how the dominant participant (E) maintains his position, despite multiple shifts of speaker. We will also analyze the unique way the sole female participant seizes a speaking turn (participant C, who although of the same military rank as the others, shows traits of marginalization in the group).

POINTING

The dominant participant, E, is the chief source of pointing but is the least frequent target of pointing by others. C and D are the least likely to point at anyone but are

* This research has been supported by the Advanced Research and Development Activity (ARDA), Video Analysis and Content Extraction (VACE) II grant #665661 (entitled From Video to Information: Cross-Modal Analysis of Planning Meetings). PIs are Francis Quek, Mary Harper, and David McNeill.

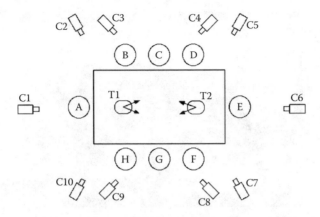

FIGURE 9.1 Layout of the testing room. The participants were in positions C, D, E, F, and G (positions A, B, and H were vacant). Illustrations in later figures are from Camera 1's vantage point.

the most likely to be pointed at by others (D is notably passive in the group). This pattern—rarely the source of pointing, often the target—may signal marginality, actual or felt, in a group setting. Table 9.2 summarizes the pointing patterns.

Figure 9.2a and Figure 9.2b illustrate two pointing events, the first showing E with his right hand rising from rest on the table to point minimally at C (and thereby authorizing—weakly—her as speaker; notice also how E's gaze reinforces the deictic action); the second is F pointing at G but in a curious way that shifts the origo or

TABLE 9.2
Pointing Patterns in the Meeting

	Source C	Source D	Source E	Source F	Source G	Total
Target C	3	2	17	8	10	40
Target D	1	4	21	11	3	40
Target E	4	0	5	2	0	11
Target F	3	2	13	0	2	20
Target G	4	4	8	7	0	124
Target Others	12	10	59	28	15	
Target All	0	0	5	0	0	5
Target Some	1	2	10	2	0	15
Target Obj	3	6	20	12	24	65
Target Abstract	5	11	8	1	1	26
Total	24	31	107	43	40	245

Note: "Target Others" excludes self-pointing.

(a)

(b)

FIGURE 9.2 (a) E (head of table) points with right hand and gaze at C (left front). Hand pointing is difficult to see in a still shot: It was accomplished dynamically, by rotating the hand toward C. Participants are festooned with motion tracking (VICON) jewelry. (b) F (right rear) points at G with origo shift toward E.

perspective base of the gesture to a locus in front of his own location, a maneuver that may unconsciously reflect the "gravitational pull" of E on his right.

GAZE

Table 9.3 summarizes the distribution of gazes during the entire meeting. Again, as in pointing, E's dominant status is registered by an asymmetry, but now with reverse polarity: He is the most frequent gaze target but the least frequent gaze source. C, the sole female present, is the least frequent gaze target but the most frequent gaze source—a pattern also seen in a National Institute of Standards

TABLE 9.3
Frequency of Gaze During the Meeting

	C Source	D Source	E Source	F Source	G Source	Total
C Target	X	38	45	59	67	209
D Target	70	X	83	112	94	359
E Target	212	136	X	144	149	641
F Target	150	107	98	X	116	471
G Target	75	52	63	68	X	258
Total	507	333	289	383	426	1938

and Technology (NIST) interaction analyzed previously (unpublished data) again involving a female participant, although not the sole female in that case, but again seemingly the marginal participant in the group.

However, gaze *duration* by E is longer—duration and shift of gaze may perform distinct functions in this tradeoff. Table 9.4 compares the frequency and duration of gazes by E to G versus those of G to E. Indeed, E looks with longer durations at G than G does at E, but this asymmetry does not hold for gazes at neutral space, the object, or papers—at these targets G's gazes are actually longer (G is one of the most active gaze shifters). E's fewer, longer gazes at people but not at objects can be explained if he uses gaze to *manage* the situation— showing attentiveness (hence longer) but feeling no pressure to seek permission

TABLE 9.4
Comparison of E's Gaze Duration (fewest shifts) to G's (more shifts)

	E's Gaze Number	E (fewest shifts) Average Duration (s)	G's Gaze Number	G (more shifts) Average Duration (s)
At C	45	5.1	67	1.1
At D	82	4.0	93	2.6
At E	—	—	149	1.9
At F	98	3.9	116	1.6
At G	63	3.1	—	—
Neutral space	150	1.0	292	1.5
At object	58	1.7	42	2.8
At papers	33	3.2	18	8.2
Others	4	2.4	8	1.9
Average	67	3.0	98	2.7

to speak (therefore fewer). Such fewer, longer gazes at people (but not at objects) are recognizably properties of a dominant speaker.

To Summarize Dominance and Marginality

Both pointing and gaze correlate with the social dimension of dominance, but in opposite directions. In *pointing*, the gesture has an active function—selecting a target; it is thus correlated positively with dominance and negatively with marginality. Marginal members may frequently be pointing targets as part of recruiting efforts.

In *gaze*, the action has a passive or perceptual function—locating the source of information or influence; it is accordingly correlated negatively with dominance and positively with marginality, especially when brief.

However, in E's case, *gaze* is also active, not passive, and this is reflected in longer durations at people only, combined with fewer shifts of gaze overall; duration thus correlates with dominance positively.

Coding Issues

Inferring gaze from video poses difficulties of coding, and it is well to say something about this. The following comments are based on notes by the coder (co-author Welji): F and G wear glasses, making it difficult to see where their eyes are and even sometimes whether the eyes are open. Often it is necessary to look for a slight movement of the eye or eyelid, which can be hard to spot. In addition, neutral space can coincide with the location of the object on the table and sometimes it is difficult to distinguish what is the target of the gaze. A third difficulty is that at some orientations it is hard to get a good view of the eyes. Finally, when coding in slow motion, a blink and a short glance away may be indistinguishable. Given the uncertainties, that no more than 8% of the gaze judgments for the glasses-wearing participants and less than 3% for the best participant were deemed tentative is perhaps reassuring.

Focus Segments

Two segments were selected for detailed analysis. Both came from the second half of the 42-minute session.

Focus 1

The first focus segment highlights a turn-taking exchange in which hyperphrases carry multiple functions. The speech is as follows:

1. E: "okay. u-"
2. G: "So it's going to make it a little tough."
3. F: "It was my understanding that the- the whole head pivoted to provide the aerodynamic uh moment. But uh I could be wrong on. That uh …"
4. G: "that would be a different design from-"
5. F: "From what-"

6. G: "from- from the way we do it."
7. F: "Okay."
8. E: "Okay so if we-"
9. G: "But we can look into that."
10. E: "If we're making that assumption ((unintel.)) as a high fidelity test"
11. F: "Yeah."

Turn Taking at Momentary Overlap of GPs

An obvious case of a GP starting with one speaker and passing to the next appears at 5, where F says "From what" and G, at 6, takes over with "from- from the way we do it." The hyperphrase package of the joint inhabitance is seen in the deployment of gaze and gesture:

> F begins with a glance at E, then gestures interactively toward G, followed immediately by gaze at G and an iconic gesture depicting the alien coffee mug (see Figure 9.3).

The hyperphrase here is a multimodal unit within which dimensions of gesture and gaze exchange places in creating the GP concerning the "way we do it," related to the imagery component depicting the object. We also see a hyperphrase being constructed by F that includes social information: E's standing as dominant speaker, in the quick glance at him at the start; G's status as current speaker, in the interactive gesture to him; and the ongoing role of the "thermos" as the discourse theme.

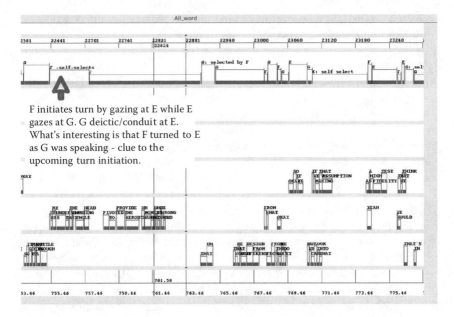

FIGURE 9.3 MacVissta screenshot of turn taking in Focus 1. Notes added on how turn taking correlated with gaze and gesture (see Chen et al., 2006 for details on the MacVissta interface).

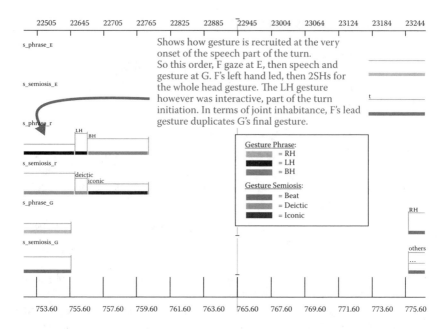

FIGURE 9.4 MacVissta screenshot of gesture in Focus 1. Notes added on how gesture correlated with gaze and turn taking.

Figure 9.4 displays how gesture was recruited at the onset of the new turn—a further component of the hyperphrase at this moment.

F-Formation Analysis

An F-formation is discovered by tracking gaze direction in a social group. The concept was introduced by Adam Kendon, who said, "An F-formation arises when two or more people cooperate together to maintain a space between them to which they all have direct and exclusive [equal] access" (Kendon, 1990, p. 209). An F-formation, however, is not just about shared space. Crucially, it has an associated meaning, reveals a common ground, and helps us, the analysts, find the units of thematic content in the conversation. Figure 9.5 shows the F-formations in Focus 1. Tracking the appearance of the same color (shades of gray here) across participants identifies each F-formation, defined as a shared focus of attention. In the focus segment, an F-formation defined by shared gaze at F (lightest gray) is replaced by one defined by gaze at G (fourth darkest gray). Interestingly, there is a brief transition or disintegration with gaze either at E or at nonperson objects—acknowledgment of E's status as dominant. But the main inference from the F-formation analysis is that speaker F was recognized as the next speaker *before* he began to speak, and this recognition was timed exactly with *his* brief gaze at E—a further signal of E's dominance. This gaze created a short F-formation with G, since both then looked

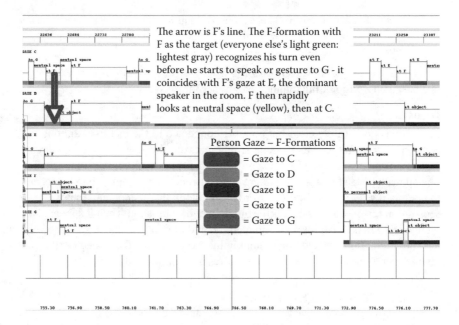

The arrow is F's line. The F-formation with F as the target (everyone else's light green: lightest gray) recognizes his turn even before he starts to speak or gesture to G - it coincides with F's gaze at E, the dominant speaker in the room. F then rapidly looks at neutral space (yellow), then at C.

Person Gaze – F-Formations

= Gaze to C
= Gaze to D
= Gaze to E
= Gaze to F
= Gaze to G

FIGURE 9.5 MacVissta screenshot of F-formations in Focus 1. Notes added on how F-formations correlated with gesture, gaze, and turn taking.

at E. This in effect signaled the turn exchange, and is another component of the hyperphrase at this moment, ushering in a joint growth point.

Back to Momentary Sharing of GPs

So, what happened here at the turn exchange was a synchronizing of inhabitance (the nonrepresentational mode of signification defined by Merleau-Ponty, 1962) by F (the next speaker) with G (the current speaker) via their joint F-formation with E the target. F's hyperphrase (a bundle of multimodal features) encompassed all these features. F's GP included the idea of his collaboration with G and with this, he could lock-step their current cognitive states. F's first GP was in fact a continuation of G's. The details appear in how gaze and gesture deployed around the table:

> Dominant E continues to gaze at designated speaker G when G gestures at object and others apparently look at the object.
>
> G gazes at the dominant participant, and makes deictic/conduit gestures in his direction (cf., McNeill, 1992 for these terms). G then shifts his gaze to the object, and then quickly shifts back to E. Nonspeaker D doesn't shift to E when G shifts but keeps gaze at G—suggesting that what we see is the speaker affirming the dominant status of E, but the overhearers are free to respond to the speaker's new turn.

Also, when F takes turn from G he waits until G finishes his ongoing sentence, but first turns to look at E in the middle of the sentence, and then starts his turn while still looking at E (only after this shifting to G).

The next example, however, displays a very different form of turn exchange, one based on *non*-joint inhabitance of a hyperphrase.

Focus 2

For reasons not entirely clear but possibly connected to the fact that, although of equal military rank, C was the sole female present, this speaker does not create a series of moves designed to synchronize idea units with any current speaker. She appears instead to wait until there is no current state of joint inhabitance, and then embarks on a turn. In other words, C exploits the phenomena that we have seen but in reverse: She waits until a break in hyperphrasing; when it appears, she plunges in. Focus 2 begins as F signaled the end of his turn, and E's gaze briefly left the interaction space. C then quickly moved to speak. The speech is the following, but to understand the action requires a multimodal picture:

> F: "to get it right the first time. So I appreciate that."
> F relinquishes turn—intonation declines.
> E gazes straight down at table (no target?), setting stage for next step.
> C intervenes with ferret-like quickness:
> C: "I'm thinking graduation exercise kind of thing. You know we might actually blow something up. Obviously we don't want to."
> E (not F, the previous turn-holder) acknowledges C's turn with gesture and gaze, but in a manner that suggests surprise—further confirming that C's strategy was to wait for a general lapse of inhabitance before starting to speak.

Figure 9.6a shows the moment C spots her chance to speak (the first line above). Figure 9.6b depicts nine frames (0.3 s) later. Note how all the participants, in unison, are shifting their gaze to C and forming in this way a multiparty F-formation and hyperphrase with C the focal point.

One has to ponder the effects of a strategy like C's that avoids shared hyperphrasing and transitional GPs. C's experience of the interaction dynamics is seemingly quite different from the others and theirs equally from hers. Whether this is due to "marginality" (as evident in pointing and gaze, Table 9.2 and Table 9.3) or is a personal trait is unclear. An all-female meeting would be of great interest, but we have not managed to assemble one to date.

COMPARISON OF FOCUS 1 AND FOCUS 2

In contrast to Focus 1, where we saw an intricate buildup of a hyperphrase out of gaze and gesture, in Focus 2 C gazes at E (even though she is following G), and E provides authorizing back channels in the form of gaze and pointing. This is the total exchange; there is no real hyperphrase or possibility of a shared transitional GP.

Taking the two focus segments together, it seems clear that speaker status can be allotted, negotiated, or seized in very short time sequences, but dominant speaker status is ascribed and changes slowly if at all.

(a)

(b)

FIGURE 9.6 (a) C leaps in. Gaze around the table is generally unfocused. (b) Nine frames (0.3 s) later, gaze generally shifts to C and E points at C.

CO-REFERENCE, F-FORMATIONS, AND GAZE

The way in which discourse coheres—how segments beyond individual utterances take form—can be observed in various ways, but we have found tracking co-referential chains in speech to be highly useful. A "reference" is an object or other meaning entity nominated in speech; a co-referential chain is a set (not necessarily consecutive) of linguistic nominations of the same referent. As a whole, the chain comprises a "topic" in the conversation. A co-referential chain links extended text stretches and, by its nature, is interpretable on the level of meaning and can be the basis of hyperphrases. An important insight is that co-referential chains also can span different speakers and so can tie together multiparty hyperphrases and shared growth points in dialogues.

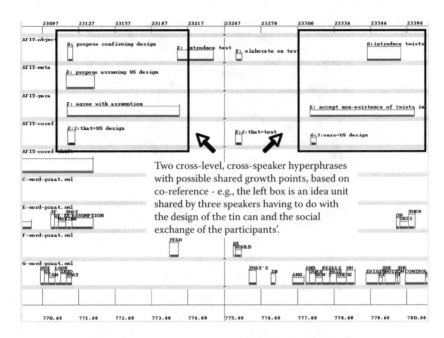

FIGURE 9.7   MacVissta screenshot of co-reference threads across multiple speakers creating F-formations.

Co-referential chains thread across different levels in the structure of discourse. A given chain might track over each of the following:

Object level: Cohesion through references to object world; for example, "a confirming design."

Meta level: Cohesion through references to the discourse itself; for example, "I propose assuming a U.S. design."

Para level: Cohesion through references that include individual participants; for example, "I agree with the assumption."

In Figure 9.7, a hyperphrase builds up between participants over each of these levels. In so doing, it unites references to the alien object by tying them to the theme of how it is designed and what should initially be assumed about this design, each contribution from a different speaker and on a different level.

Co-references also provide an overall profile of thematic content within a conversation. Figure 9.8 shows the cumulative distribution of co-references over the total 42 minutes of the AFIT session. A small number of references account for the vast bulk of cohesion in this discourse. The curve can be read from left to right as listing the dominant topics and then less dominant topics—FME people: (those who work on foreign material exploitation), operators of Air Force systems, and so forth, with the bulk of references on the long tail of single mentions.

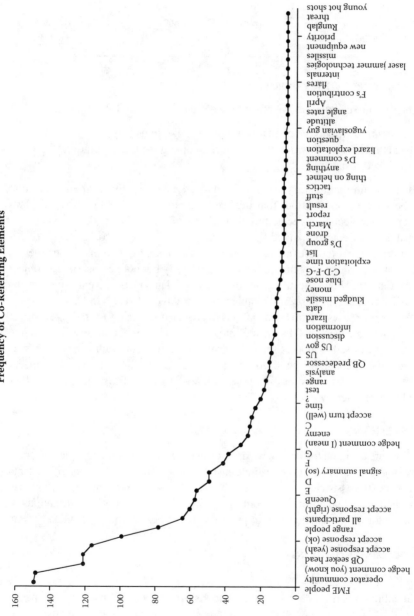

FIGURE 9.8 Distribution of co-references in the 42-minute session.

TABLE 9.5
Gaze and Level Shift

	Shift	Not Shift	N
Instrumental gaze	44%	66%	32
Social gaze	67%	33%	15

ELABORATIONS ON THE F-FORMATION

In the discourse situations we observe, we see two types of F-formation:

1. *social*, in which the elements are other individuals, and
2. *instrumental*, in which two or more people gaze at a common event or object in space.

The elaborations identify different kinds of social interactive configurations that can be seen in conversations that involve both participants and physical displays of objects (projection screens, the alien object of the AFIT session, etc.). Social F-formations are accompanied by significant shifts of the discourse levels of co-referential chains (object, meta, and para in various permutations); instrumental F-formations tend to stay on the same level (usually but not necessarily the object level). Table 9.5 shows the difference between social and instrumental F-formations in earlier data (a four-party roundtable interaction recorded at NIST).

As hyperphrases, social F-formations thus open up a variety of trading relations with which to engender GPs during interactions. This richer variety is of course significant in itself. It makes sense in terms of the stimulus value of another person in a social context. The discovery is that social gaze has an immediate effect on the cohesive structure of discourse with co-reference shifts strapped together into hyperphrases by gaze.

COALITIONS

To illustrate coalition formation, we draw on another AFIT session in which one military officer and four civilian institute instructors wrestled over (fictional) students for scholarship assistance, a process rife with coalition formation, as anyone who has served on academic admissions committees knows. We focus on manifestations of coalition formation and how to interpret these in the light of mind merging.

RECOGNIZING COALITIONS

Using Co-Referential Chains

As mentioned earlier, co-referential chains shift levels (e.g., from meta to para). Such shifts mark the negotiation of reference and often signal the formation of a coalition. Coalitions seem to show up as *clusters of paranarrative references surrounding one or more metanarrative references*. Such sandwich-like structure

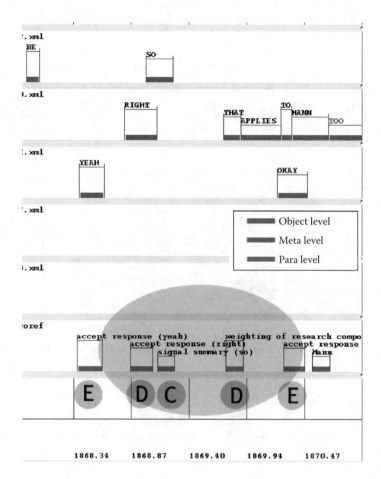

FIGURE 9.9 MacVissta screenshot of a co-referential thread tying together a coalition.

suggests that coalitions between participants end with statements related to the individual participant's roles, but also orient to focus on one or more statements whose significance relates to the discourse itself, devoid of personal identifications. In terms of "participation frameworks" (Cassell & McNeill, 1991), a coalition is a package of two such frameworks, one the activity of the task on which the coalition focuses, the other the social group joining it—the meta and para levels, respectively. By looking at who is speaking, we can detect membership in a coalition. Figure 9.9 illustrates such a case.

In this instance, D is seeking acceptance (*you know*—paranarrative), C provides it (*yeah*—paranarrative), and both refer at metanarrative level to D's previous speech (*that*). The meta comment (*weighting of research components*) is sandwiched between paras, which reflects several important qualities of these

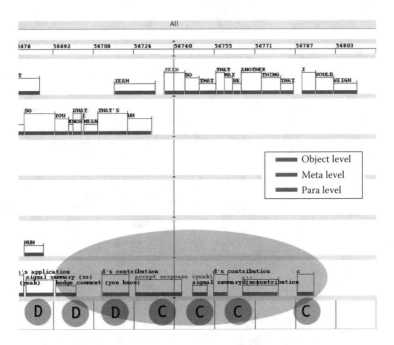

FIGURE 9.10 MacVissta screenshot of a conflict and disappearance of participant from a coalition.

coalitions—the coalition is brief, and the coalition launches from a level with some personal identification (agreement, opinion) but then fixes on a level of impersonal focus on the structure of the discourse task itself.

Identifying Conflicts

Conflicts in a group, as opposed to coalitions, can be identified as *changes across coalitions*. In the following, participant D disagrees with the system used to rank candidates. One clue to this disagreement is that he drops out of the ongoing coalition in which he had been participating (see Figure 9.10):

    Coalition 1: C, D, E
    Coalition 2: C, D
    Coalition 3: C, D, E
    Coalition 4: C, E

Thus, by the end, a new C, E coalition has formed. In terms of hyperphrases, the structure changes with the absence of D, so that any further sharing of growth points would be defined in fields to which he would not contribute. Therefore, temporarily, he would also not influence the discourse.

Summary Thus Far

Coalitions are marked by para-level comments bracketing at least one meta-level comment. This makes sense in that participants in a new coalition first indicate their allegiance to the theme (para-level) and then indicate the significance of the theme to the overall discourse (meta-level). It is possible that such a pattern is a signature of these kinds of temporary coalitions that form around specific discourse themes.

Sequence of Gaze—Another Clue

Attempts to secure mutual gaze show how coalitions are built. During a segment identified (via co-reference) as a coalition, C's gaze pattern shows how the coalition was created: the function of gaze includes deixis, C pointing (with gaze) at G, and so forth.

C tries to secure G, but is not reciprocated, then secures D, then E (arrows show direction of gaze). See Figure 9.11 and Figure 9.12.

1. C→G
2. C↔D
3. C↔E

A shared co-referential chain with C is secured when D and E return his gaze; G does not return gaze, is not part of the coalition, and might now loom as point of conflict. The important point is the alignment of the coalition with a shared field of oppositions, making possible merging GPs.

Garnering Agreement

Within a third AFIT session devoted to brainstorming a solution to pollution damage to the Lincoln Memorial, behavioral indices comprised patterns according to the acceptance or rejection of proposed ideas; these patterns in turn may be functionally

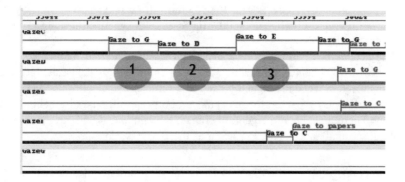

FIGURE 9.11 MacVissta screenshot of gaze recruiting members of a coalition. See Figure 9.12.

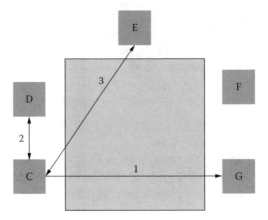

FIGURE 9.12   Map showing sequence of gaze in Figure 9.11.

related to inducing acceptance or rejection or simply overlooking some proposed ideas. Both gaze and the quantity of speaking turns appear to be crucial:

- Mutual gaze triggers a secondary turn by a listener and a possible coalition for the proposal.
- Multiple turns take place when an idea is accepted (cf., the para- and meta-level sandwich of co-references when a collation forms).
- Multiple turns by speaker supporting his own idea leads to acceptance. Thus, the cliché of the "fast talker" has some reality.
- Rejected proposals, on the other hand, do not trigger mutual gaze between speakers and listeners and thus do not initiate the above sequence.

It is noteworthy that the fate of a proposal—acceptance or rejection—is correlated with this pattern of information flow, but not necessarily with the validity of the proposal itself. In the session under study, the correct solution (in the sense that it was the one actually adopted by the Park Service) was rejected (it did not initiate mutual gaze).

The acceptance pattern can be explained in terms of the main theoretical concepts of this chapter. Acceptance includes mind merging, just as does turn exchange, and in fact it relies on the latter as a vehicle. Thus, both shared GPs and hyperphrases play a part in the acceptance of a proposal. Shared inhabitance is the key. There must be agreement, of course, but agreement without inhabitance is blind, so inhabitance is the key as far as these observations go.

CONCLUSIONS

For communication studies, the implications of this research seem clear: A multimodal approach uncovers phenomena not otherwise seen. The concept of a hyperphrase, as a group of multimodal features in trading relationships, is particularly interesting from an instrumental viewpoint—you want to pick up these interacting features if you can. We focus on floor management: who is dominant, how are turns at speaking managed, what are the ways in which someone seizes a turn, and how does the alpha participant maintain control, as well as the formation of coalitions, cleavages, and coups.

The psycholinguistic interest in these meetings lies in the apparent synchronizing of states of joint inhabitance that the turn-taking process engages. However, we see a different mode of turn taking in Officer C's case, in which her procedure was not the synchronization of, but rather waiting for, momentary lapses of joint inhabitance. While a single example cannot rule out individual style as the source of a pattern, it is the case that C's social isolation, as the sole female participant, is also a possible factor. While common ground (Clark, 1996) seems indisputable in a general sense (the officers all knew, for example, they were in the U.S. Air Force, were at AFIT, were taking part in a training exercise, had before them an alien object—in fact, assumed all the high frequency topics seen in Figure 9.8), C jumped in precisely when she sensed a lapse in the common ground—F had just given up his turn, E was drifting into the ether, no one else was starting to speak, etc. It is therefore worth considering that common ground has two orientations: a general one, which, as Clark emphasized, is a precondition for all communication; and a local one, which is not a precondition but a *product* of the interaction, and is not a given in the conversation but is constantly unfolding. From this viewpoint, C, by interjecting, created a new common ground. With the general-local common ground distinction, we can track the dynamics of the interaction.

From a psycholinguistic and social psychology viewpoint, the management of turn taking, floor control, and speaker dominance (even if not speaking) are crucial variables, and the prospect of instrumentally recording clues to these kinds of things has been the basis for valuable interdisciplinary work between psycholinguists and engineers (cf., Chen et al., 2006). These descriptive features are the reality of the meeting to which instrumental recording methods need to make reference. The automatic or semi-automatic monitoring of meetings needs to be related to the actual events taking place in the meeting at the social level, and our coding is designed to provide an analytic description of these events. The coding emphasizes the multimodal character of the meeting, attending equally to speech, nonverbal behavior, and the use of space, and the aim of the collaboration is to test which (if any) recoverable audio and video features provide clues to such events, thus warranting human inspection.

Coalition formation and maintenance follow the same meshing-of-mental-configurations principle. Like-minded partners take on demonstrably similar meanings in these materials. We can compare this interpretation to the mechanisms proposed by Pickering and Garrod (2004). We are in agreement with their overall theory that dialogue succeeds by "aligning" participants on several levels, phonetic up to "situation models." Our difference lies in the "mechanism." While they look to an automatic process of priming, so that the subsequent dialogue is causally dependent on what has gone before, we are suggesting that the metapragmatic calibration is the hyperphrase, a "reflective" process to use

Krauss and Pardo's (2004) term, whereby the elements of dialogue that inhabit the same or similar GPs across participants are interchangeable and of equal potency. In this way, dialogue is not confined to overlaps with the immediate surround; on the contrary, the "mechanism" in a hyperphrase is the *non*overlaps that meet the condition of the co-inhabiting growth points, and is ultimately dependent on thought in context. We consider this hypothesis to have inherent plausibility in its freedom and openness, as opposed to the limits of priming repetition.

In overall conclusion, we emphasize the importance of a truly multimodal perspective in uncovering interaction dynamics.

REFERENCES

Cassell, J., & McNeill, D. (2001). Gesture and the poetics of prose. *Poetics Today 12*, 375–404.

Chen, L., Rose, T., Parrill, F., Han, X., Tu, J., Huang, Z., Harper, M., Quek, F., McNeill, D., Tuttle, R., & Huang, T. (2006). VACE multimodal meeting corpus. In S. Renals & S. Bengio (Eds.), *Machine learning for multimodal interaction. Second international workshop, MLMI 2005* (pp. 40–51). Berlin: Springer.

Clark, H. H. (1996). *Using language*. Cambridge, UK: Cambridge University Press.

Kendon, A. (1990). *Conducting interactions: Patterns of behavior in focused encounters*. Cambridge, UK: Cambridge University Press.

Krauss, R. M., & Pardo, J. S. (2004). Is alignment always the result of automatic priming? *Behavioral and Brain Sciences, 27*(02), 203–204.

McNeill, D. (1992). *Hand and mind: What gestures reveal about thought*. Chicago: University of Chicago Press.

McNeill, D. (2005). *Gesture and thought*. Chicago: University of Chicago Press.

Merleau-Ponty, M. (1962). *Phenomenology of perception* (C. Smith, trans.). London: Routledge.

Ochs, E., Schegloff, E. A., & Thompson, S. A. (Eds.). (1996). *Interaction and grammar*. Cambridge, UK: Cambridge University Press.

Pickering, M. J., & Garrod, S. (2004). Toward a mechanistic psychology of dialogue. *Behavioral and Brain Sciences, 27*(02), 169–226.

Silverstein, M. (1993). Metapragmatic discourse and metapragmatic function. In J. A. Lucy (Ed.), *Reflexive language: Reported speech and metapragmatics* (pp. 33–58). Cambridge, UK: Cambridge University Press.

Slobin, D. (1987). Thinking for speaking. In J. Aske, N. Beery, L. Michaelis, & H. Filip (Eds.), *Proceedings of the 13th annual meeting of the Berkeley Linguistics Society* (pp. 435–445). Berkeley, CA: Berkeley Linguistic Society.

Section III

The Perception of
Speech and Identity

10 Spoken Expression of Individual Identity and the Listener

Robert E. Remez

To a listener, a brief phrase is sufficient to evoke a personal impression of a talker. The speech of someone familiar can have a subtle impact, and even an unfamiliar voice suggests traits, true or false, of the one who spoke. It should not be surprising that qualitative variation in speech has commonly been identified as the source of these personal impressions, and a substantial technical literature reports investigations of the acoustic correlates of regional and social group, a talker's age and sex, and a talker's affective state and arousal (classics include Abercrombie, 1967; Bricker & Pruzansky, 1976; Hecker, 1971; a recent review is offered by Kreiman, Van Lancker-Sidtis, & Gerratt, 2005). However, the custom of ascribing impressions of personal quality solely to the extralinguistic properties of speech has led to neglect of a significant dimension of individual variation that can be critical to the expression and perception of personal identity. An individual's characteristic way of producing the consonants and vowels that compose words can be distinctive even when a spoken expression is otherwise unremarkable, prosaic, and normative. Although an individual's articulation of speech is a linguistically regulated aspect of communication, personal consistency in this aspect of symbolic expression provides a rich assortment of indexical attributes. Some recent and new studies draw attention to the potential role of *idiolect*, the individual linguistic characteristics nested within dialect, in individual identification.

To expose the argument and evidence, it is useful to consider the precise circumstances in which we speak and listen. A gloss of the production of language spotlights this condition (Levelt, 1989). In a conversation, an urge to take a turn initiates a semantic aim, an intention to create an utterance of a certain dimension. This goal initiates a compositional function to choose words and to assemble them into an order with representational properties that more or less match the semantic aim. There are many ways to choose words: by shade of meaning, perhaps, or also commonness or rarity, or by alliteration or rhyme. The dimensions of variation among the words of a language include semantic properties and differential incidence, and variation is well studied in each of these. Alliteration and rhyme are characteristics of the meaningless phonological form by which words are distinguished. Phonemic form amounts to an addressing scheme for items in lexical memory, marking distinctions among words, although this dimension of variation also supplies a set of abstract criteria for articulating the word and making a private linguistic composition public.*

Through this last juncture in production, talkers and listeners within a community share the language forms that are used to compose utterances. This cheerful confluence of symbolic processes is compromised, however, by vocal dispersion when language is spoken. Classically, the population of a community is said to vary greatly in the vocal anatomy used to express the phonemic form of language phonetically (Fant, 1966; Ladefoged, 1967). Intuitively, this is evident in contrasting the voices of men, women, and children who, speaking the same words, can sound distinct. The speech of each individual gives sound to the shared linguistic forms in the unique characteristics of the person who spoke. In consequence, each individual expresses personal characteristics in an utterance.

The challenge to understand the perceptual analysis of individual expression nested within spoken language can be gauged in a recent project of talker identification by listening (Krauss, Freyberg, & Morsella, 2002). Thirty-nine opportunistically chosen strangers were recorded speaking two neutral test sentences. Each talker was also photographed, full body, against a neutral background, and was asked to report age, height, and weight. Listeners who were familiar with none of the talkers in the set were subsequently asked to identify each in a procedure that included listening to a speech sample and choosing between two photographs. One photo depicted the talker, the other a foil. Imposing the condition in which talkers were unfamiliar to listeners prevented listeners from succeeding in an identification task by remembering the vocal traits of specific individuals. Nonetheless, listeners identified talkers better than they would have by guessing alone. Which attributes of the voice did they detect? A second test calibrated a listener's ability to assess rough somatic proportions—the age, height, and weight—of talkers from the speech samples and from the photographs. Although judgments were more accurate from photographs than from speech samples, judgments from speech were still surprisingly well correlated with the actual age, height, and weight of the talkers who spoke them. Sampling the mix of attributes available in an individual's speech, listeners discern personal characteristics, and this chapter reviews the pertinent research terrain from a high altitude, observing the sources of distinctiveness in a talker's speech and the ways that a listener resolves these perceptually.

---

* This caricature of the production of an utterance might seem psychologically false, a form of assembly more apt for building a Ford than an expression. The psychological description will seem truer if the stages described sequentially here are understood as nested formal requirements satisfied in a hybrid function, part parallel. Whether the constituents are assembled in advance completely or on the fly, linguistic form is shared throughout a community of talkers, while the physical means of expression is unique to each talker and situation.

PERSONAL AND VOCAL IDENTITY

Within the technical literature on the perception of linguistic aspects of speech, individual variation among talkers has commonly been treated as a nuisance (Halle, 1985). Because the linguistic components of any message must be roughly the same for each communicating talker and listener, from this perspective the acoustic effects of the unique embodiment of each individual count as noise in a transmission line. Accordingly, linguistic perception has been attributed to the detection of canonical acoustic correlates of phonemes that are present in the speech stream regardless of the talker or the conditions under which speech was produced. In complementary fashion, the projects to describe the perceptible acoustic signature of individual talkers have largely sought to distill the durable aspects of an individual's speech that transcend the linguistic properties expressed moment to moment. In this conceptualization, the speech of an individual is treated as a composite of linguistic and personal properties, each with different acoustic correlates and each obliging a different perceptual function. Whether the goal has been identification of individuals by ear, by algorithm, or by visual inspection of spectrograms, researchers have tended to define the problem as a kind of commerce with nonlinguistic acoustic attributes as currency (Bricker & Pruzansky, 1976). In the past few years, though, the boundary between linguistic and personal aspects of speech production has been redrawn empirically. Here, a rendition of linguistic contributions to talker perception is offered; for a review of qualitative influences in the perception of spoken words, see Nygaard (2005).

To begin at the beginning, a talker can be distinctive under conditions in which an aspect of speech or constellation of aspects is unique, is produced consistently, and is resolvable perceptually by listeners. In this regard, listeners are apparently voracious for useful properties of speech, and while there is apparently no single attribute that counts as a universal indexical tag, there is a large variety that is possibly valuable. Truly, the catalog is large, and a synopsis of this literature can readily be found elsewhere (Bricker & Pruzansky, 1976; Hecker, 1971; Kreiman, 1997; Remez, Fellowes, & Rubin, 1997). Although some of the targeted properties of speech are direct consequences of vocal anatomy and physiology, others are an outcome of linguistic exposure and social role.

ANATOMICAL VARIATION AMONG TALKERS

Some aspects of individual variation seem ineluctable. The average and range of vocal pitch is associated with the mass of the larynx (Ishizaka & Flanagan, 1972). The frequency range and central tendency of the natural resonances of the vocal tract are determined by the scale of the supralaryngeal vocal tract (Fant, 1960). These characterizations are among the oldest in acoustic phonetics, appearing in the foundational monograph by Joos (1948), and the observations have had wide conceptual influence. Despite large overlap throughout the range, there are consistent differences in average fundamental frequency and glottal spectrum over the life cycle and between male and female talkers. However, variation in fundamental frequency falls short as a marker of individual identity, at least considering average frequency, frequency excursion, and most comfortable frequency, indicating that the functional states of the larynx vary more than the anatomy. For instance, there are differences in characteristic fundamental frequency reported throughout the daily cycle (Garrett & Healey, 1987) and given the brief period of these cycles, they surely must be accountable without appeal to variation in laryngeal size.

Similarly, vocal resonances vary with the length and shape of the vocal tract. Sound production governed by the linguistic properties of an utterance creates modulation of vocal resonances that constitutes the acoustic stream of speech for a listener, and the unique scale of a talker determines the frequency composition of the stream. Although vocal tract length is only weakly correlated with bodily stature, and although there is significant overlap throughout the range, again, to a first approximation, adult males tend to exhibit the lowest resonant frequencies, adult females a bit higher, and children the highest (Goldstein, 1980; Peterson & Barney, 1952). Under some conditions, perceivers act as if they were normalizing the formant variation attributable to differences in vocal tract scale (Ladefoged & Broadbent, 1957). In other words, perceptually calibrating the scale of a talker influences the apparent linguistic properties of utterances. This evidence of perceptual sensitivity to the precise dimensions of variation once suggested that vocal tract scale is a primary indexical attribute of talkers (see Pisoni, 1997). As in the case of fundamental frequency, though, the average vocal spectrum offers less in fact than in principle as an indicator of identity. One reason is that the resonant frequency is an indirect measure of vocal tract length, varying with the rounding and spreading of the lips, and the height of a mobile jaw and larynx (Fant, 1960). In similar circumstances to the larynx, the possibility of many functional states available within a single vocal tract opposes a simple conversion of sound to anatomical scale.

PHYSIOLOGICAL VARIATION AMONG TALKERS

Many degrees of freedom are available for creating qualitative acoustic variation laryngeally and supralaryngeally. Neither the exact dimensionality nor the physiology of production is understood thoroughly, although the literature contains a few meta-analyses that aim to define parameters of this multidimensional aspect of the voice. In one landmark review, Gelfer (1988) justified seventeen dimensions of qualitative variation in the voice, admittedly based in part on clinical evaluation of dysphonia and other pathology. Table 10.1 reproduces the dimensions derived in this study, and by using each of its binary dimensions as a Likert scale it is possible to parameterize the qualities of a speech sample, or of a specific talker's voice. None of the dimensions creates linguistic contrasts, at least not in English, a language often examined by researchers. The dimensions of variation can be considered aspects of personal style.

The use of the larynx to produce differences in vocal quality has a counterpart in the vocal tract. In one analytic approach to this, individual talkers are

TABLE 10.1

Dimensions Derived by the Meta-analysis of Gelfer (1988) for Describing the Qualitative Characteristics of the Speaking Voice

High pitch – Low pitch	Clear – Hoarse
Loud – Soft	Unforced – Strained
Strong – Weak	Soothing – Harsh
Smooth – Rough	Melodious – Raspy
Pleasant – Unpleasant	Breathy – Full
Resonant – Shrill	Nasal – Not nasal
Animated – Monotonous	Young – Old
Steady – Shaky	Slow – Rapid
Liked – Disliked	

characterized as adopting potentially distinctive vocal postures, each establishing a neutral articulatory state. The articulation required to produce linguistically governed gestures is constrained by assuming a consistent vocal posture of a lowered larynx, for instance, or a pharyngealized station for the tongue body, and such postural adjustments are understood to modulate the shape of the long-term integrated spectrum of speech (Nolan, 1983). A listener who is able to abstract the typical vocal spectrum of familiar talkers might then be able to recognize one from a speech sample of sufficient duration. The psychological question raised by this theory of qualitative variation is whether recognizing a supralaryngeally caused timbre* permits identification of an individual, or whether individual identity and individual style are resolved together. This aspect of individual identification deserves closer attention, although the evidence in hand does not encourage

---

* Timbre, or sound quality, is a well-established descriptive topic within auditory sensory psychology, and a classic review by Hirsh (1988) makes it possible to gauge the difficulty of creating an account of individual identification by resolution of timbre. The term itself refers to the qualitative dimension of auditory experience, and it is defined by exclusion. Namely, when two sounds of identical pitch and loudness—here, the terms refer to psychological states, not to the physical properties of frequency and power—can be differentiated by their individual qualities, the dimension of difference is timbre. Of course, timbre is a constant facet of auditory experience, and there are many studies of the acoustic causes of different timbre impressions. Hirsh notes, though, that descriptions of timbre are readily asserted, including some in Table 10.1, that pertain to the mechanical means of production rather than to the sound quality that is experienced. In other words, some claims conflate attributes of sensory quality with attributes of the object that produces it, describing a sound as "mechanical," or "oboe-like," for instance. It would be tautology to assert that the musical instruments oboe and saxophone are identified by an experience of "oboe-like" and "saxophone-like" timbre, or that a particular individual is identified by recognizing his pleasant, breathy timbre. Although attributes are subordinate to the individual who expresses them, auditory quality is sensory, primary, and uninterpreted, while vocal quality is an aspect of object perception.

the conceptualization of a listener first sampling an unknown voice to resolve the characteristic long-term vocal quality of the talker, and then identifying the person who spoke. The interval required to estimate an individual's pitch range or average vocal quality has temporal coordinates inconsistent with the fluency of perception (Pollack, Pickett, & Sumby, 1954). A second of speech might be all that is required to recognize a familiar talker, hardly a sufficient span to compile a sensory assay of variation in voice pitch and quality.

These cautions in mind, there is much evidence of the usefulness of attention to something correlated with glottal period and spectrum or consistent supralaryngeal habits, in the perceptual identification of individual talkers. The brevity of samples that evoke personal impressions, as little as 1 s, argues against a perceptual norming operation in which large-scale distributional characteristics of glottal and supralaryngeal effects are assessed preliminary to identification and then are compared to remembered characteristics of talkers who are familiar to the listener. Yet, the key features associated with the perception of voice quality and the acuity of perceptual resolution are yet to be established empirically. The facility of listeners identifying a talker from whispered samples is impaired relative to phonated speech (Pollack et al., 1954; Tartter, 1991; cf., Eklund & Traunmüller, 1997), evidence of a role of glottal period and spectrum in talker identification by ear. Supralaryngeal characteristics play a role, as shown in the successes, albeit at reduced accuracy, in the identification of talkers using an electrolarynx to substitute for the natural voice source (Coleman, 1973).

More challenging is the evidence that a talker who produced speech that was temporally reversed and presented for naming remains identifiable in many instances (Clarke, Becker, & Nixon, 1966; Van Lancker, Kreiman, & Emmorey, 1985), proof that lexical and some phonetic attributes are not necessary for the perceptual identification of talkers. In such cases, the glottal and supralaryngeal sources of quality are preserved in syllable nuclei and in consonant spectra of long duration, including fricatives, nasals, and the hold portion of liquids. The time-critical evolution of stop consonants and affricates is grossly disrupted, indicating that some critical features pertinent to a talker's traits can be available without these linguistic attributes.

LINGUISTIC VARIATION AMONG TALKERS

The articulators are a convergence point in expression. Linguistic properties might govern the abstract criteria for articulating the word heet, hoot, or hot, but a talker's age, sex, physique, vitality, attitude, and distance from the listener determine qualitative aspects of production. At least, the common assumption has been that speech incorporates all of these influences as such. Nonetheless, it would be false to conclude that the average spectral difference between talkers mostly reflects the differences due to the length of the supralaryngeal vocal tract and the language-independent bodily characteristics of specific individuals. A couple of studies indicate the nature of this complex relation.

The evidence that addresses this directly includes a cross-language comparison of the average difference in male and female formant frequency in the long vowels of twenty-six languages (Johnson, 2005). In some languages, male and female average spectra differed greatly, as if variation in resonant frequencies across talkers was the simple consequence of differences in the scale of the vocal anatomy. In this class were Wari', an Amazonian language, California English, spoken in many parts of California, and Russian. Yet, in other languages, the formant frequencies typical of one sex were highly similar to those typical of the other. In this class were Danish, spoken in northern Europe, Angami, spoken in South Asia, and Paicî, spoken in New Caledonia. This sort of comparison offers a fresh look at the interaction of linguistic and personal characteristics.

Despite differences between individuals in the anatomy of articulatory structures, the expression of speech allows wide range, and not just extralinguistically. In a hypothetical push and pull between linguistic and extralinguistic regulation of speech, this analysis of vowel resonant frequencies shows that the boundary between the two domains is movable, as if attributes of speech that are linguistically conditioned in one environment are free to vary in another. Evidently, a language can regulate phonetic compensation for intrinsic anatomical differences. This might affect vocal quality and hypothetically imperil individual identification based on this acoustic property for speakers of Danish but not Russian, although the pertinent data have not been produced.

There is evidence of other ways to mark the sex of a talker phonetically than with the height, advancement, and rounding of vowels. In one analysis, the disposition to hold or to release the final consonant of a closed syllable at the end of a sentence—for instance the t in just, the d in pursued, the k in work—was correlated with the sex of the talker (Byrd, 1994). Other evidence of linguistic and personal interchange is also observed in American English. Specifically, sex differences in vowel formant frequency are reported in juvenile subjects, well before the age of expression of secondary dimorphism in the dimensions of larynx and vocal tract (Lee, Potamianos, & Narayanan, 1999; Perry, Ohde, & Ashmead, 2001). Of course, if a talker is obliged linguistically to regulate a specific dimension of production, then when the talker shifts into the role of perceiver this aspect of speech is potentially resolvable. In addition, if it is perceptually resolvable for self-regulation, the same capacity is probably available, at least potentially, as a propensity to notice such variation in the speech of others.

Apart from apprehending the message, though, an ordinary listener—which designation includes this author as well as the reader of this chapter when we leave the laboratory—might be aware only vaguely of sex-linked phonetic expression, experiencing it as a phenomenon of character and not of phonology. Indeed, if it is a consistent feature of a talker's expression, it is no less an aspect of self than of lexical addressing. Although talker and listener alike might attend to this aspect of articulation without explicit awareness of the linguistic patterning involved, at subordinate levels of control the phonetic forms engaged in personal marking must be registered in precise detail. Without exact registration of the forms undergoing the alternation that marks sex while pointing to words, there is no consistency in production. However the compromise is struck between the shared symbolic forms and the phonetic assortment available for a specific individual's expression, a talker must produce and a listener must apprehend a legitimate allophone of a phoneme contrast in order to distinguish an intended word from other words of like composition and class (Luce, 1986; Luce & Pisoni, 1998).

The intrusion of language on the pure expression of natural bodily differences is also a feature of dialect and arguably of idiolect. In dialect, local communities drift together; in idiolect, an individual drifts distinctively, producing only a subset of the characteristics definitive of a dialect. Whether anatomy guides an idiosyncrasy of production, due to the shape and mobility of articulatory structures, or whether it is freely assigned, is a topic deserving attention of researchers. However, a provocative and informative instance is reported by Johnson and Azara (2000). In a study of the speech of identical twins, they reported that many of the utterances in the samples were so similar, comparing one twin to the other, that the interaction of linguistic exposure and biological potential crystallized largely in the same way in each. The differences they reported were no greater than is typical of a single individual producing different versions of the same utterances. Yet, twins also differed from each other consistently in other formant measures (see also Nolan & Oh, 1996), as if a subset of contrasts specifically marked the difference between the twins within a larger set of shared elements. This study offers a glimpse of the gradient from assimilation of the community standard and individual defection in rough, if not strict, analogy to social acts of different scale (see Pickett & Brewer, 2001). When an individual takes on characteristics of the dialect, sharing features of production with the local community, this minimizes individuality in phonetic expression. When an individual differs from the group extensively, this distinctiveness is purchased at the cost of easy phonetically based identification of community membership.

The research required to refine these notions with evidence would examine the interplay between dialect, idiolect, and the lexicon (for example, Clopper & Pierrehumbert, 2008). For this purpose, it would be ideal to conduct a longitudinal study of language development of monozygotic dectuplets reared together, in order to contrast inheritance, linguistic exposure to a community, and the resolution of conflicting dispositions to match the community dialect and to establish a unique idiolect within it. Failing to meet this methodological objective, there are other more approximate means of examining how language highlights and perhaps exaggerates differences between individuals in the composition of an individual's phonetic inventory.

PHONETIC IDENTIFICATION OF TALKERS

Some studies have attempted to provide a critical empirical test of the central claim that consistency in phonetic production functions indexically, independent of extralinguistic somatically correlated acoustic properties of speech (Remez et al., 1997). The method relied on tests of perceptual identification in which

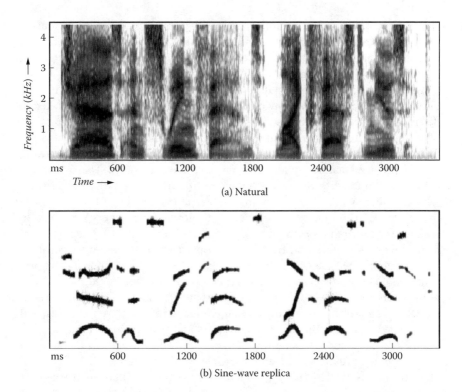

FIGURE 10.1   A comparison of the spectral characteristics of natural speech and a sine-wave replica. (a) A spectrographic analysis of the natural sentence: Jazz and swing fans like fast music. Note the broadband resonances, aperiodic constituents, and glottal pulses. (b) A spectrographic analysis of a sine-wave replica of the natural utterance. The coarse-grain spectrotemporal pattern of the natural model is preserved despite the use of time-varying sinusoids and the absence of the natural acoustic products of vocalization. From Pardo & Remez (2006).

speech was presented in synthesis. Rather than using traditional speech synthesis, which can incorporate acoustic properties that evoke natural vocal quality, the tests used drastically reduced spectral patterns consisting solely of three or four time-varying sinusoids, each set to replicate the frequency and amplitude properties of a resonance in a natural utterance. Such patterns, often designated as sine-wave speech, lack an acoustic component that exhibits the variation in fundamental frequency; it is simply omitted from the synthetic acoustic pattern. Likewise, nothing of the glottal spectrum remains, nor is the overall impoverished spectral shape more than an insinuation of the original natural utterance on which the synthetic version is modeled. Neither are the tone components related harmonically, nor are the fricative portions aperiodic, nor are the resonances broadband (See Figure 10.1). Despite intelligibility evoked by coherent spectrotemporal variation, natural vocal quality is utterly lost. These odd sounds, so different from the natural utterances on which they were based, should not have evoked an impression of an identifiable talker if the acoustic attributes that matter indexically are solely qualitative in origin and effect.

One test used ten different talkers and two groups of listeners. One listener group was not familiar with any of the original talkers, and they were asked to determine which of two sine-wave sentences had been produced by the talker who spoke a natural sentence also presented on each test trial. A second group had become familiar over a span of decades with each of the talkers whose speech provided natural models for the sine-wave versions. These listeners were asked to identify the talkers by name from remembered characteristics. Although there was a slight performance benefit exhibited by those who knew the talkers from ordinary interchange, both groups of listeners were able to identify the talkers producing the sine-wave samples without relying on vocal pitch and quality. Moreover, frequency transposition of the sine-wave constituents that eliminated acoustic correlates of vocal tract scale variation did not prevent identification of sine-wave talkers (Fellowes, Remez, & Rubin, 1997). Most telling were the errors of identification. Listeners seemed to disregard overall speech rate, a property of natural speech preserved in sine-wave sentences, and they tended to ignore the acoustic correlates and perceptual consequences of sex differences among the sine-wave talkers. Instead, it seemed as if sine-wave talkers were confused for one another when they exhibited similar segmental phonetic details, which is to say, when talkers used similar phonetic variants of consonants and vowels.

In another related study, a procedure of direct estimation of similarity showed that the pattern of perceptual contrasts among talkers was much the same whether talkers were presented as natural samples or as synthetic sine-wave versions lacking natural vocal quality (Remez, Fellowes, & Nagel, 2007). By asking listeners to weigh the attributes of talkers rather than the sound of the samples, the undeniable qualitative differences between natural and sine-wave versions were reduced in salience, presumably in favor of the subphonemic phonetic variants that remain when natural qualitative attributes are diminished or expunged.

Although the cases that produced this empirical proof used electroacoustic methods to eliminate natural vocal quality, there are more prosaic causes of qualitative distortion that probably spare the perceptual effects of linguistically controlled speech production. Phonetic patterns are simple to maintain when typical qualitative production is disrupted in laryngitis or when naturally produced qualitative effects are lost due to a poor transmission line, perhaps in an intercom or telephone. Because phonetic properties survive qualitative distortion robustly, the ability of a listener to identify a talker would gain durability if perception tracked phonetic inventory in addition to vocal quality. Certainly, this conclusion is encouraged by the mundane experience of recognizing a talker despite distortion imposed by a typical telephone, which filters the speech by band limiting the frequency range, and scrambles the phase relations among the spectral components.

A SIDEBAR ON IDENTITY

Identity is an intriguing and nuanced topic. Yet, a narrow forensic focus has governed a large portion of the research on talker identification, even when a scientific project did not entail identifying an unknown talker, or verifying that a specific detainee had self-identified honestly. The consistent axiom of this approach is the permanence of identity from cradle to grave and beyond. The forensic presumption that an individual's identity is fixed is somewhat justified by the limited time span of a legal proceeding, although the volatility of character has been a significant topic within social science since the discovery of the susceptibility of traits to circumstantial modulation. Or, perhaps longer:

> Even sound authors are wrong in stubbornly trying to weave us into one invariable and solid fabric.... Anyone who turns his prime attention onto himself will hardly ever find himself in the same state twice. I give my soul this face or that, depending on which side I lay it down on. I speak about myself in diverse ways: that is because I look at myself in diverse ways. Every sort of contradiction can be found in me, depending upon some twist or attribute: timid, insolent, chaste, lecherous; talkative, taciturn; tough, sickly; clever, dull, brooding, affable; lying, truthful; learned, ignorant; generous, miserly and then prodigal—I can see something of all that in myself, depending on how I gyrate; and anyone who studies himself attentively finds in himself and in his very judgment this whirring about and this discordancy. There is nothing I can say about myself as a whole simply and completely, without intermingling and admixture. (de Montaigne, 1574; translated and edited by Screech, 1991, pp. 373–377.)

The changes in speech that accompany these varied aspects of the self are rarely examined with the precision required to say that presenting one or another facet of character is expressed both qualitatively and linguistically. From partial treatments, it is possible to see that if this conceptualization is fair, then research that adopts the premise of immutable identity conveyed qualitatively will not make useful measures. At least part of an individual's phonetic repertoire is tied to an alternation in diction associated with social roles and registers (Labov, 1986). It is also plausible that mood is marked allophonically, although research has chiefly concerned the consequences of affect on resonance spectrum, a result of the articulation by the lips with cheer and gloom (Tartter, 1980). One alternative notion is that the expression of mood is actually performed in part, and is not simply a somatically necessary perturbation of vocal expression. If we accept the conclusion of research on clear and casual speech (Picheny, Durlach, & Braida, 1985), namely, that it is signaled in part by such alternations as /drd##ju/ → /drd͡ʒə/, then a permissible extrapolation is that other alternations in attitude might also be conveyed in the subphonemic pattern of expression in addition to qualitative effects.

One necessary consequence of a link between self-expression and phonetic expression is a perceptual cost that is already gauged, and this is the typical effect on individual perception of a known talker's use of a vocal disguise (Hollien, Majewsky, & Doherty, 1982). Even listeners who are capable of identifying a specific individual can be readily fooled when that talker attempts to mislead by affecting an uncharacteristic manner of speech. What is the source of the cost, perceptually, that results in erroneous identification? In affecting a vocal disguise, a talker might present a rare self, counterfeit or merely unfamiliar to the listener, and such changes conceivably precipitate a different allophone repertoire as well as unfamiliar qualitative mannerisms, even though disguised and undisguised talker are the same person.

CONCLUSIONS

A few simple ideas about speech production frame this chapter, which has summarized their defense, empirically and conceptually, and noted the perceptual consequences. It is fair to state them plainly as a means to identify the improvements that research can bring to this approach:

An individual expresses personal identity in speech.
Anatomy and physiology determine some acoustic characteristics of speech.
Linguistic experience regulates expression in dialect and idiolect.
Mood, motive, and situation affect the variety of linguistic phonetic properties.
A listener often falsely ascribes dialectal and idiolectal marking to qualitative attributes of an individual talker.
Linguistic differences among individuals persist across qualitative variation.

These premises are yet to be fully secured by evidence in the argument that talkers are consistent in their idiosyncratic allophonic habits and that these linguistic properties evoke impressions of personal character in listeners. Yet, there is a last argument to review here that is pertinent to the plausibility of this conceptualization. The self-regulatory goal of an individual talker poses a conflict for each language learner: to talk enough like the group to be taken as a member, yet to reserve some of the expressive potential of the linguistic phonetics to be unique within the group. Implicitly, this problem requires a talker to use phonetic perception to calibrate and to regulate articulation, fixing the center and range of the linguistic community and the centrality or eccentricity of the self—or selves. Once this capacity is developed, the perceptual sensitivity required to meet this challenge of adaptive self-regulation, linguistically, is thereafter available for another use: to calibrate the attributes of other talkers by their phonetic characteristics as well as their vocal quality.

Now, if we could only explain why it is often a pleasure to notice these subtle details about each other...

ACKNOWLEDGMENT

For many provocative, enlightening, tough, and patient discussions over a span of decades, the author is grateful to Bob Krauss. For support of this research, thanks are extended to the National Institute on Deafness and Other Communication Disorders (award DC00308).

REFERENCES

Abercrombie, D. (1967). *Elements of general phonetics.* Chicago: Aldine.

Bricker, P. D., & Pruzansky, S. (1976). Speaker recognition. In N. J. Lass (Ed.), *Contemporary issues in experimental phonetics* (pp. 295–326). New York: Academic Press.

Byrd, D. (1994). Relations of sex and dialect to reduction. *Speech Communication, 15,* 39–54.

Clarke, F. R., Becker, R. W., & Nixon, J. C. (1966). Characteristics that determine speaker recognition. *Electronic Systems Division, Air Force Systems Command Report* ESD-TR-66-638. Hanscom Field, MA.

Clopper, C. G., & Pierrehumbert, J. L. (2008). Semantic context and the Northern cities chain shift. *Journal of the Acoustical Society of America, 124,* 1682–1688.

Coleman, R. O. (1973). Speaker identification in the absence of inter-subject differences in glottal source characteristics. *Journal of the Acoustical Society of America, 53,* 1741–1743.

de Montaigne, M. (1574). On the inconstancy of our actions. [translated by M. A. Screetch, 1991, *The essays of Michel de Montaigne, II, 1*: (pp. 373–377). London: Allen Lane.

Eklund, I., & Traunmüller, H. (1997). Comparative study of male and female whispered and phonated versions of the long vowels of Swedish. *Phonetica, 54,* 1–21.

Fant, C. G. M. (1960). *The acoustic theory of speech production.* The Hague: Mouton.

Fant, C. G. M. (1966). A note on vocal tract size factors and nonuniform F-pattern scalings. *Speech Transmission Laboratory Quarterly Progress and Status Report, 4,* 22–30. Stockholm, Sweden: Royal Institute of Technology.

Fellowes, J. M., Remez, R. E., & Rubin, P. E. (1997). Perceiving the sex and identity of a talker without natural vocal timbre. *Perception & Psychophysics, 59,* 839–849.

Garrett, K. L., & Healey, E. C. (1987). An acoustic analysis of fluctuations in the voices of normal adult speakers across three times of day. *Journal of the Acoustical Society of America, 82,* 58–62.

Gelfer, M. P. (1988). Perceptual attributes of voice: Development and use of rating scales. *Journal of Voice, 2,* 320–326.

Goldstein, U. (1980). An articulatory model for the vocal tracts of growing children. Unpublished doctoral dissertation, Massachusetts Institute of Technology, Cambridge, MA.

Halle, M. (1985). Speculations about the representation of words in memory. In V. A. Fromkin (Ed.), *Phonetic linguistics* (pp. 101–114). New York: Academic Press.

Hecker, M. H. L. (1971). Speaker recognition: An interpretive survey of the literature. *ASHA Monographs,* No. 16, 1–103.

Hirsh, I. J. (1988). Auditory perception and speech. In R. C. Atkinson, R. J. Herrnstein, G. Lindzey, & R. D. Luce (Eds.), *Stevens' handbook of experimental psychology, Volume I: Perception and motivation* (pp. 377–408). New York: Wiley-Interscience.

Hollien, H., Majewsky, W., & Doherty, E. T. (1982). Perceptual identification of voices under normal, stress and disguise speaking conditions. *Journal of Phonetics, 10,* 139–148.

Ishizaka K., & Flanagan J. L. (1972). Synthesis of voiced sounds from a two-mass model of the vocal cords. *Bell System Technical Journal, 116,* 1233–1268.

Johnson, K. (2005). Speaker normalization in speech perception. In D. B. Pisoni & R. E. Remez (Eds.), *Handbook of speech perception* (pp. 363–389). Oxford, UK: Blackwell.

Johnson, K., & Azara, M. (2000). The perception of personal identity in speech: Evidence from the perception of twins' speech. Unpublished manuscript.

Joos, M. (1948). Acoustic phonetics. *Language, 24*(Supp.), 1–137.

Krauss, R. M., Freyberg, R., & Morsella, E. (2002). Inferring speakers physical attributes from their voices. *Journal of Experimental Social Psychology, 38*, 618–625.

Kreiman, J. (1997). Listening to voices: Theory and practice in voice perception research. In K. Johnson & J. W. Mullenix (Eds.), *Talker variability in speech processing* (pp. 85–108). San Diego, CA: Academic Press.

Kreiman, J., Vanlancker-Sidtis, D., & Gerratt, B. R. (2005). Perception of voice quality. In D. B. Pisoni & R. E. Remez (Eds.), *Handbook of speech perception* (pp. 338–362). Oxford, UK: Blackwell.

Labov, W. (1986). Sources of inherent variation in the speech process. In J. S. Perkell & D. H. Klatt (Eds.), *Invariance and variability in speech processes* (pp. 402–425). Hillsdale, NJ: Lawrence Erlbaum Associates.

Ladefoged, P. (1967). *Three areas of experimental phonetics.* London: Oxford University Press.

Ladefoged, P., & Broadbent, D. E. (1957). Information conveyed by vowels. *Journal of the Acoustical Society of America, 29*, 98–104.

Lee, S., Potamianos, A., & Narayanan, S. (1999). Acoustics of children's speech: Developmental changes of temporal and spectral parameters. *Journal of the Acoustical Society of America, 105*, 1455–1468.

Levelt, W. J. M. (1989). *Speaking.* Cambridge, MA: The MIT Press.

Luce, P. A. (1986). A computational analysis of uniqueness points in auditory word recognition. *Perception & Psychophysics, 39*, 155–158.

Luce, P. A., & Pisoni, D. B. (1998). Recognizing spoken words: The neighborhood activation model. *Ear and Hearing, 19*, 1–38.

Nolan, F. (1983). *The phonetic bases of speaker recognition.* Cambridge: Cambridge University Press.

Nolan, F., & Oh, T. (1996). Identical twins, different voices. *Forensic Linguistics, 3*, 39–49.

Nygaard, L. C. (2005). Perceptual integration of linguistic and nonlinguistic properties of speech. In D. B. Pisoni & R. E. Remez (Eds.), *Handbook of speech perception* (pp. 390–413). Oxford, UK: Blackwell.

Pardo, J. S., & Remez, R. E. (2006). The perception of speech. In M. Traxler & M. A. Gernsbacher (Eds.), *The handbook of psycholinguistics* (2nd ed., pp. 201–248). New York: Academic Press.

Perry, T. L., Ohde, R. N., & Ashmead, D. H. (2001). The acoustic bases for gender identification from children's voices. *Journal of the Acoustical Society of America, 109*, 2988–2998.

Peterson, G. E., & Barney, H. L. (1952). Control methods used in a study of the vowels. *Journal of the Acoustical Society of America, 24*, 175–184.

Picheny, M. A., Durlach, N. I., & Braida, L. D. (1985). Speaking clearly for the hard of hearing. I: Intelligibility differences between clear and conversational speech. *Journal of Speech and Hearing Research, 28*, 96–103.

Pickett, C. L., & Brewer, M. B. (2001). Assimilation and differentiation needs as motivational determinants of perceived ingroup and outgroup homogeneity. *Journal of Experimental Social Psychology, 37*, 341–348.

Pisoni, D. B. (1997). Some thoughts on "normalization" in speech perception. In K. Johnson & J. W. Mullenix (Eds.), *Talker variability in speech processing* (pp. 9–32). San Diego, CA: Academic Press.

Pollack, I., Pickett, J. M., & Sumby, W. H. (1954). On the identification of speakers by voice. *Journal of the Acoustical Society of America, 26*, 403–406.

Remez, R. E., Fellowes, J. F., & Nagel, D. S. (2007). On the perception of similarity among talkers. *Journal of the Acoustical Society of America, 122*, 3688–3696.

Remez, R. E., Fellowes, J. M., & Rubin, P. E. (1997). Talker identification based on pho-
    netic information. *Journal of Experimental Psychology: Human Perception and
    Performance, 23,* 651–666.
Tartter, V. C. (1980). Happy talk: Perceptual and acoustic effects of smiling on speech.
    Perception & Psychophysics, 27, 24–27.
Tartter, V. C. (1991). Identifiability of vowels and speakers from whispered syllables.
    Perception & Psychophysics, 49, 365–372.
Van Lancker, D., Kreiman, J., & Emmorey, K. (1985). Familiar voice recognition: Patterns
    and parameters. Part 1: Recognition of backward voices. *Journal of Phonetics, 13,*
    19–38.

11 Expressing Oneself in Conversational Interaction

Jennifer S. Pardo

A fundamental issue for speech perception is one that is common to all psychological accounts of perception, *perceptual constancy*. Speech perception is complicated because a given phoneme is highly variable in its acoustic-phonetic realization, yet perception of word identity is remarkably stable. A talker never repeats the same word in exactly the same way, and different talkers can produce the same word in markedly different ways. It is not obvious how a listener extracts a stable percept from such variable input, and understanding the process by which this is accomplished has been the primary goal of speech perception research (Liberman, 1996). Research on this problem has focused mainly on the perceptual processes involved in resolving relatively constant linguistic forms from variable acoustic realizations, with little systematic consideration of talker variability. However, acoustic-phonetic variability within and between talkers does not arise by chance—such variation is attributable to a variety of causes including talker physiology, dialect, affect, and social/situational factors. Among the important social functions that speech serves are marking a talker's identity and internal state, signaling a talker's orientation to an interactive situation, and indexing the situational roles of interacting talkers. Studies of conversational interaction demonstrate the influence of such functions on many aspects of spoken communication. A more complete understanding of this process would make the issue of linguistic variability more tractable because these sources converge on the same acoustic-phonetic dimensions, informing both speech perception and the perception of talker attributes.

Much of the past and ongoing research conducted in Robert Krauss's Human Communication Laboratory attempts to identify the patterns that nonlinguistic factors impose on the acoustic-phonetic form of utterances. In describing the current project, it is important to acknowledge the extensive contributions of Howard Giles and colleagues, whose communication accommodation theory provides a useful framework for grounding any work on acoustic-phonetic variation during conversational interaction. In addition, my favorite study by Krauss provides an important bridge to the current research (Bilous & Krauss, 1988). In our ongoing collaboration, we have found that interacting talkers engage in a subtle shift in their manner of expression, either becoming more or less similar in phonetic repertoire. This shift provides no help for the listener in a linguistic sense, all the utterances are intelligible, but the speech forms change nonetheless.

COMMUNICATION ACCOMMODATION THEORY

The main findings of the communication accommodation theory are extensively discussed in Giles's edited book (Giles, Coupland, & Coupland, 1991). It has been found that on many occasions, a talker will converge or become more similar to an addressee in certain attributes of speech. This pattern of convergence can move up the social scale, as when a factory worker's speech becomes more similar to the speech style of a supervisor, or it can move down, as when a doctor uses speech that is tailored to a young patient. Many of the observations reported in Giles's book center on lexical choice or on sublexical attributes such as speaking rate. However, Giles also published two interesting empirical reports that demonstrated changes in a talker's use of accent as a function of addressee identity.

In the first study, two different interviewers engaged in conversations with the same set of Bristol talkers (Giles, 1973). One interviewer spoke using Received Pronunciation (RP), the so-called Queen's English. The other interviewer spoke with his normal Bristol accent. Excerpts of 1 min duration from the Bristol speakers' responses were played to separate Bristol listeners, who rated the degree of accentedness of the speech samples. Overall, the responses to the RP interviewer were rated as less accented than those spoken to the Bristol interviewer. These findings demonstrated that Bristol talkers converged in speaking style to the RP interviewer, becoming less Bristol-accented in their speech.

The second study introduced an interesting twist (Bourhis & Giles, 1977). A set of Welsh-born adults was asked to respond to an RP interviewer whose questions were prerecorded. After collecting a baseline set of utterances, the Welsh speakers heard the RP interviewer make a negative statement about the fate of the Welsh language, "… the future of Welsh appears pretty dismal" (p. 125). A final set of spoken utterances was elicited with prerecorded questions from the same RP interviewer. Two separate Welsh speakers rated excerpts from the Welsh talkers' recordings for degree of accentedness. For those Welsh talkers who exhibited strong ties to their Welsh identity, the change from the pre- to the post-insult phase of the experiment was that of divergence—these talkers' utterances became more Welsh-accented after hearing the negative comment (one talker responded by conjugating Welsh verbs). Although much of the literature has focused on convergence, it is likely that divergence has equal prevalence in many social settings.

The story of speech accommodation is complex (for an update, see Shepard, Giles, & Le Poire, 2001). Talkers converge and diverge up and down the social scale. Many aspects of a talker's identity and social situation have been found to relate to the degree to which the markers of an accent or dialect are manifested in speech (see also Labov, 1974, 1986). Although Giles's (1973) dominance measures did not correlate with his findings on accent mobility, it is reasonable to ask whether speech variability is influenced by a very salient dimension of identity and dominance—a talker's sex.

MY FAVORITE STUDY BY KRAUSS

Krauss's Human Communication Laboratory has yielded a definitive collection of findings across a number of domains in communication. The study that has become my favorite is not cited very often relative to many of his other papers. Perhaps this is because Bilous and Krauss (1988) had an ambitious goal—to undermine the stereotype that men dominate conversational interactions with women. The findings were complex, as usual. Accommodation depended on the particular speech index that was being considered—for some indices men dominated, but for others women were dominant.

In their study, Bilous and Krauss (1988) introduced an important methodological innovation. Instead of focusing on group differences between men and women, all of the talkers first participated in a conversational task in same-sex pairs and then participated in a similar task in mixed-sex pairs. The measures of convergence/divergence were obtained by comparing the speech that was produced in same-sex pairs with the way the talkers interacted in mixed-sex pairs. The attributes they measured were total number of words, average utterance length, frequency of interruptions, frequency of short pauses (< 1 s), frequency of long pauses (> 1 s), frequency of back-channel responses, and frequency of laughter. If the male dominance hypothesis is correct, then men should not change from same-sex to mixed-sex pairings, and women should converge toward the male norm. The results showed that men and women both converged in average utterance length and frequency of short and long pauses. Women converged to male partners in total number of words and in frequency of interruptions. Men converged to female partners in frequency of back channels and frequency of laughter. However, women diverged from male partners in frequency of back channels and frequency of laughter, and men did not diverge from female partners in any of the speech indices.

This study demonstrated that accommodation is not a straightforward consequence of a talker's identity or sex—talkers converged on some speech indices at the same time that they diverged on others. This led Bilous and Krauss (1988) to conclude: "Any generalizations about the ways that men and women accommodate to each other when they interact must take into account the relevant properties of the situation in which the interaction takes place and the goals of the participants in those situations" (p. 192). Therefore, the focus of the current research is to examine the circumstances that evoke accommodation and the extent to which talkers exhibit accommodation in social settings.

A more extensive review of the literature on social interaction indicates that talkers exhibit an increase in similarity for a variety of attributes of spoken language. The findings can be organized according to the general methodology employed and the relative duration of the speech samples examined. There are a few findings that talkers who are asked to listen to spoken vowels, syllables, or words and immediately repeat what they hear are inclined to imitate the sample items; however, the imitations are not exact in acoustic-phonetic detail (Fowler, Brown, Sabadini, & Weihing, 2003; Goldinger, 1998; Namy, Nygaard, & Sauerteig, 2002; Vallabha & Tuller, 2004; Viechnicki, 2002). These findings provide evidence that speech perception might resolve phonetic forms in enough detail to support convergence in more naturalistic social settings. Studies of social interaction that include interview situations find that talkers become more similar in attributes that are at a coarser grain than lexical tokens, including increased coordination of referential terms, description schemes, and common ground (Brennan & Clark, 1996; Clark & Wilkes-Gibbs, 1986; Garrod & Doherty, 1994; Krauss & Weinheimer, 1964). When examining longer stretches of speech, researchers have found increased similarity in subvocal frequency/ amplitude contour, speech intensity, speaking rate, accent, and syntactic constructions (Branigan, Pickering, & Cleland, 2000; Giles et al., 1991; Gregory, 1990; Gregory & Webster, 1996; Natale, 1975). Finally, studies of dialect and accent change find that talkers become more similar to the standard of their most recent linguistic environment in attributes such as voice onset timing, vowel pronunciation, and referential term use (Labov, 1974; Sancier & Fowler, 1997). Such cumulative changes are assumed to result from individual social interactions. However, no one has provided empirical evidence that interacting talkers can become more similar to each other in sublexical acoustic–phonetic detail. The current project attempts to fill this void by examining changes in a talker's acoustic–phonetic repertoire before, during, and after conversational interaction.

PHONETIC CONVERGENCE

Phonetic convergence is defined as an increase in the acoustic-phonetic similarity of interacting talkers' utterances. In order to measure phonetic convergence, it is necessary to compare samples of the same lexical items spoken by each member of an interacting pair during the interaction to each other and to a set of items collected prior to the interaction. Moreover, if social settings provide the impetus for accent and dialect change, it is likely that phonetic convergence might persist beyond an individual interaction. Therefore, a corpus of speech samples was recorded from a set of talkers before, during, and after they participated in a conversational task. There were ten pairs of unacquainted talkers: six pairs of talkers formed same-sex pairs (three male and three female pairs), and four pairs of talkers formed mixed-sex pairs. To measure phonetic convergence, a combination of perceptual and acoustic measures was obtained.

In order to ensure that the talkers would produce the same lexical items during the interaction and that these items would be identifiable prior to the conversation, each pair was asked to complete six rounds of the Map Task together (developed by the Human Communication Research Center at the Universities of Glasgow and Edinburgh, Scotland; Anderson et al., 1991). The Map Task comprises paired schematic maps that contain labeled illustrated landmarks.

One member's map contains a path drawn from a starting point, around various landmarks, to a finishing point, and the companion's map contains only a starting point and landmarks. A crucial component of the Map Task is the distinction in role—one member is the instruction giver and the other is the instruction receiver. The goal of the task is for both talkers to communicate effectively enough so that the giver's path can be duplicated on the receiver's map, despite the fact that the talkers cannot see each other or each other's maps. Completion of the task requires active involvement of both participants, and spoken samples of the landmark labels can be collected both before and after the conversational interaction, to compare to those that are produced by both participants over the course of conversation.

After all pairs of talkers had completed five or six pairs of maps together, the recordings were coded for between-talker repetitions of the same landmark label phrases. These task repetitions and a set of pre- and post-task versions of the same lexical items were excised from the recordings to create a sensitive test of phonetic convergence. The perceptual assessment of phonetic convergence comprised a listening test that used an AXB design. On each trial, a listener heard three samples of the same lexical items. The middle or X-item was always an utterance of the phrase produced by one of the two members of a pair. The A and B items were always repetitions of the phrase produced by the other member of a pair. The task for a listener was to choose which item, A or B, sounded more like the middle item in terms of its pronunciation. On some of the trials, the flanking items to be compared to the middle item included the repetition from the task session and the pre-task session item. On other trials, the flanking items comprised the pre-task session item and the post-task session item. The order of presentation of the items was counterbalanced so that all items had a 50% chance of being presented in A or B.

If a listener judged the task repetition to be more similar in pronunciation to the partner's task sample item than the pre-task session item, then the talker has converged in pronunciation from the pre-task session to the task session. If a listener judged the post-task session version to be more similar in pronunciation than the pre-task session item, then the talker has persisted in phonetic convergence beyond the task session. If a listener is unable to express a preference, then the responses will occur randomly across the trials, leading to a 50% preference for the task repetition or the post-task session item. Therefore, the perceptual assessment of phonetic convergence can be quantified as a greater than chance (50%) judgment of the task repetition or post-task session items as more similar in pronunciation than the pre-task session items. Moreover, the degree of phonetic convergence was compared across the factors of *Timing* in the Map Task session (early vs. late), *Talker Role* (giver vs. receiver), and *Pair Sex* (male vs. female, or male givers vs. female givers). Thirty listeners provided judgments for the same-sex pairs, and twenty-one listeners judged samples from the mixed-sex pairs of talkers.

Overall, the AXB perceptual assessments of phonetic convergence confirmed that paired talkers became more similar to each other in their pronunciation of repeated landmark label phrases during performance of the Map Task. For the same-sex pairs, listeners judged the task repetition or post-task session items to be more similar on 62% of the trials. Mixed-sex pairs also yielded a significant effect, with listeners finding the key items more similar on 53% of the trials (both measures were statistically different from chance, 50%, $p < 0.05$). However, the AXB protocol for the mixed-sex pairs required that a listener choose among items produced by a female talker in comparison to an item from a male talker and vice versa. Perceptual comparisons between male and female speech are particularly difficult and may have affected the ability of listeners to detect phonetic convergence with mixed-sex pairs of talkers. Alternatively, it could be the case that men and women do not converge as readily as they do when in same-sex pairs, but this speculation awaits further research.

Phonetic convergence is not an all-or-none phenomenon. A number of factors influence it. For the same-sex pairs, convergence was found to occur relatively early (62%), increase in the second half of the conversations (68%), and persist into the post-task session (62%). Overall, receivers converged more than givers. When givers provided the sample items repeated at short delay by receivers, the receivers' repetitions showed phonetic convergence (62%), but not as great as when the receivers provided the sample items that a giver repeated (68%). Furthermore, female pairs of talkers converged less than male pairs of talkers (58% female; 75% male). Finally, the role of the talker interacted with the sex of the pairs—female receivers did not converge to female givers (47%), female givers converged to female receivers (62%), male receivers converged to male givers (71%), and male givers converged to male receivers (64%). These data and analyses are reported in much more detail in Pardo (2006). For mixed-sex pairs, there were similar trends in the data, but the effects were not as pronounced, and some cells failed to reach significance. The effect of role showed an interesting pattern. Male receivers also failed to converge to female givers (51% n.s.), but female receivers converged to male givers (55%). Taken together, there is no evidence that receivers converged to female givers, whether in same-sex or mixed-sex pairings. These findings echo those found by Bilous and Krauss (1988)—accommodation is influenced by a talker's sex in ways that are not attributable to hypothetical male dominance. Furthermore, these findings provide the first indication that phonetic convergence is also influenced by the role that a talker has in a structured task situation.

ACOUSTIC MEASURES OF CONVERGENCE

Although a listener under these circumstances makes a global judgment of an utterance based on multiple acoustic-phonetic dimensions, it is useful to ask whether any single acoustic dimension is driving these judgments. For example, pitch and speaking rate are relatively salient attributes of speech. If listeners were basing their judgments of similarity on fundamental frequency (F0, roughly heard as pitch) or utterance duration (related to speaking rate), then the variability in the AXB judgments should be related to the variability in these acoustic attributes. To determine the extent that variability in the AXB data are accounted for by variability in the degree to which a task repetition or post-task session item matched a task sample item in average F0 and/or duration, multiple regression analyses treated these factors as predictors of the AXB data from the same-sex talker pairs.

First, the acoustic measures were converted into measures reflecting the acoustic similarity between a task sample item and its task repetition or post-task session item—the absolute values of the differences for each pair of label phrases in average F0 and duration were computed for each AXB comparison type. These data were entered into the multiple regression analysis, which found that the linear combination of average F0 and duration was related to the AXB similarity test data, accounting for 28% of the variance in the AXB scores (adjusted $R^2 = .279$, $F(2,69) = 14.756$, $p < .001$). Moreover, each acoustic factor predicted the AXB similarity data over and above the other factor, with average F0 accounting for 12% and duration 20% of the variance in the AXB similarity data (average F0: adjusted $R^2 = .117$, $F(1,70) = 10.363$, $p < .002$, R^2 change = .085 $F(1,69) = 8.350$, $p < .005$; duration: adjusted $R^2 = .204$, $F(1,70) = 19.151$, $p < .001$, R^2 change = .171, F change $(1,69) = 16.809$, $p < .001$; correlation between duration and average F0, $r = .154$, $p = .098$). Although average F0 and duration were linearly related to listeners' judgments of similarity, there is a great deal of variability in the AXB data that is not accounted for by these acoustic measures.

Because there was an interaction between the effects of Talker Role and Pair Sex in the AXB similarity data, analogous multiple regression analyses were performed separately for female and male talkers. For female talkers, the linear combination of average F0 and duration was related to the AXB data, accounting for 41% of the variance, but not for male talkers, for whom the acoustic measures were only marginally related to the AXB scores [females: adjusted $R^2 = .411$, $F(2,33) = 13.210$, $p < .001$; males: adjusted $R^2 = .069$, $F(2,33) = 2.295$, $p = .117$]. In separate regression analyses for each acoustic factor, the only significant finding was that duration predicted the AXB scores for the female talkers over and above average F0 [duration: adjusted $R^2 = .413$, $F(1,34) = 25.611$, $p < .001$, R^2 change = .351, $F(1,33) = 20.851$, $p < .001$; average F0: adjusted $R^2 = .067$, $F(1,34) = 3.516$, $p = .069$, R^2 change = .015 $F(1,33) = .891$, $p = .4$ n.s.; males all adjusted $R^2 < .03$, n.s.].

Overall, the regression analyses found that perceived phonetic convergence is somewhat related to similarity in duration and is weakly related or unrelated to similarity in average F0. However, the relationship appears to be obtained only for female talkers. Because similarity in duration did not predict variability in male AXB data (nor perfectly for the female AXB data), there must be additional dimensions that listeners use when judging similarity, and possibly there are different standards applied to male and female talkers.

ANALYSES OF PRE-TASK AND POST-TASK VOWEL SPACES

The acoustic analyses of the items from the conversational task indicated that unidimensional acoustic parameters, such as average F0 or item duration, bore a small to moderate relationship to perceivers' judgments for female talkers. The next set of acoustic measures assessed whether the persistence of phonetic convergence could be due to changes in vowel pronunciation and estimated the extent to which changes in a talker's vowel space aligned with an individual partner and a talker's role. Because vowels are exposed to a variety of influences, a talker's vowel repertoire is a likely domain of phonetic convergence. These influences include changes in resonant frequencies related to speaking register, dialect, and ideolect.

In order to characterize acoustic variability among vowels, early research on the production and perception of speech (e.g., Peterson & Barney, 1952) settled on a two-dimensional representation using the lowest resonant components, the first and second formants (F1 and F2). This representation also follows linguists' classifications of the vowels as high versus low (jaw height, roughly the inverse of F1) and back versus front (tongue position, roughly F2). The vowels in *heat* and *hoot* (/i/ and /u/) are high (with low F1), and the vowels in *hat* and *hot* (/æ/ and /a/) are low (with high F1); /i/ and /æ/ are more fronted than /a/ and /u/ (having higher versus lower F2). In general, these four point vowels sit at the periphery of the vowel space, with other vowels in intermediary steps between them. Vowels are highly variable acoustically, and perceptually, vowels yield a greater degree of within-category discrimination than consonants (Pisoni, 1973, 1975). On these grounds, vowels are likely candidates for convergence—there is both acoustic room for and perceptual resolution of variability among vowel tokens. Moreover, Labov (1974, 1986) has described vowels as central to sound change and dialectal differences among talkers of American English.

Recent evidence suggests that a talker cannot match his or her own vowel productions exactly, with mimicked productions falling to the center of sample items (Viechnicki, 2002) or following idiosyncratic biases in variation (Vallabha & Tuller, 2004). Therefore, exact matching of vowel spectra is not expected either within or between talkers, but partners may still converge in vowel formant frequencies. The vowel measures were taken from subsets of the speech collected in the pre-task and post-task sessions. For each session, three repetitions of the point vowels, /i/, /æ/, /a/, and /u/, each embedded in hVt words in the carrier sentence, "Say again," comprised materials for acoustic analysis. The vowel sets were digitally analyzed using Praat, a freeware acoustic analysis software package designed by Paul Boersma and David Weenink at the Institute of Phonetic Sciences at the University of Amsterdam. Measures of F1 and F2 were taken at the midpoint of each vowel token from linear prediction spectrographic analyses. Figure 11.1 illustrates the F1 × F2 vowel spaces in the pre-task and post-task sessions for all of the talkers in the same-sex pairs. The acoustic analyses of vowel space indicated that none of the talkers matched average F1 × F2 vowel spectra from the pre-task to the post-task session. Statistical analyses of vowel spectra found that there were differences in F1 and F2 from the pre-task to the post-task sessions for both male and female talkers and indicated that these differences were influenced by a talker's role and vowel identity.

To quantify the differences in vowel dispersion more precisely with respect to phonetic convergence, the acoustic measures were converted to Euclidean

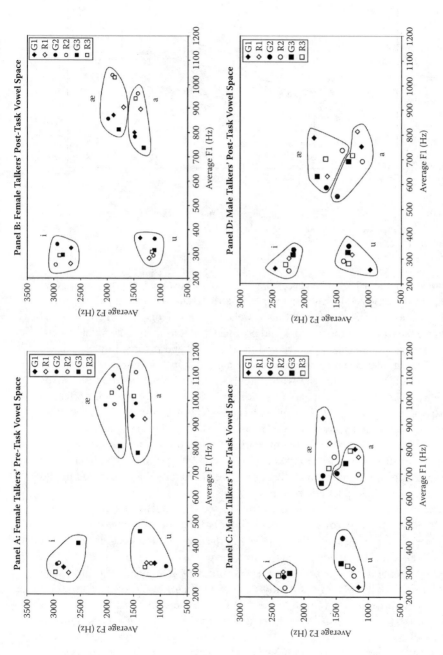

FIGURE 11.1(A–D) Plots of the F1 × F2 vowel spaces for same-sex pairs of talkers. Panels A and B comprise pre-task and post-task vowel measures for female talkers, and panels C and D contain the same measures for male talkers. Filled bullets correspond to givers and open bullets to receivers. Bullets of the same shape correspond to talkers who were paired in the intervening Map Task session.

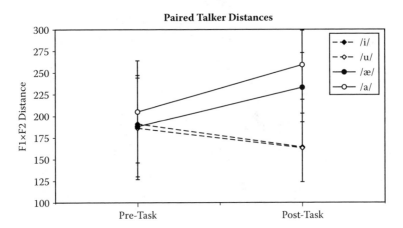

FIGURE 11.2 Vowel convergence measures for paired talkers with 95% confidence intervals. Each point corresponds to the average of the inter-talker distances for the same vowel in the pre-task and post-task sessions.

distances in the F1 × F2 space. The first set of distance measures assessed phonetic convergence by comparing pre-task differences between paired talkers with post-task differences for all four vowels. Figure 11.2 displays the inter-talker distance measures for the pre-task and post-task sessions across the point vowels, showing that paired talkers converged in /i/ and /u/ and diverged in /æ/ and /a/. These inter-talker distance measures were analyzed in a mixed design analysis of variance (ANOVA) for the within items effects of *Session* (pre-task versus post-task), *Sex* (female vs. male), and *Pair* (1–3), and the between items effect of *Vowel* (/i/, /æ/, /a/, and /u/). The mixed design ANOVA confirmed the interaction between *Session* and *Vowel* ($F(3,8) = 5.346, p < .027$), and these factors also interacted with *Pair* and *Sex*, verifying the earlier observations of unique convergence patterns for different pairs of talkers ($F(6,16) = 4.247, p < .011$). The inter-talker distance measures demonstrated that talkers both converged and diverged in distinct aspects of their phonetic repertoire.

The measures of vowel centralization assessed the tendency for each talker to produce more central vowels by calculating distances between the front vowels (/i/ to /æ/) and the back vowels (/u/ to /a/) in the pre-task and post-task sessions. The talkers centralized vowel spectra from the pre-task ($d = 786$) to the post-task ($d = 728$) session, and givers' vowel spectra ($d = 694$) were more central than receivers' ($d = 820$). More importantly, as shown in Figure 11.3, givers centralized vowel spectra from the pre-task to the post-task sessions more so than receivers did. A mixed design ANOVA on the centralization measures for the within items effects of *Session* (pre-task vs. post-task), *Talker Role* (giver vs. receiver), *Sex* (female vs. male), and *Pair* (1–3), and the between items effect of *Comparison Type* (/i/ to /æ/ and /u/ to /a/) confirmed the main effect of *Session* ($F(1,4) = 33.054, p < .006$) and the main effect of *Talker Role* ($F(1,4) = 119.470, p < .001$) and the

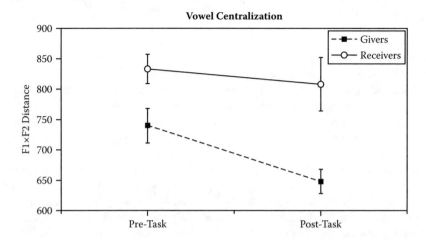

FIGURE 11.3   Vowel centralization measures for high versus low vowels with 95% confidence intervals. Each point corresponds to the average of the inter-vowel distances (/i/ to /æ/ and /u/ to /a/) for the givers (filled bullets) and receivers (open bullets) in the pre-task and post-task sessions.

interaction between *Session* and *Talker Role* ($F(1,4) = 10.567$, $p < .04$); the three-way interaction with *Sex* was not significant ($p = .9$ n.s.). Despite the fact that all talkers centralized from the pre-task to the post-task sessions and givers' vowels were more centralized overall than those of receivers, givers exhibited greater centralization across the pre-task and post-task sessions than receivers. Combined with the finding that the high vowels converged between talkers and the low vowels diverged, it appears that givers differed from receivers mainly in the centralization of the low vowels, /æ/ and /a/.

Taken together, it appears that givers diverged from receivers in the low vowels, /æ/ and /a/, and these vowels centralized more for givers than for receivers. Although definitive proof is difficult to establish, the measures of vowel spectra seem to indicate a shift toward centralization for givers' low vowels. Receivers, on the other hand, largely maintained the peripheral expression of their low vowels. This phenomenon could be a starting point for the kinds of shifts in vowels that Labov (1974, 1986) described for dialectal changes, in which the back vowels shift to more fronted positions in the vowel space. The high vowels showed some convergence, but again, this has not been demonstrated unequivocally. These measures indicate that talkers differ in their use of vowel variants, and the pattern may be consistent with their role in conversational interaction. These findings of co-occurring convergence and divergence indicate that some attributes are free to vary with the partner, but others are reserved for individual expression, perhaps to mark a talker's approach to his or her role. Because vowel centralization is often related to a casual speech setting, it is possible that givers were attempting to soften their distinct role by signaling a casual attitude at the same time that they converged to their partners in other regions of the vowel space.

194   Expressing Oneself/Expressing One's Self

This project establishes the phenomenon of acoustic-phonetic convergence in a spontaneous social setting. Convergence occurred early, increased over the course of an interaction, and persisted beyond the conversational setting. More importantly, the social constraints of role and talker sex modulated the degree of acoustic-phonetic convergence. Acoustic measures demonstrated that these subtle changes are not universal—the perceptually salient acoustic dimensions of pitch and speaking rate were mostly unrelated to perceivers' global assessments of phonetic convergence, and some vowels converged at the same time that other vowels diverged. A more complete understanding of the extent, means, and purpose of acoustic-phonetic convergence awaits future investigations. This phenomenon does not appear to serve any linguistic aims; indeed, all utterances were intelligible and the talkers performed the task with relative ease. It is likely that these changes served other nonlinguistic purposes, as proposed so eloquently by Krauss and Chiu (1998):

> Linguists regard language as an abstract structure that exists independently of specific instances of usage…, but any communicative exchange is situated in a social context that constrains the linguistic forms participants use. How these participants define the social situation, their perceptions of what others know, think, and believe, and the claims they make about their own and others' identities will affect the form and content of their acts of speaking. (p. 41)

ACKNOWLEDGMENTS

This chapter is based on a talk given by the author at the Festschrift for Robert M. Krauss on June 10, 2006. Completion of this chapter was supported in part by a grant from the National Science Foundation to Jennifer Pardo at Barnard College. The author thanks Ezequiel Morsella for his hard work in organizing the Festschrift for Robert Krauss and in editing this volume. The author is also indebted to the following people for their role in the completion of this paper: Robert Krauss, Isabel Cajori Jay, Robert Remez, Deniz Cebenoyan, Yi-Ting Chang, Katrina del Fierro, Alexandra Suppes, and George Ton.

Anderson, A. H., Bader, M., Bard, E. G., Boyle, E., Doherty, G., Garrod, S., Isard, S., Kowtko, J., McAllister, J., Miller, J., Sotillo, C., Thompson, H. S., & Weinert, R. (1991). The HCRD Map Task corpus. *Language & Speech, 34*, 351–366.
Bilous, F. R., & Krauss, R. M. (1988). Dominance and accommodation in the conversational behaviours of same- or mixed-gender dyads. *Language & Communication, 8*, 183–194.
Bourhis, R. Y., & Giles, H. (1977). The language of intergroup distinctiveness. In H. Giles (Ed.), *Language, ethnicity and intergroup relations* (pp. 119–135). London: Academic Press.
Branigan, H. P., Pickering, M. J., & Cleland, A. A. (2000). Syntactic co-ordination in dialogue. *Cognition, 75*, B13–25.

Brennan, S. E., & Clark, H. H. (1996). Conceptual pacts and lexical choice in conversation. *Journal of Experimental Psychology: Learning, Memory, & Cognition, 22,* 1482–1493.

Clark, H. H., & Wilkes-Gibbs, D. (1986). Referring as a collaborative process. *Cognition, 22,* 1–39.

Fowler, C. A., Brown, J., Sabadini, L., & Weihing, J. (2003). Rapid access to speech gestures in perception: Evidence from choice and simple response time tasks. *Journal of Memory & Language, 49,* 396–413.

Garrod, S., & Doherty, G. (1994). Conversation, co-ordination and convention: An empirical investigation of how groups establish linguistic conventions. *Cognition, 53,* 181–215.

Giles, H. (1973). Accent mobility: A model and some data. *Anthropological Linguistics, 15,* 87–109.

Giles, H., Coupland, J., & Coupland, N. (1991). *Contexts of accommodation: Developments in applied sociolinguistics.* London: Cambridge University Press.

Goldinger, S. D. (1998). Echoes of echoes? An episodic theory of lexical access. *Psychological Review, 105,* 251–279.

Gregory, S. W. (1990). Analysis of fundamental frequency reveals covariation in interview partners' speech. *Journal of Nonverbal Behavior, 14,* 237–251.

Gregory, D., & Webster, S. (1996). A nonverbal signal in voices of interview partners effectively predicts communication accommodation and social status predictions. *Journal of Personality & Social Psychology, 70,* 1231–1240.

Krauss, R. M., & Chiu, C-Y. (1998). Language and social behavior. In D. Gilber, S. Fiske, & G. Lindzey (Eds.), *Handbook of social psychology*, Vol. 2 (4th ed., pp. 41–88). Boston: McGraw-Hill.

Krauss, R. M., & Weinheimer, S. (1964). Changes in the length of reference phrases as a function of social interaction: A preliminary study. *Psychonomic Science, 1,* 113–114.

Labov, W. (1974). Linguistic change as a form of communication. In A. Silverstein (Ed.), *Human communication: Theoretical explorations* (pp. 221–256). Hillsdale, NJ: Lawrence Erlbaum Associates.

Labov, W. (1986). Sources of inherent variation in the speech process. In J. S. Perkell & D. H. Klatt (Eds.), *Invariance and variability in the speech processes* (pp. 402–425). Hillsdale, NJ: Lawrence Erlbaum Associates.

Liberman, A. M. (1996). *Speech: A special code.* Cambridge, MA: The MIT Press.

Namy, L. L., Nygaard, L. C., & Sauerteig, D. (2002). Gender differences in vocal accommodation: The role of perception. *Journal of Language & Social Psychology, 21,* 422–432.

Natale, M. (1975). Convergence of mean vocal intensity in dyadic communication as a function of social desirability. *Journal of Personality & Social Psychology, 32,* 790–804.

Pardo, J. S. (2006). On phonetic convergence during conversational interaction. *Journal of the Acoustical Society of America, 119,* 2382–2393.

Peterson, G. E. & Barney, H. L. (1952). Control methods used in a study of the vowels. *Journal of the Acoustical Society of America, 24,* 175–184.

Pisoni, D. B. (1973). Auditory and phonetic memory codes in the discrimination of consonants and vowels. *Perception & Psychophysics, 13,* 253–260.

Pisoni, D. B. (1975). Auditory short-term memory and vowel perception. *Memory & Cognition, 3,* 7–18.

Sancier, M. L., & Fowler, C. A. (1997). Gestural drift in a bilingual speaker of Brazilian Portuguese and English. *Journal of Phonetics, 25,* 421–436.

Shepard, C. A., Giles, H., & Le Poire, B. A. (2001). Communication accommodation the-
    ory. In W. P. Robinson & H. Giles (Eds.), *The new handbook of language and social
    psychology* (pp. 33–56). New York: Wiley.
Vallabha, G. K., & Tuller, B. (2004). Perceptuomotor bias in the imitation of steady-state
    vowels. *Journal of the Acoustical Society of America, 116*, 1184–1197.
Viechnicki, P. D. (2002). Composition and granularity of vowel production targets.
    Dissertation Abstracts International. 63(4-A), 1320.

12 Perceptual Prosody and Perceived Personality
Physiognomics Precede Perspective

Julian Hochberg

> Many years ago, my maternal grandfather told me a story about two men in his hometown, Vitebsk, Belorussia, walking down a road on a bitterly cold winter day. One man chattered away animatedly, while the other nodded from time to time, but said nothing. Finally, the man who was talking turned to his friend and said: "So, nu, Shmuel, why aren't you saying anything?" "Because," replied Shmuel, "I forgot my gloves." At the time, I didn't see the point of the story. Half a century later it has become a primary focus of my research.
>
> **Krauss (1998, p. 59)**

That anecdote indeed reflects one of Robert Krauss's major scientific concerns, an area in which he and his colleagues have made and continue to make major contributions: exploring causal relationships between real-life variables important in real-life communication, in real-life interactions, and in real-life judgments. Characteristically, instead of setting up theories that are friendly to being tested via detection or retention of alphanumerics or of Gabor functions but that have no known consequences outside the laboratory, he used animated cartoons to evoke the gesture-accompanied spoken descriptions that he wished to analyze, and he digitized photographs and voices of strollers recruited in Central Park in order to compare those two sources of judged personae. Moreover, that kind of ecological relevance has not garnered trivia: For example, most recently Krauss and his colleagues have formulated an approach that, with its consequences, could help lead the body of psychological science more generally—and the ways in which we use the pervasive media that enhance our lives—in a new direction and to a new status. In the sections titled "Motor and Lexical Gestures" and "Gestural Feedback Model (GFM)," I describe which of his papers are most central to my discussion; in the section titled "Looking and Other Anticipatory Behaviors: Sustaining the Purpose," I sketch the related aspects of the current field of perceptual psychology (as I see it), and in what ways its prospects could be affected by Krauss's treatment of gestures as the sustaining medium for speech and as a category of anticipatory multipurpose behaviors. In the section titled "Why the Need for Humanoids, and How Might They Help Us?", I gape at the enormous field of potential

197

Expressing Oneself/Expressing One's Self

applications, in the arts and media and in the communication and service industries, for this field of research.

SOME OF WHAT GESTURES SAY ABOUT OUR MINDS' EYES, EARS, AND PURPOSEFUL BEHAVIORS

MOTOR AND LEXICAL GESTURES

To Krauss (1998), motor gestures support speech prosody ("beat"), and lexical gestures retrieve word forms, as Chawla and Krauss (1994) showed by using professional actors in both spontaneous and rehearsed modes. Gestures precede lexemes by approximately 1000 ms, as found by Morrel-Samuels and Krauss in 1992, and they occur five times as often when accompanying spatial as opposed to nonspatial phrases, as Rauscher, Krauss, and Chen (1996) demonstrated by having the speakers describe to listeners the content of animated cartoons that only the speakers had seen. Moreover, when speakers were prevented from gesturing, they took longer to describe the cartoons if the latter had spatial content. This is well in line with Krauss's overall argument: Gestures are made not only to assist the listener; instead (or rather, *in addition*), they are made to help the speaker to speak, in ways that depend on the circumstances. (Note that Krauss frequently uses the communication/entertainment media in conducting his innovative laboratory research, a noncoincidental point to which I will return shortly.)

These are just three of the many ingenious studies performed by Krauss and his colleagues in exploring why gestural movements are made (for a survey of his work prepatory to that discussed here, see Krauss, Chen, and Chawla, 1996). They have been contested by studies from other laboratories arguing that gestures are made by the speaker in order to serve the listener or are made in order to serve the speaker in some way other than what Krauss had proposed (for example, to help conceptualize what is being spoken), but a recent judgment by Morsella and Krauss (2005) both sums up the present state of the field quite reasonably and introduces their newest proposal, which may have very far-reaching promise for the rest of psychology and its related technologies, and which motivates the present chapter:

> That these movements may be accomplishing several things at once is a problem for theories that strive for simplicity, but theories of the role of gestures must allow for this possibility. We believe that the GFM provides a good account of one of the functions gestures serve, but a complete account of all of these functions is not yet within our grasp.

I certainly agree that achieving complete accounts of any psychological processes by *simple* theories is not a plausible hope, whether in relation to the purposes of conversational gestures or to explain any other cognitive phenomenon, but I do believe that their gestural feedback model (GFM), introduced next, has very powerful predictive, explanatory, and economic potential. I also suggest that it not only serves more than one function, it also refers to multiple overlapping systems.

GESTURAL FEEDBACK MODEL (GFM)

According to the GFM approach, a major way in which gestures help the speaker is by sustaining the speaker's anticipations of the structure of his or her upcoming speech; for example, by contributing to the anticipation of the semantic components of what is to be spoken. Such assistance is needed because the relevant inherent supporting processes are by themselves otherwise very transient and might therefore well be unavailable by the time the speaker needs to instantiate them (from Krauss & Morsella, 2002; Morsella, 2002; Morsella & Krauss, 2004, 2005). In addition, it is important for us to remember that the speaker does not know precisely when a particular fragment of speech will come due, or the precise time at which the other person—that is, the intended listener—will have finished some utterance and be ready to hear the speaker. However, that temporal uncertainty can be buffered or bridged by anticipatory gestures or by other effector dispositions that serve the speaker as what I will here call *memoranda,* by reactivating semantics through feedback from those effectors or motor commands. Supporting evidence is drawn from the finding by Morsella and Krauss (2004) that more gestures are obtained with noncodable visual objects than with readily codable ones (e.g., Figure 12.1a as opposed to Figure 12.1b), and that electromyography (EMG) evidence shows that nonvisible forearm activity occurs during speech preparation (Morsella & Krauss, 1999, 2005)—*even though that action would not be a visible gesture or offer assistance to any listeners.*

Subsequently, Hostetter, Alibali, and Kit (2007) and Hofstetter & Alibali (2008) have presented findings that are not in fact inconsistent with those of Figure 12.1a,b in order to support a theory that differs somewhat from the GFM (which they do not address) but which does not oppose it. They propose that gestures help the speaker in conceptualizing the speech. In contrast, in the Krauss/ Morsella proposal, the function of gestures that GFM addresses is that of reactivating semantics through feedback from effectors or motor commands. The latter

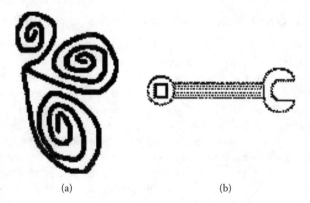

(a)   (b)

FIGURE 12.1   (a) Noncodable, (b) codable visual objects from Morsella and Krauss (2004).

proposal reveals an extremely powerful implication that expands the potential applications of the GFM beyond those it has addressed thus far; that is, GFMs sustain the speaker's purposeful activity *in advance*, which is the feature that I wish to emphasize in this discussion.

In particular, I want to suggest that the internal feedback from the effectors involved in the anticipatory or preparatory movements of the eyes, eyebrows, head and mouth positioning, etc., that are used in our social interactions, comprise a very early and lasting part of our real and virtual *environments*. Such anticipatory functions, needed to sustain behavioral intentions for which the relevant perceptual content is otherwise only briefly retained, are not unique to speech. They are certainly needed for very many human (and other species') activities. However, they must be particularly needed for coping with the animate and inanimate targets that swim before the moving head and eyes of the very early anthropomorphizing pretoddler. GFM must underpin the overt and covert looking behaviors that are so critically involved in personal relations, whether using the eyes or other effectors to dog-ear the immediate future. Nevertheless, it must also lie behind our expectations of how fluid pours, how bottles roll, how people move, even though we adults do not think everything is equally alive.

Let us consider some of the implications that the Krauss/Morsella insight about GFM in gesture-accompanied speech might have for visual perception and looking behavior more generally as well as direct our attention to the prespeech period during which so many of our gesture-supported behaviors and our visuomotor planning must originate. Finally, I point out how our science and our society are likely to be seriously affected as human/humanoid (computer) interaction expands.

The characteristics of looking behaviors, and of the multiple demands on the systems that guide and generate those behaviors, cannot be reduced to simple systems that guide and generate those behaviors, cannot be reduced to simple retina-to-oculomotor formulae, for reasons that call out for GSM-like superordinate mechanisms, as considered next.

LOOKING AND OTHER ANTICIPATORY BEHAVIORS: SUSTAINING THE PURPOSE

Gestures usually precede the speech they support. In the work of Morrel-Samuels and Krauss (1992), the gap was approximately 1000 msec, which means about four words or syllables at normal rate. (Those numbers will be important to the rest of this section.) In such utterances, and even more so in any other discourse in which the words are not scheduled in advance, some arrangement is needed to monitor (or at least to sample) the syllables, words, or phrases as they are uttered. Something like a "marching song" is needed in order to sustain attention to the utterance being planned, something like a memorandum is needed to keep in mind the utterance or gesture that should soon come due, just as visual momentum is needed to profit from the movie cuts that are so important to cinema (e.g., Hochberg & Brooks, 1978) and is surely needed for computers interacting with humans (see Woods, 1984). Such anticipatory plans must serve as useful accompaniments to all extended purposeful transient behaviors, not just to the behavior of speech-and-gesture. That is, the transitory nature of the lexical plans, which is what makes something like GFM necessary, is not only a feature of speaking behavior, it also characterizes listening and looking and many other purposive behaviors, as well—playing a tune or a game, tracking a ball or a deer, studying a painting or driving a car, etc. All such actions usually involve *transient* goals or subgoals, and therefore require some relative of GFM.

Visual perception in the human must share some of the needs of speech perception, essentially being a purposeful goal-oriented behavior in which the attention shifts relatively rapidly and relatively briefly, to some place at which an answer to some visual question is anticipated. That answer is usually a foveal input, corroborating or modifying an anticipation held by the perceiver (see Hochberg, 1968) which was based, in part, on what the periphery had hinted at undetailedly when in the previous view. Unless the viewer has the proper visual question prepared when the glimpse is finally obtained, the answer may never be obtained and encoded, part of a diverse class of phenomena now known as inattentional blindness and change blindness (Simons & Levin, 2007). Think of a glance directed toward the place at which some rapidly moving person or object is due to cross the field of view, and for which the answer needed might concern expression, license number, etc. That is, the expansive and apparently continuous world that we think we see is very different from the succession of brief and constricted samples we receive through sequences of eye move- ments and directed attentional deployments. The eye receives only a very small amount of foveal information within each brief glance (usually about 200 ms in duration, and < 50 ms in transit time for the next saccade). Each such glance is, *by choice* (cf., Hoffman & Subramaniam, 1995; Kowler, Anderson, Dosher, & Blaser, 1995), usually aimed at some specific new place that had previously been glimpsed only by unclear extrafoveal or unattended vision. The encoding time is very brief and after it is over the viewer is left with only very sparse and sim- plistically encoded (that is, visually categorized) memories of what was where. Therefore, attentive perceptual inquiry is not a passive reception of retinal dots, a sweep of pixels each signaling the wavelength and intensity of the light it has received (which was the dominant view when I was in graduate school). It is a sequence of motivated rapid and *transient* acts, with some equivalent of memo- randa and marching songs to maintain the landmarks and targets in living and moving environments.

As noted earlier (Morrel-Samuels & Krauss, 1992), gestures lead lexemes by some 1000 ms, or 4 × 250 ms syllables; note now that music measures center around 1000 ms and 4 × 250 ms beats; fast strides (at my age) are about 300 ms; and sequences of saccades themselves normally take around 250 ms per glance (as much as 50 ms of that time spent in moving). The tiny fovea (ca. 2°), which brings the only detail obtained in each glance, does so in answer to whatever question motivated the inquiry. Lacking detail, the extrafoveal information often survives in the field of view from one glance to the next, and obviously can normally serve as a landmark or a framework within which to enter the foveal information, so that studies of eye movements or attentional shifts (which are not the same thing) often treat attention as a moving spotlight in a stable scene. However, the objects of attention are not always stationary scenery, as GFM reminds us.

With GFM in mind, I have undertaken two kinds of experiments on retrieving visual information from moving objects or persons. (Tangent velocities ranged from 10 to 30 deg/sec.) The first (Figure 12.2A,B) probed the time needed for a gaze to shift from a stationary point to arrive at a moving target just as the latter displays the letter or number that is to be reported. With circular paths and with dancers as shown, 200 to 500 ms (and three to five practice trials with the overall task) sufficed. The second (Figure 12.2C) moved nonsense shapes (a–c) and familiar shapes (g, h) behind an aperture, presenting a brief probe at some point in the 10- to 16-step sequence, and testing how well the viewer could retain the shape and location of the probe, with differing conditions for the test (c, h) and for the extra-aperture presentation (i). With no disclosure of the extra-aperture shape (as in d–f), performance was at chance, but otherwise (a, c), behavior was essentially perfect when rates fell between 200 ms and 500 ms per view. Both kinds of experiments require the viewer to prepare for information to come; the rates of the inputs are in the range noted earlier that characterizes so much of our behavior, and they may provide a step toward extending the Morsella/Krauss GFM model beyond speech to extended perceptual behavior.

In visual perception, such planning, and even looking ahead to check on from what one intends to retrieve information later, is now in fact being documented by recording actual eye movements (Hayhoe, Shrivastava, Mruczek, & Pelz, 2003), but we should remember that attention and fixation are not the same thing, and that the memorandums used in sustaining the speech events assisted by GFM are not necessarily themselves part of those events (Morsella & Krauss, 2005). Indeed, such visual anticipatory glances (and their cortical accompaniments) have been found and can be studied at a very young age, well before speech as such is acquired. So research can potentially be directed at very young infants during what we may take as their gesture-acquisition period, a point I return to in the following.

Glances are of course themselves potentially gestural components of the act of interaction, and that is especially true before infants achieve speech. Questions about how acts of looking are part of the social process, and how such acts themselves serve to direct the other person's attention and contribute to judgments of personality, certainly now receive some research (e.g., Bayliss & Tipper, 2006; Mason et al., 2004, 2005), but because glances are important gestures as well as information-seeking actions, the points made by Krauss and his colleagues about speech-accompanying gestures apply as well to the glances we make in social interaction (whether the interaction is real or virtual). When the speaker looks offside at some object, that act might be intended to serve the listener (e.g., by indicating what the speaker is referring to) or, alternatively, it might be made to serve the speaker (by confirming the object's presence, by maintaining some rhythm, by breaking visual contact, or by establishing a behavioral bond).

Head-centered gestures certainly serve the audience or recipient, and are certainly long known and studied. They also must serve the actor in a GFM capacity

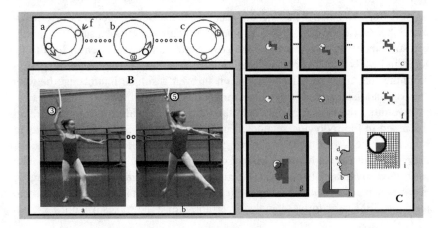

FIGURE 12.2 Probing perceptual anticipation and assembly: (A) In movie sequences excerpted in (a-c), a forecast, f, is shown of where a moving target will later show a letter; the viewer is to jump ahead and catch it foveally when the time comes. (See Note Figure 12.2a). (B) A similar task, using short ballet sequences. (C) Assembling shapes without eye movement: Sequences of 10-12 slides reveal shapes through a stationary aperture and in silhouette (a, b, g), or only through the aperture (d, e). After each sequence, the entire shape (c, f, h) tests the viewer as to where a probe had appeared earlier (b, e). This procedure allows us to test the contributions of different extrafoveal contributions (h, i). See text.

Because it takes time to move our eyes, perceptual actions very often require us to direct our attentive gaze proactively, aiming it toward something that is not yet where it will be when our moving gaze grasps it; such anticipatory visual behavior involves extrafoveal attentional deployment, and not just recordable eye movements. Moreover, if multiple glances are needed, their order and the target's future relative motion should have to be taken into account. Figure 12.2A shows a first step toward one method of exploring such parameters of presequenced multi-glance looking.

In the experiment of Figure 12.2A, a set of X adjacent small rings (1.7" dia.) were presented sequentially on a circular path (7.8" dia.), clockwise or counterclockwise (as per arrows in 12.2Aa). A few (2 or 3) alphanumeric symbols (e.g., u and b), 0.4" in height, were each presented singly within nonadjacent rings for the observers (n=2) to detect. (Separate tests had shown that the symbols used were correctly reported (>.99) if fixated within 1.7" in a single 10ms unmasked presentation.) In each trial of the experiment of Figure 12.2A, a set of signals (like arrow f, in 12.2Aa) forecast where the symbols would later appear. The forecasts' timings and the symbols' exposure durations and the rings' presentation rates (2, 4, 6.6, 10, and 20 per sec.), were varied over 200 trials. Both viewers correctly (>.99) identified series' of two or three successive symbols variously positioned around the circle, if rates allowed at least 100ms per symbol and at least 150ms for each of the presignaled glances.

There were no relevant nearby landmarks, but truly no-landmark (dark) displays, and longer memory spans, remain to be explored; experiments on more complex but familiar paths, and the contribution of extrafoveal input to preprogrammed glances, are currently in progress (Figures 12.2B,C).

as well (for example, if the speaker has raised his or her eyebrows in order to remember that some question is to come next). It also seems plausible, but hard to measure unobtrusively, that there are covert effector responses equivalent to the forearm EMGs found by Morsella and Krauss (2005). A great deal of the gesture planning that must usually be going on in even a simple interchange between speaker and listener most probably cannot be measured.

Two other domains that may help the burgeoning field of human gesture are discussed in the following sections. The point at which communicative interactions originate—the time in which our gestures and our GFMs (and our personae) arise—is noted as ready for the kind of media-based study that Krauss has used to such good advantage. In addition, the growing field of computer-run and computer-scripted media—and the incipient field of human–humanoid interaction—may push the GFM issue forward and will certainly raise the stakes if it does.

WHERE IT BEGINS: GESTURES IN MOMMY'S ARMS

We know that most infants enter the world having already heard the melody and prosody of mother's and others' speech and song and seem already set at birth to respond to the rhythm and tonality of the exaggerated speech-related behaviors that seem common to mothers of all origins (Grieser & Kuhl, 1988). However, we also know that all newborns must enter our scene having seen nothing and remain unable to focus much beyond mother's face for a long while thereafter. While they may be able to distinguish depth cues as distinctive patterns almost immediately (Bower, 1971), they almost certainly do not see distance and space from cues such as texture-gradients and linear perspective (Yonas, Elieff, & Arterberry, 2002; Yonas, Granrud, Arterberry, & Hanson, 1966), as measured by reaching responses, until they are some 5 months old (which may help to explain why a human child does not need special training to recognize three-dimensional objects in two-dimensional visual media [Hochberg, 1997], and hints at what that recognition consists of). As measured by VOE (increased looking time that occurs with violation-of-expectation), inconsistencies in such depth cues are detected in drawings by some 3 months of age (Durand, Lécuyer, & Frichtel, 2003). Moreover, at such ages, infants certainly cannot validate cues to visual distance beyond a foot or so by reaching and touching.

So for at least 3 months, neonates can see and concentrate on nearby Mommy (or her surrogate), and on studying what her face and voice are doing, and they certainly do so before acquiring any need for the depth cues that have received so much attention in experimental psychology and epistemological philosophy. From what I have seen, much of most mothers' behavior when holding the infant is designed to excite and reward the latter's active looking and anticipating and to recruit its interactive behavior (and that certainly agrees with what mothers are advised to do). Mother's actions and vocalizations are therefore heavily endowed with rhythm and melody and with pauses that act as signals of payoffs-to-come (rather than, as one alternative, signals of disengagement).

As noted previously, by 3.5 months, if not earlier, infants have been found to make glances that anticipate events yet to come (Canfield & Kirkham, 2001). Previously, Zingale and Kowler (1987) had found multisaccade planned sequences in adults and, like these, which surely comprise clear instances of task-sustaining behavior, the anticipatory looking in the infant must reveal at least some of that ability to hold and therefore sustain an effector plan for the future. It must also comprise an informative gestural behavior when viewed by the object of inspection (Mommy), and—comprising still more social consequence of such early looking behavior—when taken with the protracted gazes that result from violated expectations, noted earlier, should provide an early form of nonimitative prosody on the infant's part. It seems likely to me that during this period the infant is already learning to anticipate some (perhaps simplified) version of what the mother's prosody and gestures portend; is learning to emit gestures, expressions, and sounds appropriate to the mother's actions; and has already come to sustain the supporting poses and goal-saving effector actions that underlie GFM. That is to say, this period allows the infant to initiate a self-establishing personality that has learned some content of heard/watched speech and only starts to speak almost a year later.

In short, it is while playing with and exchanging looking behaviors with Mommy that the infant learns to employ various anticipatory actions (not just fixations-as-gesture), which serve to enable and sustain other more overt actions (such as gestures of head and hand and voice) until they come due and which, when correctly executed, bring the awaited joyous responses from Mommy. At a later age, such planned-in-advance actions support imaginary interactions with synthetic surrogates or replacements for Mommy, like favorite toys and animated cartoons, whose fancied responses are provided by the anticipating child itself while playing both sides of the interaction. (Note that children do in fact respond as early as 1, 3, and 5 months to animations [Sherrod, 1979] and to what we have had long before animations, namely illustrated story books.) Still later, these interaction-supporting abilities help sustain various social interactions and their substitutes—including virtual interactions, as in video presences and video games. However, it is the first year or so of prespeech interactions that may be so important for the lives that follow—and for the enormous involvement our species has with anticipation-rewarding and GFM-like plan-sustaining activities such as music, games, art, dance, and movies.

Research on gestural interaction and on GFM during this important period would seem desirable for even a rudimentary understanding of purposeful human behavior and its development, but it is complicated by the need for a controllable research collaborator with whom the infant is to interact. Fortunately, as noted previously, it might be possible to substitute facial animations for the mother during research sessions (assuming that this has no bad effects, e.g., that infants are not upset by the absence of cuddling during the research periods). More fancifully, computer-generated displays will probably soon become available which will interact with the infant's gestural behavior. (There already are such setups that reward infant articulations; cf., Fel et al., 2004; visiBabble, 2004). In fact, computer-driven devices that simulate human appearance and behavior (wannabe "humanoids") are already with us, and are beginning to be able to interact with humans and even respond to some of the latter's more common gestures and prosodies. Examples of the former are to be found primarily in programs like computer-run telephone receptionists and information dispensers, which employ prosody.

Such (implausible) devices would certainly make the required interaction research easier, but careful use of whatever existing animation procedures are now available should also serve while we await the humanoids. However, why is such computer-based imitation and response to human gestural behavior being actively pursued?

WHY THE NEED FOR HUMANOIDS, AND HOW MIGHT THEY HELP US?

Aside from thoughts about surplus value, globalization, security forces, etc., there are certainly various uses for computer-based simulations of humans and their behaviors—computer animation software to replace some or most of the intensive labor previously needed for both line and three-dimensional animation is now a major commodity, and there have even been plans to simulate specific people in two- and three-dimensional versions. Designs that mass-produce software, which in turn produces games with which players avidly interact, are also readily available. Surveillance software that can recognize faces is of obvious use. Most important are devices that replace human telephone and videophone operators. To improve their interaction with humans requires either that human callers drastically flatten their speech and discard their dependence on prosody when listening or that the software is given the ability to emit and absorb such information itself and become humanoid (which is surely implausible at the high end) or that some compromise is reached that is mutually acceptable. That last point, which seems the most plausible, means that we need a great deal of quantitative versions of the kinds of research introduced by Krauss and his colleagues, with Bayes and tensor analysis both being built into the humanoids, and specific tolerances being taught to humans

One can see why society and industry might be impelled in this direction. But why should serious psychological scientists pay attention to such tinsel?

One reason was noted previously—to help in research with real humans. Another obvious reason is the support from a growing set of industries. If we add to the humanoid phone and service staff the other economic players (media, games, instruction, etc.) mentioned previously, surely clinical psychology is no longer the dominant economic player in psychology. But the most important reason, in my opinion, is this: In order to be comprehensible to human-interactive computers and their makers, anything we say about the mechanisms that underlie humanoid and machine gestures and about human social interaction, and anything about how GFM and similar memoranda work their ways in humans, has to be written in a language that both predicts and illuminates our behavior, and is also objective, quantitative, and science-friendly (as a sampling, see Ogando, 2007; Sims, 2007; Weinberg & Driscoll, 2006). That means that we will have come a long way toward a real science of psychology. Admittedly, that body of knowledge would still leave out a lot. But it will give us a lot more than we have had up to now and should not be any less friendly to the investigation of brain processes, etc., except insofar as it offers alternative rewarding avenues of research.

Meanwhile, remember to bring Schmuel's gloves, but with Wi-Fi.

REFERENCES

Bayliss, A. P., & Tipper, S. P. (2006). Predictive gaze cues and personality judgments. *Psychological Science, 17*, 514–520.

Bower, T. G. R. (1971).The object in the world of the infant. *Scientific American, 225,* 30–38.

Canfield, R. L., & Kirkham, N. Z. (2001). Infant cortical development and the prospective control of saccadic eye movements. *Infancy, 2*, 197–211.

Chawla, P., & Krauss, R. M. (1994). Gesture and speech in spontaneous and rehearsed narratives. *Journal of Experimental Social Psychology, 30,* 580–601.

Durand, K., Lécuyer, R., & Frichtel, M. (2003). Representation of the third dimension: The use of perspective cues by 3- and 4-month-old infants. *Infant Behavior and Development, 26,* 151–166.

Fell, H., Cress, C., MacAuslan, J., Ferrier, L., Sterup, G., & Heinrich, A. (2004). visiBabble for reinforcement of early vocalization. *www.unl.edu/barkley/present/cress/visiBabbleASHA04.pdf*

Grieser, D. L., & Kuhl, P. K. (1988). Maternal speech to infants in a tonal language: Support for universal prosodic features in motherese. *Developmental Psychology, 24,* 14–20.

Hayhoe, M. M., Shrivastava, A., Mruczek, D., & Pelz, J. (2003). Visual memory and motor planning in a natural task. *Journal of Vision, 3*, 49–63.

Hochberg, J. (1968). In the mind's eye. In M. A. Peterson, B. Gillam, & H. A. Sedgwick (Eds.), *In the mind's eye* (pp. 70–99). New York: Oxford University Press.

Hochberg, J. (1997). The affordances of perceptual inquiry: Pictures are learned from the world, and what that fact might mean about perception quite generally. In M. P. Friedman & E. C. Carterette (Eds.), *Cognitive ecology* (pp. 151–204). San Diego, CA: Academic Press.

Hochberg, J., & Brooks, V. (1978). Film cutting and visual momentum. In J. W. Senders, D. F. Fisher, & R. A. Monty (Eds.), *Eye movements and the higher psychological functions (*pp. 293–313). Hillsdale, NJ: Lawrence Erlbaum Associates.

Hoffman, J. E., & Subramaniam, B. (1995). Saccadic eye movements and visual selective attention. *Perception & Psychophysics, 57*, 787–795.

Hostetter, A. B., & Alibali, M. W. (2008). Visible embodiment: Gestures as simulated action. *Psychonomic Bulletin and Review*, *15*, 495–514.

Hostetter, A. B., Alibali, M. W., & Kit, S. (2007). I see it in my mind's eye: Representational gestures reflect conceptual demands. *Language and Cognitive Processes, 22,* 313–336.

Kowler, E., Anderson, E., Dosher, B., & Blaser, E. (1995). The role of attention in the programming of saccades. *Vision Research, 35*, 1897–1916.

Krauss, R. M. (1998). Why do we gesture when we speak? *Current Directions in Psychological Science 7*, 54–59.

Krauss, R. M., Chen, Y., & Chawla, P. (1996). Nonverbal behavior and nonverbal communication: What do conversational hand gestures tell us? *Advances in Experimental Social Psychology, 28,* 389–450.

Krauss, R. M., & Morsella, E. (2002). The gestural feedback model. Unpublished manuscript, Columbia University.

Mason, M. F., Hood, B. M., & Macrae, C. N. (2004). Look into my eyes: Gaze direction and person memory. *Memory, 12,* 637–643.

Mason M. F., Tatkow E. P., Macrae C. N. (2005). The look of love: Gaze shifts and person perception. *Psychological Science, 16,* 236–239.

Morrel-Samuels, P., & Krauss, R. M. (1992). Word familiarity predicts temporal asynchrony of hand gestures and speech. *Journal of Experimental Psychology: Learning, Memory and Cognition, 18,* 615–623.

Morsella, E. (2002). The motor components of semantic representation. (Doctoral dissertation, Columbia University, 2002). *Dissertation Abstracts International: Section B: the Sciences & Engineering, 63 (4-B).* (University Microfilms No. AAI3048195).

Morsella E., & Krauss, R. M. (1999, October). *Electromyography of arm during the lexical retrieval of abstract and concrete words.* Poster presented at the Annual Convention of the Society for Psychophysiology, Granada, Spain. *Psychophysiology, 36,* S82.

Morsella, E., & Krauss, R. M. (2004). The role of gestures in spatial working memory and speech. *American Journal of Psychology, 117,* 411–424.

Morsella, E., & Krauss, R. M. (2005). Muscular activity in the arm during lexical retrieval: Implications for gesture-speech theories. *Journal of Psycholinguistic Research, 34,* 415–427.

Ogando, J. (2007). Humanoid robots put best faces forward. *Design News,* Feb. 26.

Rauscher, F. H., Krauss, R. M., & Chen, Y. (1996). Gesture, speech, and lexical access: The role of lexical movements in the processing of speech. *Psychological Science, 7,* 226–231.

Sherrod, L. R. (1979). Social cognition in infants. *Infant Behavior and Development, 2,* 279–294.

Simons, D. J., & Levin, D. T. (2007). Ideas of lasting influence. In M. A. Peterson, B. Gillam, & H. A. Sedgwick (Eds.), *In the mind's eye* (pp. 557–561). New York: Oxford University Press.

Sims, E. M. (2007). Reusable, lifelike virtual humans for mentoring and role-playing. *Computers & Education, 49,* 75–92.

Weinberg, G., & Driscoll, S. (2006). Robot-human interaction with an anthropomorphic percussionist. *Computer Human Interaction Proceedings Social Computing, 3,* 1229–1232.

Woods, D. (1984). Visual momentum: A concept to improve the cognitive coupling of person and computer. *International Journal of Man-Machine Studies, 21,* 229–244.

Yonas, A., Elieff, C. A., & Arterberry, M. E. (2002). Emergence of sensitivity to pictorial depth cues: Charting development in individual infants. *Infant Behavior & Development, 25,* 495–513.

Yonas, A., Granrud, C. E., Arterberry, M., & Hanson, B. L. (1966). Infants' distance perception from linear perspective and texture gradients. *Infant Behavior and Development, 9,* 247–256.

Zingale, C. M., & Kowler, E. (1987). Planning sequences of saccades. *Vision Research, 27,* 1327–1341.

Author Index

Subject Index